# Cotton Mills
# in Greater Manchester

Frontispiece. In the late 19th century the former cotton town of Mossley developed a characteristic landscape of terraced housing built alongside large steam-powered mills. The last surviving large mill in the town was Brunswick Mill (959), which had typical features of an 1890s spinning mill but also incorporated parts of an earlier mill which stood on the same site. The mill was demolished in 1990.

# Cotton Mills in Greater Manchester

Mike Williams

*with*

D. A. Farnie

The Greater Manchester Archaeological Unit
in association with
the Royal Commission on the Historical Monuments of England

Carnegie Publishing Ltd., 1992

**Front cover illustration**

The cotton-spinning mills of Ancoats, built between 1798 and 1912, perhaps the finest surviving group of early textile mills in Greater Manchester. Early mills in Manchester were distinguished by their large size, their dependence on steam power and their concentration in closely-packed groups alongside the canal system. From left to right are Brownsfield Mill (315*), Royal Mill (370*), Sedgwick Mill (372*) and Old Mill (362*).

**Back cover illustration**

*Coming from the Mill, 1930*, L. S. Lowry's depiction of a typical Lancashire cotton town. The widespread loss of such traditional landscapes in the 20th century has been matched by an increasing appreciation of the historical significance of mills and related buildings.

---

Cotton Mills in Greater Manchester
by Mike Williams with D. A. Farnie

Published by Carnegie Publishing Ltd., 18 Maynard Street, Preston PR2 2AL

Copyright © Carnegie Publishing Ltd. 1992

Text copyright © The Greater Manchester Archaeological Unit and the Royal Commission on the Historical Monuments of England, Crown copyright 1992, except for Chapter Two, copyright © D. A. Farnie 1992

All photographs copyright © the Royal Commission on the Historical Monuments of England, Crown copyright 1992, except for City of Salford Arts and Leisure Department, Figure 13; Mrs C. A. Danes, Figure 15; Manchester Central Library, Figures 14, 18, 21, 24, 25, 29, 31, 33, 34; Bolton Archive and Local Studies Service, Figures 20, 23; *Bolton Evening News*, Figure 22; Oldham Local Studies Library, Figures 27, 28; Rochdale Libraries, Local Studies Collection, Figure 36; Birmingham Library Services, Figures 39, 56, 63, 65, 66, 67; City of Salford Art Gallery, back cover

All drawings copyright © The Greater Manchester Archaeological Unit and the Royal Commission on the Historical Monuments of England, Crown copyright 1992

Designed and typeset by Carnegie Publishing Ltd., Preston

Printed and bound in the UK by The Alden Press, Oxford

**British Library Cataloguing-in-Publication Data**
Williams, Mike
 Cotton Mills in Greater Manchester
 I. Title   II. Farnie, D. A.
 338.4767721094273

 **ISBN 0-948789-69-7** (Casebound)
 **ISBN 0-948789-89-1** (Softback)

This publication has been assisted by a grant from the Royal Commission on the Historical Monuments of England

# Contents

# Forewords

GREATER MANCHESTER is widely renowned as one of the great centres of the Industrial Revolution. It is associated in particular with the cotton industry, as first Manchester and later other towns within the modern county developed mass production methods in textile mills of huge scale. The decline of the industry in the 20th century has caused the loss of many mills, but still these buildings give the area its unique character. The historical importance of the mills and the serious threat which they face in the modern world led the Royal Commission on the Historical Monuments of England (RCHME) to join with the Greater Manchester Archaeological Unit (GMAU) in a survey intended first to identify and then to record the remains of the textile industry. The results of the survey constitute an archive held in complete form at the John Rylands University Library, 150 Deansgate, Manchester M3 3EH, and in selective copy form in the National Monuments Record, RCHME, Fortress House, 23 Savile Row, London W1X 2JQ, and the Greater Manchester Archaeological Unit, University of Manchester, Oxford Road, Manchester M13 9PL.

The Royal Commission has undertaken or supported two other mills surveys, in Yorkshire and East Cheshire, and the three projects represent a substantial response, in terms of record, to the crisis faced by old industrial buildings in a period of rapid economic change. It is hoped that the three surveys will provide a greater understanding of one important class of industrial monument. The Royal Commission has a continuing commitment to recording the country's industrial heritage, for the circumstances which prompted action on northern textile mills apply in equal measure to a wide range of buildings associated with other industries.

The Royal Commission has welcomed its association with the Greater Manchester Archaeological Unit. Commissioners would like to thank in particular its Director, Phil Mayes, for his willingness to join in the survey and provide many of the facilities that brought it to completion. The Commission also recognises the excellent work of the survey officer, Mike Williams, who conducted the fieldwork, compiled the archive and wrote the bulk of the present book, and of Bob Skingle, Principal Photographer with the Royal Commission, who took all the photographs used here. Commissioners join with Mr Williams in thanking members of the working party which steered the survey during its course and Unit and Royal Commission staff involved at different stages of the work. Special thanks are recorded to Dr D. A. Farnie, who was a member of the working party and who contributed a chapter to this volume. Finally, the Commission thanks owners and occupiers of mill property for allowing access to their buildings.

PARK OF MONMOUTH

*Chairman, Royal Commission on the Historical Monuments of England*

---

IN 1984 the County Councils of Greater Manchester and West Yorkshire commissioned the report *Mills in the 80s.* This was carried out by Roger Tym and Partners who identified an enormous volume of vacant space in old industrial buildings in the two counties and analysed the economic pressures on their owners. The report's recommendations included proposals for refurbishment and re-use but also defined a policy of grant-aided demolition. Mills, which still dominate many urban and rural landscapes in Greater Manchester, were under threat. A shared interest in industrial heritage brought the Greater Manchester County Council and the Royal Commission on the Historical Monuments of England together, through the good offices of the Greater Manchester Archaeological Unit. Within a very short period a programme of survey and record had been formulated and supporting finance agreed. The survey officer, Mike Williams, was appointed, and in 1985 the work began. From the outset two objectives were clearly identified, namely the creation of an archive of the results of field survey, photography, map-work and documentary research and, arising from these, a comprehensive publication. Initially, support for the programme was divided equally between the Royal Commission and the Greater Manchester Council (GMC), but during the latter stages the level of the Royal Commission support steadily increased. The Association of Greater Manchester Authorities, successor to GMC, gave continuous support to the work and the University of Manchester generously provided both accommodation and extensive facilities. The Manpower Services Commission recognised the inherent value of the project and supported the appointment of survey assistants over a number of years. Dr D. A. Farnie was an active participant in the survey working party and his unrivalled, incisive knowledge of the history of the industry is demonstrated in his contribution to this volume.

The scale of the survey at times seemed overwhelming. Some 2,400 sites were identified from the map sources alone and of these over 1,000 were surveyed. For the first time the loss of mills was quantified: in

Manchester, for example, less than a quarter survived. The very process of survey heightened the interest of many individuals, in the public and private sectors, best able to influence the future of these outstanding monuments, which, by their sheer scale, are so costly to turn to new uses. This publication of the results will focus attention on buildings which epitomise the county's industrial legacy. Month by month mills are demolished. For many, a brief drawn and photographic record is all that will survive, yet for others, profitable re-use has been achieved. These twin processes, and the debate they encourage, will continue, but now in a climate informed by survey, synopsis and publication.

The survey brought local and national interests together to good effect and this well researched, balanced publication represents a major contribution to our understanding of the history and architecture of the most important single group of buildings in the county.

COUNCILLOR H. D. STACHINI
*Chair, Greater Manchester Planning and Transportation Committee*
*Association of Greater Manchester Authorities*

# Acknowledgements

THIS BOOK and the archive on which it is based are the result of years of enthusiastic work by a wide range of people. The author would like to thank everyone who worked on the project, in particular Phil Mayes, Director of the Greater Manchester Archaeological Unit, and Colum Giles of the Royal Commission on the Historical Monuments of England, without whose continual support and advice the project would not have been possible. Thanks are also due to all the owners and occupiers of the mills of Greater Manchester for allowing access to their buildings. The Greater Manchester Textile Mill Survey was jointly funded by the RCHME, initially with the Greater Manchester Council (GMC) and latterly with the Association of Greater Manchester Authorities. Support was also received from the University of Manchester and the project was based at the offices of the Greater Manchester Archaeological Unit on the university campus.

The project was monitored and advised by a Working Party comprising at different times J. T. Smith, Dr John Bold, Professor R. A. Buchanan, Tom Hassall, Colum Giles and Dr Ian Goodall of the RCHME, Phil Mayes, Adrian Tindall and John Walker of the GMAU, Chris Makepeace of the GMC and, from the University of Manchester, Dr D. A. Farnie of the Department of History and Dr R. W. Brunskill of the School of Architecture.

Many employees of the GMAU made an invaluable contribution. Documentary research was carried out by Claire Hunt, Jane Bryan, John Dodds, John Davies, Magella Egan, Gill Freer, Alison Jones, Gabriella Petter and Nicola Swords. Archive and publication drawings were produced by Paul Clayton, David Rawson and Jim Thompson. The Gazetteer was compiled from the county Sites and Monuments Record database by Peter Arrowsmith and Mark Blackler.

Of the staff of the RCHME, Tony Berry trained the survey team and worked on the publication drawings; Bob Skingle took the publication photographs; Roger Featherstone of the Air Photography Unit organised aerial photography; Davina Turner and Fran Brown edited the text; Jean Craven provided secretarial and clerical support; Diana Hale gave advice relating to the archive; and Dr Bridgett Jones carried out extensive documentary research. Advice on editorial and publication issues was provided by Kate Owen.

Local Studies Libraries, record offices and archive departments throughout the region were helpful and supportive throughout the project, and district planning departments kindly allowed access to Building Control Plans. The late Frank Wightman, millwright and engineer, made available his annotated drawings of textile mills and provided first-hand knowledge of mill engineering.

Every effort has been made to discover and acknowledge the copyright relating to illustrative material. Any omission is regretted and information regarding copyright in any such cases is welcomed.

MIKE WILLIAMS

# Editorial notes

The structure of this book is outlined in the Introduction. The numbers following the names of mills throughout the text refer to the Gazetteer. Numbers which include an asterisk indicate that the mill is described and illustrated in more detail in the Inventory. Drawings follow the conventions outlined in *Recording Historic Buildings: a Descriptive Specification* (2nd edition, RCHME 1991), 5–8. A few conventions specific to industrial buildings have been used, namely:

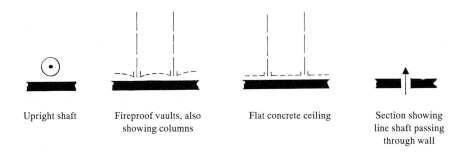

Upright shaft        Fireproof vaults, also        Flat concrete ceiling        Section showing
                     showing columns                                            line shaft passing
                                                                                through wall

# 1

# Introduction

TEXTILE MILLS have been central features of industrial landscapes in northern and western England for over two centuries. Consequently mills are now perhaps the most characteristic type of historic building in many northern towns. In Greater Manchester the prolonged importance of the textile industry resulted in the construction of mills in great numbers. Textile mills and their machinery were the subject of continual development and improvement, so the surviving buildings include a wide variety of dates and architectural types. The early mills included advanced structures which were at the forefront of technology during the Industrial Revolution. The huge scale of mills built a century later reflected both the international importance of the Lancashire textile industry and the extent to which building techniques, mechanical engineering, power systems and production methods had developed.

The county of Greater Manchester was created in 1974 with boundaries enclosing what was traditionally known as south-east Lancashire, along with parts of north Cheshire and west Yorkshire. The conurbation included the 'cotton towns' which had grown around the commercial centre of the Lancashire textile industry (Fig 1). Over 2,400 mills and cloth-finishing works were built in an area measuring approximately 25 miles north to south by 30 miles east to west. By the 1980s the decline of traditional industries had resulted in the loss of over half of these mills, while many of the remainder were derelict or awaiting grant-aided demolition. One effect of the widespread loss of mills, however, was increasing public interest in industrial heritage, in mill architecture and in the sensitive re-use of industrial buildings.

This book is the product of a survey begun in 1985 by the GMAU and RCHME.[1] It aims to provide an interpretation of the development of cotton-spinning and weaving mills, which form over 70 per cent of the extant textile mills in Greater Manchester (see Gazetteer). Cotton mills in Greater Manchester differ considerably from textile mills in other regions, for example in their size, date range, architectural details and degree of economic specialisation. Readers wishing to make direct comparisons with other areas can refer to the RCHME publication *Yorkshire*

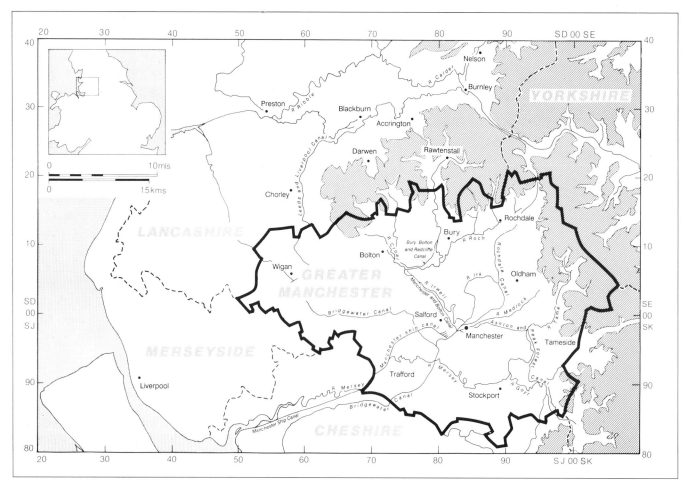

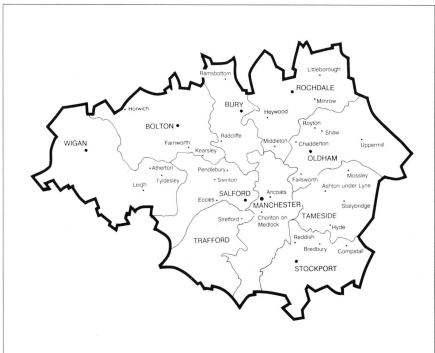

Figure 1.
Above: the regional setting of Greater Manchester. Topography and climate both influenced the concentration of the textile industry in the area.

Left: the county's metropolitan districts, with most of the major cotton towns.

*Textile Mills 1770–1930* and the joint publication *The Textile Mills of East Cheshire*.

In this book the development of the cotton mill is subdivided into four chronological stages which form the subject of Chapters 3 to 6. The approach adopted is to consider mill building as being dependent on a range of interrelated factors, such as the development of construction techniques, machinery and power systems. Each of these chapters begins with a summary followed by sections on the size, shape and external features of mills in that period. Methods of construction are then discussed and related to the ways in which machinery was organised internally and to the development of power systems. It is hoped that this discussion will lead to a greater understanding of the features of mill architecture and to an appreciation of the way in which mill building developed over the whole period. The Inventory section of the book provides individual case studies of most of the mills mentioned in the text. The Gazetteer contains brief details of all the textile mills which were extant in Greater Manchester between 1985 and 1987. In the text the name of a mill is followed by its Gazetteer number in parentheses: an asterisk after the number indicates that the mill is described in the Inventory.

## The origins of cotton mill building in Lancashire

In the middle of the 18th century south-east Lancashire was predominantly an agricultural area of isolated settlements and market towns with, at its centre, the growing town of Manchester. Cloth manufacture had long been an important industry. By the 1780s the national demand for textiles, particularly cotton, had begun to increase. In the following decades a range of natural and economic advantages in south-east Lancashire resulted in a dramatic increase in mill building and transformed the area into a great centre of the factory-based cotton industry.[2] Topographically the area comprised an undulating lowland basin containing the River Mersey and its tributaries which was bounded by the Pennine uplands to the east and to the north (Fig 1). The area was open to prevailing winds from the west and the south, thus ensuring a high annual rainfall with high humidity. The domestic textile industry which pre-dated the first factories had benefited from the availability of water-powered sites in the uplands while the humid atmosphere made it easier and cheaper to spin cotton yarn.[3] When steam became more important than water power, local coal reserves were exploited. Also of great importance was the development of the port of Liverpool in the 18th century and the completion by 1776 of the Bridgewater Canal. Extending from its terminus at Castlefield in Manchester to the Liverpool area, the canal was used for the transportation of coal and raw materials, effectively linking Manchester to international trade routes and the sources of raw cotton.

## The raw material

The Lancashire cotton industry was dependent on imported raw material, making it subject to fluctuations in international trade. Economic downturns had drastic effects on the mill communities, while mill building often took place in relatively prosperous boom periods. Until the 1860s most cotton was obtained from the slave plantations in the United States of America.[4] The huge consumption of cotton led to the development of close links between Lancashire and the southern states in the early 19th century.[5] After the disruption caused by the American Civil War, however, additional sources of cotton were developed, notably Egypt and India. Cotton from different sources had particular characteristics which were carefully exploited by spinning mills producing different yarns.[6] From as early as the 1790s mills in different parts of Greater Manchester were specialising in the production of certain types of yarn. The most important characteristic of the yarn was its fineness, which was traditionally measured as the 'count'.[7] Manchester and later Bolton specialised in the finer yarns, which sold for the highest price, while in the Oldham area hundreds of mills were built to produce coarse yarns.

## Processes and machinery inside a cotton mill

Mills for spinning and weaving cotton were primarily functional buildings designed to accommodate a range of machinery as efficiently as possible. The external form of cotton mills was influenced by both the type of machinery used and the internal organisation of processes. By the late 19th century the efficient distribution of machinery was one of the main concerns of mill architects, and mills increasingly followed similar basic principles of internal layout (Fig 2). The machinery in mills was itself subject to gradual improvement and varied with both the type of raw cotton used and the nature of the final product. The following account is a summary of the main processes and machinery which influenced the form of mill buildings.[8]

In a spinning mill, which was usually a multi-storeyed building, there might be over a dozen groups of powered machines carrying out the successive stages of yarn production. In summary, however, there were just three main stages of production which were located in different parts of the mill. The first stage involved the opening and initial preparation of the bales of raw cotton. The second stage concerned carding and the production of a roving, a thick cord of cotton fibres. In the third stage the roving was stretched and twisted on the spinning machine to produce the yarn.

In the 18th century the initial processes were carried out by hand in separate workshops, but after the mid 1790s they tended to be located in the mill and became mechanised. The compressed bales of raw cotton were opened, the impurities removed and the fibres formed into a continuous sheet of wadding known as a lap. In the 1790s the raw cotton was opened and cleaned by spreading it on to a mesh and beating it with sticks, a process known as willowing or batting (Fig 3). This was later mechanised with a machine sometimes called a willow.[9] After about 1800 an

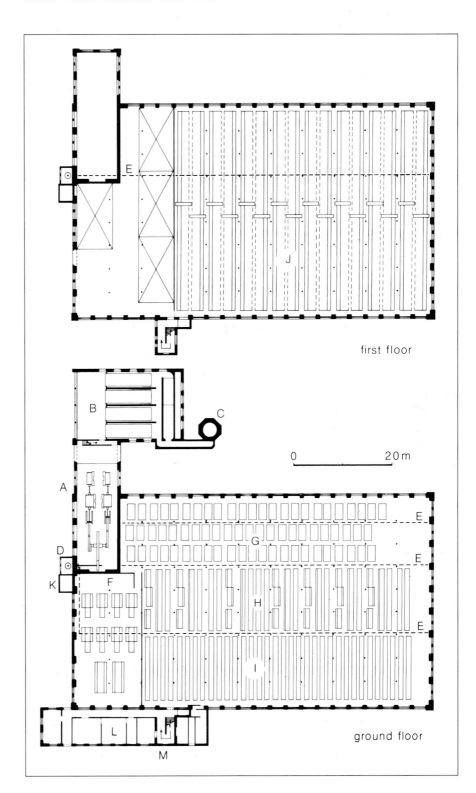

first floor

ground floor

0              20 m

Figure 2. The power system and machinery layout of a typical late 19th-century spinning mill (adapted from plans published in *The Textile Manufacturer*, 1891, 341–3).

A:  engine house
B:  boiler house
C:  chimney
D:  upright transmission shaft
E:  line shafts
F:  blowing room containing scutchers
G:  carding engines
H:  draw frames
I:  roving frames
J:  self-acting mules
K:  dust flue
L:  offices
M:  stair tower

Figure 3. In early mills hand-powered batting or willowing removed impurities from the raw cotton (Tomlinson 1854, 7).

Figure 4. A typical scutcher manufactured in the late 19th century. Such machines were a more efficient method of removing impurities and formed the cotton into a lap ready for carding (*The Textile Manufacturer*, 1887, 88).

additional machine known as a scutcher began to be used in which a spiked drum rotating at high speeds worked in conjunction with a fan to separate the impurities and mix the cotton fibres. The cotton was formed into a lap by rollers at the back of the machine (Fig 4). These initial processes liberated large quantities of cotton dust posing a serious fire hazard, and in early mills they were carried out in attached buildings. Later they were located in a segregated fireproof room inside the mill, often known as the blowing room, which was equipped with a ventilation system to extract the cotton dust.

The second stage, involving carding and the production of a roving, was carried out on carefully arranged groups of machines located in the ground floor of the mill (Figs 2, 5). The mechanisation of these processes, principally by Sir Richard Arkwright, was one of the most significant steps in the development of the cotton factory in the late 18th century. The

Figure 5. Carding engines (left), belt-driven from an overhead line shaft in a spinning mill of around 1830 (Baines 1835, plate 6).

carding engine basically consisted of a wide drum with a surface of wire spikes rotating within a close-fitting casing which was also lined with spikes. The cotton lap was fed into the machine where the combing action of the wires made the fibres parallel, producing a thin sheet of fibre which was formed into one or more untwisted slivers.

After carding the sliver was fed into a nearby machine called a draw frame, in which it was further attenuated by being passed through sets of rollers rotating at different speeds, a process known as draughting. Slivers from several different carding engines were combined, or 'doubled', into a single sliver in the draw frame to eliminate irregularities in thickness. Depending on the counts to be spun, the doubled slivers might be doubled again in a further draw frame. In the next machine the sliver was again stretched by draughting rollers and given a slight twist to form the roving. Without the twist it would have been too weak to be handled. In Arkwright's mills the roving was produced on a single machine, but by the late 19th century the process had been subdivided and involved a sequence of three separate machines. In mills spinning the finest yarns rovings were produced on five successive machines.

Cotton mills were designed to contain one of two general types of spinning machine. The type of spinning machine influenced a mill's external form and internal organisation. Spinning was usually sited in the

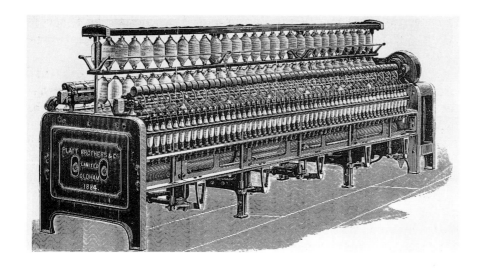

Figure 6. A typical ring-spinning frame of the 1880s. Such machines operated at higher speeds than the earlier throstles and water frames but were of similar proportions. They were a derivative of the water frame used in Arkwright mills in the late 18th century (*The Textile Manufacturer*, 1887, 375).

upper storeys with the machines located transversely across the floor. The first type of spinning machine used in cotton mills was the water frame, developed and patented by Arkwright, in which the roving was stretched by draughting rollers and twisted by the action of winding it on to the spindle. The water frame could be used only on a relatively large scale in powered factories and at first could not produce yarn of sufficient strength to be used as warp. It could achieve a continuous high output, however, and did not require highly skilled operatives demanding high wages. It was gradually improved during the 19th century, leading to the development of two derivative machines. The throstle, introduced in the early 19th century, worked on the same principle but was better engineered and could be driven by steam power. The ring frame, a later development, was invented in the United States of America in 1829 but was not widely used

Figure 7. Two partially powered mules of the 1830s. In this example the machines are arranged longitudinally, but it was more common for spinning machines to be located transversely, occupying most of the width of a mill (Baines 1835, plate 11).

in Britain until the late 19th century (Fig 6). It worked at higher speeds and was continually improved to become the standard spinning machine in use by the mid 20th century.

The second type of spinning machine, the mule, was invented by Samuel Crompton of Bolton in 1779.[10] The mule was much more widely used than the water frame and its derivatives and had more influence on the expansion of the Lancashire cotton industry. It was a hybrid design, combining the roller draughting of the water frame with the salient features of an earlier machine, the spinning jenny. It was a long machine with bobbins containing the roving arranged along the back and the spindles containing the spun yarn along a movable parallel carriage. The carriage was mounted on wheels and moved about 1.5 metres away from the bobbins, so pulling out the roving (Fig 7). At this stage the roving was twisted into yarn, and was wound on to the spindles as the carriage moved back in.

The mule was partly powered by the mid 1790s, but still required both skill and strength on the part of the operative. Unlike the water frame its output was intermittent, spinning yarn in lengths of about 1.5 metres at a time, but the yarn it produced was finer yet strong enough to be used for warp. In its favour the mule was a more adaptable machine which initially could be hand-powered and, unlike the water frame, its use was not restricted by patents. Mules were used in large numbers in late 18th-century Manchester and many detailed improvements continued to be made to Crompton's original design. In 1830 Richard Roberts of Manchester introduced the self-acting or automatic mule, which permitted the whole cycle of operation to be powered. The number of spindles, and hence the size of each machine, was increased from about 200 in 1790 to over 1,300 in 1890 (Fig 8).

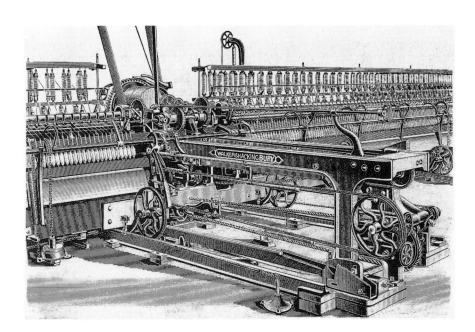

Figure 8. The central section of a much larger automatic or 'self-acting' mule of the 1880s. Most of the components are of cast iron; the belt drive is taken from an overhead line shaft (*The Textile Manufacturer*, 1884, 465).

After spinning, the yarn might be subject to further processes. By the mid 19th century it was stored for a few days in a conditioning cellar in the basement of the mill. The floor of the cellar was flooded with water and the yarn allowed to absorb moisture in the humid atmosphere to improve its handling qualities. Spinning mills often included yarn-winding machines for transferring the yarn from the spindles on to bobbins before despatch from the warehouse (Fig 9). Yarn doubling involved combining two or more yarns from the spinning machines to form a stronger thread, used for lace-making or for sewing cotton. It was carried out on a machine similar to a ring frame. From *c.*1840 mills were built to specialise in yarn doubling. The dyeing of yarn and any other finishing treatments usually took place at a separate works.

Weaving was usually carried out in a separate mill, often a single-storeyed shed, although 'integrated' mills with both spinning and weaving were common in the mid 19th century. Yarn was prepared for weaving in two main stages. First the warp threads were wound on to a beam, which was fitted on to the head of the loom. Second, the warp had to be protected from abrasion during weaving by the application of a starch mixture, known as size. The weft might have to be wound on to special

Figure 9. Yarn-winding machinery in an early 20th-century spinning mill (*The Textile Mercury*, 1910, 339).

Figure 10 (opposite). Plan and elevation of a cast-iron powerloom of about 1830. After the 1820s the widespread use of the powerloom influenced both the internal organisation of mills and the geographical distribution of the industry (Baines 1835, plate 12).

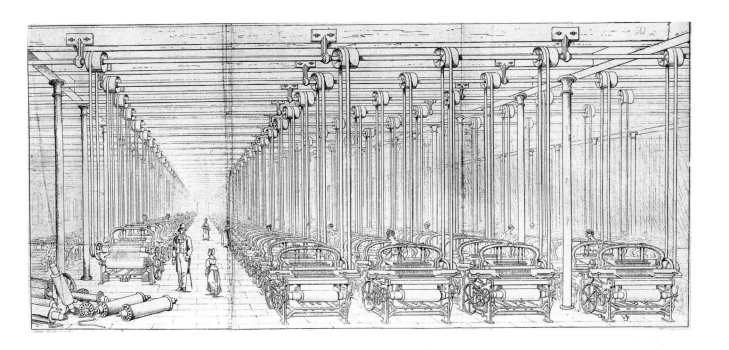

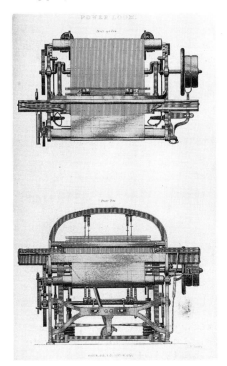

Figure 11 (above). 'Power Loom Weaving Factory of Thomas Robinson Esqr., Stockport', *c.*1830. The weight and vibration of powerlooms, together with the need for good internal lighting, encouraged the construction of weaving sheds from an early date (Ure 1835, facing p. 1).

bobbins to fit into the shuttle. Weaving was performed on handlooms in domestic workshops until about 1820, having benefited from the invention of the flying shuttle by John Kay in 1734. The first powerloom was patented by Edmund Cartwright in 1785, but successful powerlooms were not used until the second decade of the 19th century. The main development was Richard Roberts' introduction in 1822 of a cast-iron powerloom, adopted rapidly thereafter in Lancashire (Figs 10 and 11).

## The development of mill building

The machines and the processes which they performed were contained in mills, and as machines changed in size and complexity so mill architecture developed in response. The evolution of the cotton mill is studied in detail in Chapters 3 to 6, but here it is important to stress the relationship between buildings, machinery and the nature of the power system used to drive the machines.

Mills are essentially functional and utilitarian buildings and thus their form is dictated primarily by the processes which they were intended to contain. Other more formal architectural considerations were at play in the design of some buildings but even in the most ornate of mills these influences were subservient to the need to house machines and accommodate processes in the most efficient manner. Thus the spinning mill changed to permit mules of increasing size to be housed in the best way, and the weaving shed was developed to provide efficient accommodation for powerlooms. An important influence on mill form was the development of new methods of construction, enabling ever-larger structures to be built and permitting economies of scale in operating costs. The contrast between the non-fireproof timber-floored mills of the late 18th century and the much larger steel and concrete-floored mills of the early 20th century is only the most obvious of the changes represented by the development of structural technique. Power, too, played an important role in determining mill form, for as the size and quantity of machines grew so too did the demand for power. The growth in the size of mills was in part made possible by the development of better prime movers, first water-wheels, later steam engines and lastly electricity. The architectural evidence shows this story clearly. In Greater Manchester, surviving cotton mills show particularly good evidence of the development of steam power and of methods of fireproof construction during the 19th century.

If mills were only the product of these salient forces – mechanisation, methods of construction and power systems – they might lack individual quality. Within certain bounds, however, textile mills are a distinctive and clearly identifiable class of building. Their architectural character is due partly to the craftsmen responsible for the construction of new building types, partly to the owners, many of whom took the opportunity to express their wealth and status in their buildings, and partly to the architectural profession, which in Greater Manchester came to develop a strong specialism in mill construction and which may also have brought with it an awareness of the aesthetic qualities of mills. The story of the various influences at work in the design of mills – largely but not exclusively functional – forms the subject of this book.

# 2

# The cotton towns of Greater Manchester

We have been frequently amused at seeing a factory described by one class of writers as somewhat worse than a Pandemonium, and by another as a trifle better than an Elysium. The descriptions of each party are equally unlike the truth.

Lamb 1848, 9 (*A judgement made by the rector of the parish which included Ancoats, the industrial heart of Manchester*)

To one born in a cotton town a cotton factory is not a factory nor a works, but a mill. There are historic reasons for this. The first generation of the factory system was an age not of steam but of water.

Unwin 1924, 21 (*A judgement made by the first British Professor of Economic History and a native of Stockport*)

The word *mill* continued to mean a factory long after steam had almost everywhere taken the place of water power.

Mantoux 1961, 224

## The age of expansion, 1771–1926

THE rapid expansion of the British cotton industry remains one of the most astonishing episodes in history. The new machine-based industry expanded in two distinct phases, dominated by different sources of power in the waterwheel and the steam engine. In 1771 Arkwright established at Cromford on the River Derwent in Derbyshire the first water-powered cotton-spinning mill equipped with roller spinning frames holding about 1,000 spindles.[1] His example was imitated and 208 similar mills had been established by 1787, wherever sites could provide the power to turn a waterwheel and especially in the river valleys of the Midlands, the Pennines and Scotland.[2] During the Arkwright era, however, strict limits were imposed upon the pace of industrial expansion.

Those limits were transcended with the widespread adoption of the spinning mule and the steam engine in a new wave of dynamic expansion which from the 1790s effectively transferred the new industry from the Midlands to Lancashire.[3] In that second era of development the growth of the industry unleashed an avalanche of productive power and detonated a demographic explosion as population multiplied in direct proportion to the increased import and consumption of raw cotton. Between 1775 and 1911 Lancashire and Cheshire together increased their population more than tenfold. Of that increase almost one-third was attributable to the combined growth of Manchester and eight of its mill towns, Ashton under Lyne, Bolton, Bury, Oldham, Rochdale, Salford, Stockport and Wigan. Such rapidity of growth made Lancashire seem like 'the America of England'[4] and Manchester like 'the Chicago of the 19th century',[5] not only a great city in itself but also 'the heart of a system of cities' comprising the domain of 'Cottonia'.[6]

During the same period the industry achieved successive peaks of influence within the British economy. By 1830 it had attained its maximum share, 51 per cent, of the export trade. In 1871 it attained its maximum share, 32 per cent, of the world's total consumption of cotton goods. During the last great mill-building boom of 1900–10 some 200 new mills were built in Lancashire and the trade press first began to publish photographs, as distinct from engravings, of the new mills.[7] It was then that the industry reached the zenith of its national importance. The MP for East Manchester was A. J. Balfour, Prime Minister from 1902 to 1905, while the General Election of 1906 produced a landslide victory for the Manchester creed of free trade. In 1913 the British cotton industry, with 39 per cent of the world's spindles and 29 per cent of its powerlooms, reached its maximum volume of production and exports. During the boom after the war of 1914–18 Manchester reached the zenith of its career as 'the hub of the universe',[8] serving an area with 104 separate local authorities and some 700 trades dependent upon the cotton industry. During the year 1920 production, exports, profits and dividends all reached their maximum value, at an inflated level of prices. The turnover of Manchester's banks accounted for 46 per cent of the total provincial bank clearings and the number of members of the Manchester Royal Exchange reached an all-time maximum of 11,539. The influence of the cotton industry extended throughout much of the economic world, although its share of the world's consumption had shrunk since 1871 to only 8 per cent. That influence was magnified by its role as the pioneer of machine production, factory organisation and a new industrial era. 'The last century has witnessed many revolutions . . . So far as our country is concerned, the greatest revolutionists have been steam, machinery and cotton.'[9] After 1920 Lancashire entered upon a prolonged depression which was largely unexpected and without any true parallel in previous industrial history, serving as a sombre precursor of the world economic depression of 1929–32. Cotton-mill companies were, however, insulated from market pressures by their loan accounts and continued to pay dividends between 1921 and 1926 whilst a few new mills were built.

## The role of small-scale enterprise

During the heyday of expansion the industry attracted new entrants during successive waves of prosperity and provided pasture for a multitude of small businesses, so that firm and mill tended to remain broadly identical. The tally of firms engaged in the cotton industry of Greater Manchester reached its peak, at 1,069, only in 1892[10] but even after this date they still remained more numerous than the member firms of any other basic manufacturing industry. During the long era of expansion before 1892 the industry had undergone several changes in organisation, passing through successive phases, characterised by the respective dominance of:

1   the spinning mill and the handloom weaver, from the 1770s;

2   the combined firm which from the 1820s added to its spinning trade weaving upon the basis of the new powerloom in a new and distinctive type of single-storeyed shed;

3   the specialised spinning and weaving firms, from the 1850s, such single-process firms becoming typical from the 1870s in expanding centres of production while combined firms remained typical of such older districts as Tameside and Glossop;

4   the informal group of firms under unified direction – businessmen broke through the limits imposed by the single mill or the single site by adding new mills, by floating new associated joint-stock companies and, above all, by organising from the 1890s informal groups of separate companies under a common chairman;

5   the formal large-scale amalgamation from the 1930s.

The growth in the size of mills was reflected in an eightfold increase in the amount of capital per operative between 1795 and 1914, before the great inflation of prices in 1919–20. The increase in the size of mill and of firm did not follow a general pattern. Some towns proved more hospitable than others to large-scale enterprise while others supplied all the facilities required by smaller employers. Big business found a congenial environment in Manchester, Ashton, Mossley, Bolton, Leigh and Wigan while small firms tended to remain typical of such towns as Stockport, Oldham, Rochdale, Bury and Heywood. From the 1870s the joint-stock company with limited liability transformed the business structure of the new metropolis of cotton spinning in Oldham but elsewhere encountered opposition to its spread, unless it assumed the guise of the private limited company. Such resistance proved to be especially marked in towns like Bolton, Farnworth, Wigan, Radcliffe, Manchester, Salford, Tameside and Glossop. Thus 'the Oldham limiteds' remained highly exceptional units of production across the full spectrum of business. The representative form of company within the industry as a whole became from 1885 the private limited company.

Only during the era of decline in the 20th century did the industry pass under the influence of a few giant combines, especially from the 1930s onward. The rationalisation of the industry's atomistic structure began in the 1880s and 1890s with the creation of informal groups of spinning companies in Rochdale, Oldham and Ashton. That trend was carried further by the three waves of formal amalgamation which took place in 1898, in 1918–20 and in 1929.[11]

## The emergence of specialised spinning and weaving areas

As separate spinning and weaving firms emerged under the powerful stimulus of the Oldham limiteds, the industry's two main processes of production became segregated into different areas of Lancashire, with spinning in the south-east and weaving in the north-east. Weaving did not, however, decline in the spinning district to the same extent that spinning did in the weaving district. Rather it continued to expand down to 1914, only two years before the powerlooms of north-east Lancashire reached their maximum number. It did, however, undergo a significant shift in location as it decreased in the major centres of production and expanded in the smaller towns where sites for sheds were cheaper. Between 1884 and 1914 six towns, including the major centres of Manchester, Rochdale, Oldham and Glossop, substantially reduced the number of their looms. That loss was more than counterbalanced by a large increase in the number of looms in the seven centres of Bolton, Radcliffe, Wigan, Farnworth, Leigh, Bury and Hyde. The process of regional specialisation began in the 1850s and lasted until the 1940s. The peak proportion of the industry's looms located in north-east Lancashire, 79 per cent, was attained in 1945 while the corresponding peak proportion of spindles in south-east Lancashire, 90 per cent, was registered in 1951. Not only did the south retain a much higher proportion of looms than the north did of spindles, it also became the main theatre of technical advance as its firms adopted the American innovations of the ring frame and the automatic loom. Those firms and districts failing to adopt the new technology suffered inevitable decline.

## The climacteric of 1926

The year 1926 proved to be a climactic one in the economic history of Lancashire. In that year what were to be the last cotton mills in Lancashire were completed, at Astley Bridge to the north of Bolton and at Royton to the north of Oldham: both the Holden (10) and the Elk (443) mills (Fig 12) were mule mills. The cotton industry had reached its maximum productive capacity, with Liverpool unloading 3,300,000 bales per annum, or one-quarter of world imports, and 575,000 Lancashire operatives employed on 57,300,000 spindles and 767,500 looms, with 80 per cent of capacity working for the export trade. Sixty-one per cent of the

Figure 12. The Elk Mill, Royton, Oldham (443). This mill was built by Shiloh Mills Ltd., which had been incorporated in 1874. It was designed by the architect Arthur Turner and commissioned by T. E. Gartside (1857–1941) as Shiloh Mill No. 3. Gartside had created the Shiloh group of eight companies and built the new mill out of accumulated reserves. The Elk Mill was the very last mule mill to be built in Lancashire: it housed 107,240 spindles, with an external cardroom and engine house. Since the 1890s many mills had come to prefer a short name comprising three letters, such as Era, Ena, Orb, Rex, Roy and Wye. Such brevity had an economic function, fulfilled when the name was inscribed upon mill skips as well as upon a water tower or a chimney.

industry's labour force were women and 61 per cent were union members, distributed among 167 unions.

In the same year, 1926, the cotton-spinning industry of Greater Manchester reached its zenith, with 51,000,000 spindles or 88 per cent of the total number in Lancashire and with 205,500 powerlooms or 27 per cent of the total in Lancashire in about 2,000 mills operated by 1,000 firms in a score of towns.[12] Manchester's bank clearings still accounted for 42 per cent of all provincial clearings. The year 1926 proved, however, to be one of severe trade depression, accentuated by a major coal dispute and by the general strike. Gross profits in the cotton industry sank to 23 per cent of their 1920–5 level.[13] As the limited companies suffered large withdrawals of their loans they made compensatory calls upon their part-paid shares to the unprecedented and unwelcome extent of £4,700,000: cotton-mill shares declined in aggregate market-value by an estimated £10,000,000 upon a total paid-up capital of £50,000,000. Most spinning companies paid their last dividends in 1926, a year which was followed by eight years (1927–34) of losses. Holden's never built the seven other mills which had been intended to raise capacity to 1,000,000 spindles. The region of Greater Manchester began to reduce its spindleage from 1927 whilst the cotton industries elsewhere in the world ceased to expand their productive capacity during the world depression of 1929–32.

## The era of decline

During the fifty years following the climacteric of 1926, what had been the world's greatest manufacturing industry was quietly but effectively dismantled. The cotton industry lost its primacy both in Britain and in the outside world, where the United States of America had been expanding its productive capacity more rapidly than the United Kingdom from as early as the 1820s. Primacy in the cotton industry of the world had passed unnoticed to the United States of America in the 1890s when it first surpassed Britain in the total volume of production: in 1929 the United States of America surpassed the United Kingdom in the number of its looms, in 1959 in the number of its spindles. Cotton textiles lost their primacy in British exports after 140 years (1803–1943). The British balance of trade in textiles became adverse for the first time since the 18th century. The United Kingdom became a net importer first of cotton manufactures from 1960, then of textiles in general from 1970 and finally of textile machinery from 1984. Then India surpassed the United States of America in spindleage in 1972 and was in turn surpassed by China in 1977. The cotton industry which had originated in India had returned, on a factory basis, to Asia which had supplied Lancashire with its two largest markets – India and China – for cotton manufactures for almost sixty years (1869–1926). In the 1960s Manchester seemed to be 'the very symbol of a city in long and unremitting decline',[14] whilst in the surrounding factory towns 'where the mills still stand they remain as the totems of the old Lancashire'.[15]

The following sections illustrate the diverse industrial history of the main spinning towns of Greater Manchester.

## Manchester and Salford, with Trafford

For two centuries Manchester has served to polarise opinion and has evoked extreme views, which have often reflected the outlook of the observer as much as any external reality. The importance of the city may indeed have been exaggerated by contemporary social observers, politicians, novelists and foreign visitors. Its industrial significance was epitomised by Mrs Gaskell, when she christened the city 'Milton' (or Milltown) in *North and South* (1854). Surprisingly no history of the cotton industry of Manchester proper has ever been written: no reference is made to the mills of Manchester in the standard gazetteer of the city's buildings.[16] Contemporary guide books to Manchester usually excluded any detailed survey of the city's industrial districts. That particular bias may have been due to the failure of factories to make any aesthetic appeal to a society accustomed to regard the Lake District as the acme of beauty. The visual impact of mills seems to have been greatest where they lay in a rural setting, were built of stone and were illuminated by night – all factors discriminating against the brick-built factories of Ancoats during daylight hours. Those mills were rarely eulogised and tended to be described as 'huge, black, inelegant, unpicturesque' and as 'mere brick boxes', most like unto prisons.[17] Only the recent work of Bailey (1985) and of Lloyd-Jones and Lewis (1988)[18] has begun to reveal the true contours of the history of Cottonopolis, city of one hundred mills and market for the products of another two thousand.[19]

The history of the cotton industry in Manchester undoubtedly remains distinctive in several respects. First, cotton mills were built there relatively late, after they had been set to work elsewhere in Lancashire in

1776–9 on riverside sites where water power was much more abundant than in Manchester itself. Even during the first phase of construction of Arkwright-type mills, during the 1780s, their number remained small. Secondly, the building of mills was powerfully influenced by the ebb and flow of business confidence and was concentrated into short and intense bursts of investment. The greatest of those booms, in 1800–2, followed on the boom in canal building during the 1790s and coincided with the Peace of Amiens between England and France, which opened the markets of Europe to Manchester spinners. During those three years the number of cotton-spinning firms in the township of Manchester doubled from fifty-one in 1799 to 111 in 1802, while their rateable value trebled.[20] Never again did the town experience such an intense mill-building boom.

Thirdly, the high price of land largely influenced both the location and the structure of mills. Thus the new steam-powered mule mills were built upon the outskirts of the established nucleus of the town, first in Ancoats from the 1790s and then in Chorlton on Medlock from the 1800s. The high capital cost of mill construction was spread over the maximum amount of productive capacity by building multi-storeyed mills surpassing the mills of Derbyshire in height and rivalling the warehouses of Liverpool.[21]

By 1798 a record height of eight storeys had been reached by A. & G. Murray's mill (358*), beside the new Rochdale Canal in a district where the factories appeared to Robert Southey 'as large as convents without their antiquity, without their beauty, without their holiness'.[22] The products of those mills tended to be high in value in order that their price might cover the high fixed costs of production. Thus the immigrant Scots established a secure niche in the spinning and doubling of fine counts of yarn, especially for export. That position they maintained by resisting protectionist clamour, by encouraging technical innovation, by patenting new inventions, by fixing prices from 1803 and ultimately by forming a combine.

The spinning mills of Manchester were therefore large, their average size sextupling between 1795 and 1820.[23] Their high profile made a profound impression upon all visitors to the city. Manchester became not only the largest but also the most highly concentrated centre of cotton spinning in the world. Sophisticated foreign observers found the phenomenon to be one without any precedent in their own experience, especially when reinforced by the strong diurnal ebb and flow of the operative population of Ancoats. Thus the Swiss engineer, Hans Caspar Escher, noted in 1814 that 'in a single street in Manchester there are more spindles than in the whole of Switzerland'.[24] The observation was correct because the mills of Murray's and McConnel's on Union Street altogether mustered 169,300 spindles or 12 per cent more than the 151,000 spindles in Escher's homeland in 1814. Those mills equalled in length the royal palace in Berlin.[25] Their size was often taken to be representative of the size of mills in the cotton industry as a whole. That conclusion was misleading but nevertheless became widely diffused especially in so far as Manchester became identified with Lancashire and fine spinning with the whole of the industry.

Fourthly, Manchester's role as the commercial capital of the cotton industry reduced the relative importance of its own manufacturing sector within the economic life of the city as a whole. Its unchallenged supremacy as the central market of the region had been a major influence in stimulating the development of manufacturing throughout the 18th century and in attracting foreign merchants from the 1780s, so opening up the markets of the world to the cotton industry. That function was reinforced by the development of its communications network, its transport services and its financial facilities, so making the city into the great centre of printing and publishing, of commercial and technical education and of trade associations. The whole district might appear in 1844 to be 'one huge town, almost one huge factory'[26] but a clear division of labour existed between the commercial functions fulfilled by Manchester and the industrial functions fulfilled by the surrounding mill towns. Within a radius of 12 miles from the Royal Exchange lay 280 cotton towns and villages, all dependent upon the one great central market as colonies were dependent upon their mother country. Those towns remained 'satellites of a central luminary, tributary cities of a great capital of industry . . . The Manchester Exchange is their sovereign mistress.'[27] The city's commercial function rather than its industrial production earned it the designation of Cottonborough in 1851, of Cottonopolis in 1854 and of Yarndale in 1872.[28]

Finally, Manchester's importance as a centre of the cotton industry began to decline after 1853. That decline may be detected in the annual statistics which are available for the number of cotton firms in Manchester for the years 1795–1820 and for the number of cotton mills for the years 1820–60.[29] The city remained the leading centre of cotton spinning for fifty years from the 1800s. As the nucleus of the whole cotton industry it harboured representatives of all of its branches and especially of the most profitable ones, including fine spinning and doubling, and the manufacture of thread, smallwares and clothing, especially waterproofs. Its highly diversified economy embraced representatives of all the ancillary trades, including the finishing industries and the engineering trades. Its most typical trade remained, however, the spinning of fine counts of yarn. McConnel's remained the world's finest spinners until the 1830s, having raised their maximum counts from 170s in 1795 to 250s in 1812. Murray's raised their maximum counts to 300s by 1828 while Houldsworth's at their Newton Street Mills (1796) raised theirs from 300s in 1828 to 460s by 1840 and to 600s by 1851. Local engineers served the spinners of Lancashire as well as those of Manchester. They developed the self-acting mule (1825–32) and introduced the combing machine from Alsace in 1852 as well as the ring-spinning frame from Massachusetts in 1872.[30] Manchester spinners introduced the private limited company into the cotton industry in 1864 and the amalgamation in 1898, creating in the Fine Cotton Spinners' and Doublers' Association what remained for thirty years the industry's most successful combine.

After the boom of 1848–53 detonated by the repeal of the Corn Laws the number of cotton mills in Manchester reached a peak at the close of 1853 when they totalled 108 or 6 per cent of the 1,683 warehouses within the city. Thereafter the number of mills began to decline under the pressure of the continuing inflation of land values as commerce competed more keenly for sites with manufacturing industry. Millowners were saddled not only with high rents but also with high rates and high gas bills because of the haziness of the atmosphere. They also found water to be in short supply. Their opportunities for recruiting cheap labour were limited by the independent spirit of the local operatives, by the preference of girls for employment of higher social standing than was offered by the mill and by their own reluctance to adopt the half-time system instituted in 1844, so reducing the influence of heredity in the recruitment of hands and cutting off a reserve of trained children.[31] The industry tended to develop increasingly in the suburbs where costs were lower and became decentralised from its base in the central township. Thus mills were established in Gorton and Newton in 1825, in Beswick in 1828, in Eccles in 1835, in Weaste in 1837, in Reddish in 1845, in Swinton in 1850, in Pendlebury in 1855 and in Patricroft in 1867.[32]

Manchester had been a great centre of handloom weaving, of loomshops and even of handloom factories, one of which was built to a height of six storeys.[33] Apparently it only began to adopt the powerloom from 1820,[34] almost a generation after Stockport, but nevertheless became by the 1830s the largest weaving centre in south Lancashire. It was, however, surpassed as a centre of cotton spinning by Bolton in the 1850s and by Oldham in the 1860s. It had become by the 1840s the metropolis of the building trades and its long-sustained building boom, as reflected in the sales of real property, reached its zenith in 1872–7 without any contribution from mill building. From 1883 both the spindles and the looms hitherto operated within the central township experienced a process of absolute decline. One old mill was even converted into model dwellings.[35] That symptom of industrial decay was invoked in order to justify the construction of the Manchester Ship Canal. Five years after the opening of the canal in 1894 the cotton industry began to expand anew in the suburbs, adding 1,000,000 spindles during three years of the Edwardian boom (1906–8). Expansion was most rapid in Eccles, Patricroft and Failsworth: the last mills of the conurbation were then established in Pendlebury, Monton (Fig 13) and Barton in 1905, in Droylsden in 1906 and in Failsworth in 1907, followed by the last mill of all, built in 1924 for W. H. Holland and Sons at Miles Platting. From the 1860s the city retained its position as the third largest centre of cotton spinning for ninety years. It was then surpassed by Leigh and Rochdale from 1952, by Preston from 1959 and by Wigan from 1961, so declining to the seventh place (see pp. 46–7). The clothing industry surpassed the cotton industry as an employer of labour first within the city itself by 1900 and then, by 1935, within the whole Manchester region of fourteen boroughs.[36]

Salford became 'Manchester's Cinderella'[37] and suffered from the submergence of its history within that of its larger neighbour. Indeed its

Figure 13. Monton Mill (836), Eccles, in 1968. The location of this mill is significant in relation to its date of construction, 1905. It was built beside a canal, seventy years after the advent of the railway age. Canalside sites long continued to be favoured for mills. Monton Mill lies beside the historic Bridgewater Canal; it was one of the last mills to be built in the Manchester conurbation.

close proximity to Manchester assimilated its function to that of a thoroughfare and made it more dependent on Manchester for services than any other town. Salford also acquired an even more negative image than that of Manchester, perhaps influenced by five local interpreters of the industrial scene in the persons of L. S. Lowry, Walter Greenwood, Shelagh Delaney, Robert Roberts and Ewan MacColl.[38] Salford was, however, noteworthy in several other respects. First, its textile tradition was based upon weaving and finishing, using the relatively pure water of the Irwell, especially in Pendleton, for bleaching. From that river it could draw much

Figure 14. Acme Mill (807), Pendlebury, in 1906. The Acme Mill was a hybrid mill of 80,000 spindles (half ring, half mule), designed by the leading mill architect P. S. (Sydney) Stott (1858–1937). It was the first spinning mill in Lancashire to use electric power to drive the machinery: thus its most distinctive feature was the absence of any factory chimney. The Acme Mill was demolished in 1984 but remains assured of an after-life longer than that of other mills. It inspired Lowry's most famous painting which embodied a distinctive view of industrial civilisation (*The Textile Manufacturer*, 1906, 233).

more power than could Manchester. Thus it acquired before 1783 in the factory of William Douglas (1746–1810) beside the Irwell at Pendleton one of the earliest water-powered mills in Lancashire, making Douglas by 1795 the proprietor of the largest firm in the Manchester district.[39] Secondly, Salford became the site of one of the earliest of showcase mills in the seven-storeyed Salford Twist Mill (849) of Phillips and Lee (1799–1802). That mill was one of the first buildings with a fireproof iron frame but does not seem to have been imitated locally until the mill-building boom of 1823–6, which doubled the number of mills in Salford to ten.

Thirdly, Salford became a notable seedbed of enterprise as well as of philanthropy.[40] Its millowners carved out remarkably profitable niches for themselves within the trade, especially the four firms established between 1833 and 1839.[41] As in Manchester, their position remained unchallenged by any joint-stock limiteds. Their ranks included E. R. Langworthy (1797–1874), who became the first cotton millionaire generated by the Manchester district.[42] The book-cloth trade carried on at the Victoria Mills, Weaste, which had been taken over from Ermen and Engels in the 1870s, created two more millionaires in William D. Winterbottom (1858–1924) and George H. Winterbottom (1861–1934). The cotton industry of Manchester proper does not seem to have generated comparable individual fortunes. That prosperity percolated downwards to the operatives, as Manchester firms competed for their labour.[43] Fourthly, the industries of Salford became almost as diversified as those of Manchester and included the finishing trades and engineering, especially the manufacture of machine tools and finishing machinery. Fifthly, Greater Salford reached the acme of its industrial development with the building in 1905 of the six-storeyed Acme Mill (807), at Pendlebury (Figs 14 and

Figure 15. Lowry's 'Pendlebury Scene' shows the Acme Mill (807), 1931. The millfolk in the foreground are typically creatures of minimal substance, in contrast to the massive mill in the background, which looms over both houses and people. It may be noted that Lowry still remains excluded from most biographical dictionaries of artists.

15), which was the first Lancashire mill to be driven solely by electric power and inspired Lowry's most famous painting 'Coming from the Mill' (1930).[44] Finally, the rate of growth of Salford's population proved to be the highest of any cotton town between 1775 and 1911, under the general stimulus afforded by Manchester and finally by the Ship Canal. The expansion of its population was greatest in Pendleton (1861–1911) and continued until 1927, or for over a decade after most other cotton towns had reached their peak level of population in 1914. Thereafter its population declined (1927–71) faster than any other cotton town, at a rate almost treble that of Oldham or Burnley.

Trafford, or Stretford as it was known until 1974, acquired the world's first industrial estate in Trafford Park, which was developed from 1896 along the southern bank of the new Ship Canal. That great waterway had been intended to rescue the cotton industry from the deep depression of 1877–9 but the new industries attracted to Trafford Park did not include cotton. The single-storeyed model mills designed by the architect Theodore Sington (1848–1926)[45] for construction beside the Ship Canal and incorporating a continuous flow system for the processing of material were never built. Only a single textile firm established itself in the park, Textilose Ltd in 1911, for the exploitation of a foreign patent of invention.

## Stockport and Tameside

(Tameside includes Ashton under Lyne, Dukinfield, Stalybridge, Hyde, Denton and Mossley)

'The glorious epic of Stockport' was originally to have been penned by George Unwin[46] but still awaits its chronicler. That story is distinctive and instructive. The primary natural advantage of the locality lay in the abundant, swift and soft waters of the Tame and Goyt, which merged into the Mersey, whose banks supplied numerous sites for mills. Perhaps its greatest acquired advantage lay in the enterprise of the first generation of cotton masters who replaced the established staple trade of silk by that of calico. Their initiative developed the putting-out industry within the surrounding countryside. They also made Stockport into a notable cradle of technical innovation. They endowed the town with the region's only wind-powered cotton mill.[47] From 1780 they transformed it into the classic seat of water-powered industry, ushering in fifty years of expansion. From 1790 they built the first of three showcase mills.[48] From 1791 they pioneered the application of steam power to their operations.[49] The swelling output of cheap machine-spun yarn created a boom in handloom weaving and ushered in the golden age of domestic textile manufacture in the surrounding countryside, as described by William Radcliffe in a much-quoted passage relating to the period 1788–1802. By 1800 population had increased to surpass that of Chester, so dethroning the county town for the first time from its historic primacy. By 1811 the town ranked second only to Manchester as a spinning centre: its manufactories rose in tiers above each other from the river bank and mustered more spindles than those of Bolton. Well might it seem to promise to develop into 'a second Manchester'.[50]

The leading firm was that of Peter Marsland who had become the largest spinner in the whole region, with 87,172 spindles in 1811 or more than either McConnel and Kennedy or Murray's. Stockport also had an important finishing industry [51] and some firms integrated the full range of their operations from carding and spinning to finishing. Generally, however, firms remained small and numerous, like those of Oldham and Rochdale, supported by the survival of jenny spinning and by the development of a substantial doubling trade. Above all, Stockport pioneered from 1803 the development of the steam loom, accomplished for power weaving what Arkwright had done for machine spinning and became the first great centre of powerloom weaving, as Cromford had been of machine spinning.[52] Local manufacturers undertook the weaving of fine and fancy cloth, especially muslin, as well as of India shirtings. They survived an outbreak of Luddite loom breaking in 1812, and the first recorded strike by powerloom weavers in 1818. They also expanded their activity into the townships to the north, especially from the 1830s.

The first era of the town's expansion came to an end in the 1830s. Relations between masters and men deteriorated with the failure of strikes in 1802, 1829 and 1844 and despite the rise in wages to the highest level in the industry.[53] The family firms suffered from a high turnover after the second generation. 'The genealogy of Stockport mills would yield as

Figure 16. Broadstone Mill No. 2 (871), Reddish, Stockport. The mill was constructed in 1907 and was the largest spinning mill completed in the industry to that date. Its 138,000 spindles, added to the 124,500 of Mill No. 1, raised the company's total capacity to 262,500 spindles. In 1908 it was surpassed in size by the Times Mill No. 2 at Middleton.

good a lesson as any, perhaps, of the hereditary visitation of sin.'[54] The town enjoyed its peak decade of population growth for the whole of the 19th century during 1831–41 but its population remained virtually stable between 1841 and 1871. The inhabitants suffered severely during the depression of 1837–41 and again during the Cotton Famine.[55]

The revival of 1880–1920 was initiated by private employers forming joint-stock limiteds from 1881 (the Vernon Cotton Spinning Co) and ring-spinning companies from 1891.[56] The town never adopted the limited company with the same enthusiasm as Oldham but did build two of the industry's largest mills, for mule spinning in 1907 (Broadstone Mill No. 2 (871) (Fig 16), with 138,000 spindles, raising total capacity to 262,504 spindles) and for ring spinning in 1906–9 (Stockport Ring Mill No. 2 (921), with 72,000 spindles).[57] Private employers raised the standing of Stockport as a spinning centre from the rank of seventh in 1884–1900 to that of sixth in 1914–54 (see pp. 46–7). Its doubling mills pioneered the use of the gas engine[58] whilst a disastrous fire in 1901 at the Kingston Mill (900) stimulated the wider adoption of the sprinkler system.[59] Stockport reached the absolute peak of its spinning capacity in 1920. Its weaving industry may have reached maximum capacity, in terms of looms installed, by 1853, but it nevertheless led the whole region in the 1930s in the adoption of the more-looms system, so raising productivity.[60] Thanks to the diversification of its economy it remained 'a city of balance, proportion and harmony'[61] and enjoyed a positive expansion in population during the 20th century, in sharp contrast to the cotton towns of Lancashire.

The group of 'five municipal boroughs strung in gloom along the banks of the Tame', in the phrase of W. H. Barker, and conjoined in 1974 as Tameside, were distinctive in two respects. First, they included the region's original cradle of Dissent from the Anglican Church in Dukinfield and became a nursery of prosperous cousinhoods of Dissenting millowners. Secondly, they supplied a notable example of town planning, undertaken by the Earl of Stamford in Ashton under Lyne, the natural metropolis of the district.[62] The presence of water power had been the main factor attracting mills to the district and had enabled relatively unknown Stalybridge to acquire in 1776 one of the earliest mills in Lancashire.[63] Tameside remained, with Rochdale and Rossendale, the last stronghold in the region of the waterwheel and it became the headquarters of the Ashton under Lyne Millowners' and Mill-Occupiers' Water Works Company (1846–1904), with all of its capital contributed by local cotton spinners and manufacturers. The introduction of the steam engine and the mule in the 1790s and of the steam loom from 1806 accelerated the pace of industrial expansion and gave rise to a remarkable growth of population in the 1820s, especially in Stalybridge and Hyde. The area then became a cradle of integrated firms which carried on both spinning and weaving by power and developed a profitable trade in the manufacture of high-quality printing cloths. The whole district became 'the headquarters of the powerloom'[64] after its introduction by the Ashtons of Hyde in 1806. By 1845 Hyde mustered more powerlooms than either Ashton or Stalybridge.

The expansion of Mossley's capacity was remarkable in its rapidity and was achieved, especially from the 1830s, by a relatively small number of specialised spinning firms. There John Mayall (1804–76) built Britannia Mills (956) in 1849–50,[65] and established what remained for thirty-four years (1857–91) the largest cotton-spinning firm in the world, operating 444,000 spindles at its peak in 1893–6. Outside Mossley integrated firms remained more typical of Tameside than were specialised spinners or weavers. Such firms grew to substantial size and remained under the control of the same families for generations, providing continuity in employment similar to that enjoyed in Bolton and Bury. The most notable of those firms was Ashton Bros who made a large portion of their workers into freeholders.[66] In Hyde married women did not work in the mill because local wages were so high and there was no tradition of strikes such as existed in Ashton and Stalybridge, diffusing the blessings of peace as well as prosperity.

Tameside became the worst afflicted district in all Lancashire and Cheshire during the Cotton Famine and the only one to suffer a net loss of population by migration during the decade 1861–71.[67] In Stalybridge 'the finest . . . cotton mill in England', the square-built Clarence Mill (968), was constructed in 1862–4 (Fig 17), in part as a relief measure.[68] The Cotton Famine seems to have stimulated some diversification of industry through the development of hatting in Hyde and Denton as well as in Stockport. The population of Ashton, Stalybridge and Dukinfield never-theless increased more slowly during the fifty years 1861–1911 than that of the rest of Lancashire and Cheshire. Local integrated firms faced a challenge upon two fronts. In weaving they experienced competition from the towns of north-east Lancashire, which proved especially keen during the strikes of 1883 and 1887: the centre of gravity of the weaving trade shifted northwards and Tameside's looms reached their all-time maximum number in 1883. In the spinning trade the joint-stock company made

Figure 17. The Clarence Mill (968), Stalybridge. This square type of mill, with an increase in width beyond that customary, dates back at least to 1819, when Charles Grant built 'the Square Mill' at Ramsbottom, but was very rarely imitated. The average ratio of length to width was typically 3:1 in the Arkwright type of mill, 1.8:1 in the Fairbairn type of mill of the 1830s and 2:1 in the mill of the Edwardian era.

Figure 18. The Texas Mill, Ashton under Lyne. This rare view of a mill in the process of erection shows the construction of the iron and steel framework within the four-storeyed mill. Designed by P. S. Stott, the Texas Mill was the last of seven mills built by an Ashton syndicate. With four other mills it became part of Atlas Mills Ltd in 1920, was transferred to the Lancashire Cotton Corporation in 1931 and destroyed by fire in 1971 (*The Engineer*, 28 December 1906, 652).

an appearance in Ashton from 1874 (with the Whitelands Twist Co) and in Stalybridge from 1881 (with the Stalybridge Cotton Mill Co). Ashton became the leading centre of the joint-stock movement in Tameside and introduced the spinning of Oldham counts from 1875. A syndicate of local businessmen built seven mule mills, usually comprising four storeys, between 1891 and 1905 (Fig 18).[69] Their enterprise staved off the threat of industrial decline and introduced into Ashton the spinning of Bolton counts from Egyptian cotton in 1892. The borough rose in rank from the eighth largest spinning town in 1884 to the rank of sixth in 1903 (see pp. 46–7).

Mossley was not rejuvenated by the limited company. In 1882 its century of expansion came to an end and it began to decline in population from 1891. Its last mill was built for Wrigley's in 1900 and no more were added during the Edwardian boom. Mossley's stagnation seemed to presage the fate of its neighbours. Successive peaks of spindleage were

Figure 19. Bayley Field Mill (952), Hyde. This mill was claimed to be one of the first to use a steel framework for the floors. A strong structure was required because the mill was built above a colliery, which was filled in by the owners, Ashton Bros, when the mill was built in 1890.

reached in Ashton and Mossley in 1907, in Stalybridge and Denton in 1912 and in Hyde as well as in Dukinfield in 1916. Thereafter the spinning capacity of Tameside, as measured by its spindleage, declined more rapidly than that of any other district in Lancashire. Ashton reverted to its rank as the eighth largest spinning town in 1913–29, declining further to the position of tenth in 1939–54 (see pp. 46–7). Between 1861 and 1911 Stalybridge's rate of population growth remained the very lowest of twenty mill towns and one-tenth of the rate in the rest of Tameside: it was surpassed in population by Hyde during the 1880s.

Hyde had been threatened in its prosperity by the closure in 1885 of the Hibbert Mills.[70] Its remarkable renaissance from 1903 was inspired by the firm of Ashton Bros.[71] That firm pioneered the use of steel in the construction in 1890 of Bayley Field Mill (952) (Fig 19).[72] It also pioneered the introduction into the British cotton industry of the highly productive Northrop automatic loom from 1904.[73] That innovation in weaving was a timely response to the competition of Burnley and helped to raise the number of looms in Hyde by almost a half (1904–21). Hyde had never been a major spinning centre, but it became a major weaving centre, rising in rank from the twelfth largest in south Lancashire in 1904 to the tenth in 1917 and to the fourth in 1934–63. The town simultaneously diversified its occupations and, unlike the rest of Tameside, experienced a rapid growth in its population (1861–1911), a growth which continued throughout the 20th century. Hyde also adopted the private limited company more extensively than any other cotton town, reflecting the creative role played by the family firms of the locality.

## Bolton, Farnworth and Leigh, with Wigan

During the era of the industry's maturity the spinning trade was dominated by two towns. Bolton and Oldham acquired their first mills in 1776 and 1777 respectively but they never assumed the high profile of Manchester. They became the main centres of cotton spinning only in the mid 19th century, reaching their industrial zenith together in the year 1926. Both towns lay close to the industry's central market and both enjoyed a high degree of the humidity essential to cotton spinning. Both became major centres of mule spinning, with a lower than average proportion of ring spindles. Both expanded in population faster between 1775 and 1911 than any other cotton town apart from Salford.

Bolton was an old market town, unlike Oldham. It had an old textile tradition and carried on a fine trade in both spinning and weaving. It became the seat of a high-quality fustian industry and the source of the largest contingent of 'country manufacturers' attending the Manchester market in the 18th century. Bolton was the home of Crompton, the inventor in 1779 of the most important of all 'the Great Inventions', the mule designed for fine spinning: it remained the main centre of the hand mule as well as of the handloom. Its economy was well balanced and diversified, with a bleaching trade and a machine-making industry. Bolton surpassed Stockport in productive capacity during the 1820s and

Manchester during the 1850s, when a mill-building boom transformed the town briefly into the leading spinning centre of Lancashire. In that decade it secured full access to a new source of supply of raw material in long-stapled Egyptian cotton, a staple fibre which proved invaluable when the American Civil War cut off the supply of cotton from the Southern States of the United States of America. The main trade of the district remained the spinning of medium counts (i.e. counts of 60s, or Bolton counts) from long-stapled cotton for the quality trades, greatly enhancing the value of its raw material and producing quality where Oldham produced quantity. In total population Bolton may have been surpassed by Oldham during the decades 1861–81 but its population of cotton operatives always remained larger than that of Oldham because its cotton industry was labour-intensive in spinning, in weaving and in finishing. Its spinning trade adopted self-actors in place of hand mules in the 1860s and 1870s but its mules remained typically shorter than those

Figure 20. Irwell Bank Mills in 1907 at Stoneclough, near Farnworth, Bolton. The Irwell Bank Spinning Company Ltd was formed in 1891 as a contractors' company, i.e. a company promoted by tradesmen with a direct material interest in building, equipping and supplying a new mill. Such companies had a compelling interest in increasing the size of a mill to a maximum. The new company enjoyed powerful support from the machine makers J. H. Hetherington of Manchester but aroused the hostility of Bolton spinners. It took over an existing mill at Prestolee, rebuilt it and transformed it by 1894 into the largest spinning mill in the world, equipped with the largest of steam engines, one of 2,000 horsepower. Out of its profits the company was able to build two more giant mills, in 1903 and 1907. The illustration shows Mill No. 3 in the left foreground with the windows of the upper four storeys still unglazed. Mill No. 1 is in the background on the right, with Mill No. 2 adjoining Mill No. 3.

Figure 21. Beehive Mill No. 2, Great Lever, Bolton. The Beehive Spinning Company Ltd was registered in 1894, the only mill-building company to be formed in the industry during a year of depression. Originally the company planned to build three identical mills, each with 118,000 spindles. In the event it built only two mills, the first in 1895 with 130,000 spindles and the second in 1902 with 131,000 spindles. The photograph shows Mill No. 2 with its six storeys, stair tower and engine house. Such illustrations were used as advertisements by both machine makers and architects (*The Textile Mercury*, 1904, 65).

of Oldham. Those mules were operated at slower speeds and required closer supervision so that Bolton spinners employed more assistants (or piecers) than their counterparts in Oldham.[74]

The town, christened Spindleton in 1892, Northtown in 1938 and Worktown and Throstleton in 1943,[75] remained the great citadel of private enterprise in sharp contrast to the joint-stock stronghold of Oldham. Its family firms furnished the aristocracy of the spinning trade and the industrial elite of Lancashire. As employers they maintained harmonious relations with their operatives and concluded in 1853 the first joint piece-rate list in the cotton trade: that list equalised labour costs between mills of different efficiency and so preserved firms from excessive competition. Bolton's employers built more first-class mills than their peers in any other mill town: they introduced such innovations as the rope drive in 1875[76] and the sprinkler system in 1885. Only one local notable seems to have left an estate above £1,000,000 – John P. Thomasson (1841–1904), who had inherited the mills established *c.*1814 at Mill Hill (101). The greatest achievement of Bolton's cotton magnates was to build up the largest firms within the industry and so to establish the pattern emulated by later joint-stock companies. Thus between 1862 and 1888 Musgrave's had installed 350,000 spindles in their six Atlas mills (12–17, see Inventory), while Crosses and Winkworth, based at Gilnow Mill (71*), had installed 325,000 spindles between 1864 and 1887. In 1892–5 the Irwell Bank Spinning Co built what was then the largest mill in all Lancashire at Stoneclough, Kearsley, with 132,408 spindles: in 1903 and 1907 the company added two more giant mills and raised its total capacity to 335,752 spindles (Fig 20).[77] The Swan Lane Spinning Co (138*, 139) massed 330,000 spindles in the three mills built in 1902, 1905 and 1914: it claimed that the 210,000 spindles in two of the three mills were sited under a common roof and therefore constituted the largest mill in the world.[78] Such immense structures exerted a powerful influence upon both their workfolk and outside observers (Fig 21). Their sheer size impressed Lowry as he took his regular Saturday evening walks through Kearsley and Farnworth to Bolton from Pendlebury, where he lived for forty years (1909–48). The prosperity of the local operatives was reflected in the purchase in 1886 of the massive Spinners' Hall (Fig 22) and in the acquisition of one of the highest proportions of home owners in the country.[79] Their indomitable spirit, even in hard times, was vividly portrayed in a popular film of 1934 (Fig 23).[80]

Bolton remained a great centre of fine weaving as well as of medium fine spinning, unlike Oldham. It preserved into the 1890s one of the last surviving groups of handloom weavers in the county. As it expanded its weaving industry on the basis of the powerloom it rose in status from the fifth weaving town in south Lancashire in 1884–90 to the fourth in 1891, when it first surpassed Oldham in the number of its looms. It became the centre of an extensive weaving belt reaching from Wigan and Leigh across the county to Rochdale, Bury and Radcliffe. Bolton surpassed both Rochdale and Bury in the number of their looms from 1907 and then surpassed Manchester itself in 1914, to become the premier weaving town

Figure 22. Spinners' Hall, St. George's Road, Bolton. The hall was built in 1880 for the Junior Reform Club by the borough's leading architect, J. J. Bradshaw (1837–1912). It was bought at a bargain price in 1886 by the Bolton Operative Cotton Spinners' Association, which was the wealthiest society of its kind in the country. The association used the building as their headquarters and permitted four other unions to share its facilities. An enlargement completed in 1912 included three separate assembly halls and endowed the association with more prestigious offices than the local headquarters of either political party (*Bolton Evening News*, 25 July 1973).

Figure 23. Bolton Union Mill No. 2, built in 1885. The Bolton Union Spinning Co Ltd was registered in 1874, with strong support from local machine makers Dobson and Barlow, as the town's first joint-stock limited company. It built a mill of 50,000 spindles on the Oldham model, survived eight years of depression and built Mill No. 2 in 1885, trebling its spindleage to 145,000 and adding a third mill in 1902 for 40,000 spindles. It was renamed in 1920 the Denvale Spinning Company, was taken over by the Lancashire Cotton Corporation in 1929 and was used, according to Leslie Halliwell, in the 1934 film *Sing As We Go.*

of south Lancashire. It continued to expand its loomage until 1922 while its satellite town of Leigh increased the number of its looms until 1927. Bolton ranked as the ninth weaving town in all Lancashire (1891–1939) and even surpassed Darwen in 1941 and Accrington in 1942 to assume the sixth rank in the years 1942–51.

Bolton extended its influence over the second largest network of manufacturing villages in Lancashire after Manchester itself, especially as the steam engine was adopted in the flat Lancashire plain where water power was unavailable. Amongst the newest of those satellites were Farnworth and Leigh. Farnworth enjoyed a century of unbroken expansion from 1827 to 1931, including a great mill-building boom in the 1860s. A meteoric ascent raised it in status from the nineteenth spinning town in 1884 to the ninth in 1909–29 and to the seventh in 1945–54 (see pp. 46–7). Leigh acquired a similar medium fine trade and enjoyed a similar rapid rise in standing, especially after the opening in 1864 of the Eccles–Tyldesley–Wigan Railway. It rose from the position of ninth spinning town in 1884 to that of fifth in 1914–34. Its specialised spinning firms became by the 1880s larger in average size than those of Bolton, Manchester, Ashton or Oldham, with an average spindleage of 76,000 in 1884, of 138,700 in 1914 and of 165,100 in 1928. Those firms were largely created upon a joint-stock basis, because Leigh was a late developer. There the Howe Bridge Cotton Spinning Co was registered in 1868 and built four mills at Atherton (1082) in 1870–1900. It raised its spindles to 250,000 by 1891, so becoming the fourth largest cotton-spinning firm in

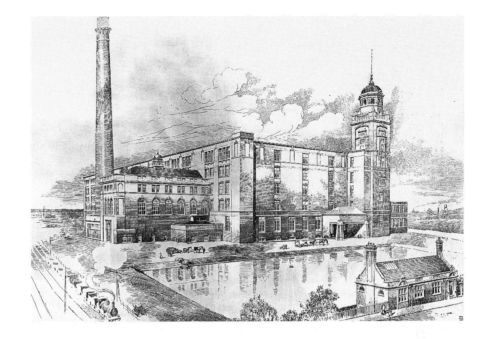

Figure 24. The Laburnum Mill at Atherton, Leigh, in 1905. This mill represents the perfected form of the Lancashire cotton mill, with its six storeys in the centre, a separate cardroom at the front and a massive engine house supplying power via a rope race. In the foreground is the mill lodge, or reservoir. The mule rooms housed ninety-six mules with an aggregate of 118,800 spindles (*The Textile Mercury*, 1905, 333).

Lancashire, after those of Mayall, Musgrave and Crosses and Winkworth: by 1922 it had almost trebled its capacity, to 700,000 spindles. Atherton also acquired the Laburnum Cotton Spinning Co in 1905 (Fig 24). That company increased its spindles from 118,800 in 1905–13 to 238,464 in 1914–18, after adding a new mill for 130,000 spindles, and grew further to 343,944 in 1920,[81] so ranking as the sixth largest cotton-spinning firm.

Leigh furnished the cotton industry with its final frontier for expansion, increasing its looms faster than any other town in south Lancashire and extending its capacities in weaving until 1927 and in spinning until 1936 (see pp. 46–7). There were built in 1902–24 the region's last large cohort of cotton mills, all containing mules and averaging 100,000 spindles each.[82] In their elegance those mills embodied the final culmination of the regional mill-building tradition. There was established in 1929 the seat of a new combine, the Combined Egyptian Mills formed by sixteen companies with thirty-four mills, including the Howe Bridge and Laburnum Spinning Companies as well as the new all-electric Holden Mill (10) at Astley Bridge. That combine mustered 3,200,000 spindles and ranked as the second largest cotton-spinning firm in the world: it was the first amalgamation to locate its headquarters outside Manchester, siting its head offices at the Howe Bridge Mills (1082), but did not achieve financial success. Farnworth reached its peak capacity in 1920 while Bolton attained its own apogee in 1923–6, when Bolton Wanderers twice won the FA Cup and the district's spindles reached 7,800,000, or 13.5 per cent of the total in Lancashire. During the subsequent era of decline Bolton was cushioned by its high-quality trade and increased its share of the industry's spindles from 12 per cent in 1914 to 21 per cent in 1960.

Like Leigh, Wigan lay upon the geographical margin of the industry but emphatically not upon its economic margin. From an early date it had

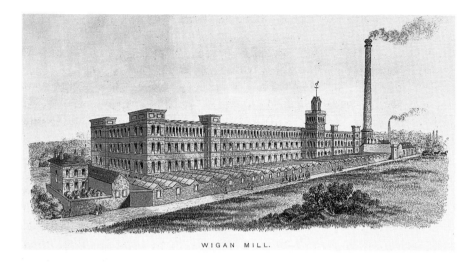

WIGAN MILL.

Figure 25. Ever since its construction Gidlow Works (1078) has remained one of the most notable buildings in Wigan; in 1984 it became the centre of a conservation area. The interior design was essentially functional: unusually, the raw cotton was received on the top storey, passed downwards by gravity flow through successive processes and was finally woven into Dacca-brand calico in the single-storeyed sheds in the foreground (Leigh 1873, 196–7).

Figure 26. Gidlow Works (1078). This view of one corner of the mill explains why the Earl of Derby in 1865 praised it as 'a pleasure to the eye to rest on, so well has architectural effect been studied in its construction'. The architect, George Woodhouse (1829–83) of Bolton, was a leading mill architect of his time. He made deliberate use of white and blue Staffordshire brick in order to relieve the monotony created by the use of ordinary red fired brick. The mill remains a permanent memorial to John Rylands and embodies a triumph for aesthetic over utilitarian considerations: as such it may be compared with the John Rylands Library in Manchester. It was, however, one of the most expensive mills ever built: costs were raised by the use throughout of fireproof modes of construction and by the need to insert massive iron reinforcing ties, three of which are clearly visible on the tower in the centre.

developed the twin industries of coal and cotton, becoming from 1789 the main centre of coal production in Lancashire and electing in 1802 the county's first cotton MP in the person of John Hodson (1758–1828). Its employers developed the putting-out trade throughout the surrounding area. In 1811 it still employed a high proportion of jennies in a trade which spun coarse counts and wove stout coarse cloths, including 'wigans': Wigan remained the only cotton town to bestow its name upon an all-cotton fabric.[83] Perhaps its collieries helped to entrench the negative image of the town,[84] even after it had become a major rail junction in the

1830s. There coal, water and, above all, labour were cheaper than elsewhere in the county: low wages were a product of a low cost of living, low productivity, lack of union organisation and the strength of the masters' association. The tradition of family ownership remained strong. The firm of Rylands and Sons (1819–1989) had been first established in St Helens but had moved to Wigan in 1820. That firm built their model three-storeyed Gidlow Works (1078) in 1863–5 and then became the leading firm in the cotton trade (Figs 25 and 26).[85]

Wigan used the joint-stock company in order to introduce the new technique of ring spinning through the May Mill of 1887. A private firm, Ffarington, Eckersley & Co Ltd nevertheless became for three decades the largest ring spinners in Britain from 1888, with 160,000 spindles at their Western Mills (1108), and was renamed Eckersleys Ltd in 1901. Wigan acquired a higher proportion of ring spindles than any other spinning town and proved that the key to survival lay in the adoption of the latest technology, reducing its spindles after 1918 more slowly than any other town. Its employers could adopt such a strategy only because the town had the weakest trade unions in all Lancashire and could employ cheap female labour: its mule spinners were exceptional in the 1880s in that half were reported to comprise ununionised women.[86] Wigan built fewer mills than other towns and reached its peak capacity in loomage in 1915, three years before its peak spindleage. It had, however, increased its looms twice as fast as its spindles between 1884 and 1914 and rose in status from the ninth weaving centre of south Lancashire in 1917 to the sixth in 1963 as its firms adopted the automatic loom. From the 1920s it rose in status from the rank of the fourteenth largest spinning town in 1919 to that of eleventh in 1934–54 and to that of fifth in 1963, in a notable triumph for modern textile technology (see pp. 46–7).

## Oldham and Middleton

Oldham became not only the main centre of cotton spinning in Lancashire but also the leading mill town of the world. It played only a minor role during the classic period of the Industrial Revolution (1780–1850), although it led all other cotton towns in the rate of its population growth between 1775 and 1821 when it became a great centre of handloom weaving. By the 1920s Oldham had built three times as many mills as Bolton but in the service of a fundamentally different industry. Oldham remained a centre of the coarse-spinning trade, consuming American cotton, spinning coarse counts of 32s (Oldham counts) and producing cheap yarn in swelling volume. Its employers were typically small masters and often shared mills through the old-established system of renting 'space and turning': they generated no millionaires. Its operatives became noted for their productivity and earned by 1841 the highest gross pay in Lancashire: they benefited from the excellent facilities for technical education, which became more extensive than those in Bolton and were crowned by the growth of mutual technical classes, organised by the operatives themselves. Their purchases from the local co-operative stores surpassed from 1872 the retail sales of the Rochdale Pioneers. The highest paid of all were the mechanics employed by Platt Bros, who exceeded Dobson and Barlow of Bolton in capacity from the 1840s and so became the largest machine makers in Lancashire.

During the crisis of the Cotton Famine, Oldham successfully adapted its mules under the guidance of Platt's in order to spin Surat yarn in place of American. In that decade the borough surpassed both Manchester and Bolton in spinning capacity to become the metropolis of cotton spinning and mill building: with Bolton it then established a diarchy within the industry which endured for another century (see pp. 46–7). Its cost-cutting ancillary industries expanded to include the cotton-waste trade, the trade in second-hand machinery and the publication of textile directories. Its contributions to the technique of mill building began with the construction from 1860 of the Sun Mill (553) (Fig 27) and Melbourne Mills, which were 30 metres wide and double the width of the new model mills of the 1830s.[87] Those contributions were notably enhanced in the 1870s when Oldham became the main centre of the formation of joint-stock companies in the spinning trade. As 'Diviborough' (1877) or as 'Shareopolis' (1880),[88] the town acquired its own share market which enjoyed from 1874 a century of independent existence. Seventy new Oldham limiteds, established in 1873–5 by local investors with the help of loans, built thirty-seven new mills and took over thirty-three existing firms. Oldham added 2,200,000 spindles in 1870–7, with more capacity created by mill-building companies than in any other town, and so enhanced the competition faced by older family firms. In 1870 the firm of Samuel Radcliffe had been the country's largest consumer of cotton, at their seven mills sited in Oldham and in Rochdale. By 1875, however, the Sun Mill (553), pioneer of the limiteds, had become the largest firm in the district, with 142,000 spindles (Fig 28). The average size of the new mills rose dramatically from 50,000 spindles in the 1870s to 75,000 in the 1880s and to 100,000 in the 1900s. The Lion Mill (487) was built in 1889 at Royton with a record number of 107,472 spindles[89] and then the Pearl Mill at Glodwick in 1890 with 116,352. The width of new mills increased by one-fifth from 38 metres in the Abbey Mill (391) in 1875, to 39 metres in the Lion Mill (487) in 1890, and to 45 metres in the Durban Mill (440) in 1905, or to fivefold the width of the original Arkwright-type mill. Oldham architects acquired Manchester offices and became the main builders of factories throughout the region.[90] As the most efficient centre of yarn spinning in the world, Oldham helped to create the new geographical division of labour in Lancashire, with spinning centred in the south and weaving in the north. The Oldham spinning list of 1875 regulated the payment of wages and, unlike the Bolton list, penalised employers who retained short and slow mules instead of installing longer, faster and more productive machines. Oldham specialised in spinning to a higher degree than other towns. Its consumption of cotton increased from one-sixth of the total used by British mills in 1868 to one-third in 1877: it trebled its share of the industry's spindleage in twenty years (1866–86) and allowed its looms weaving velveteens to decline from the peak number reached in

Figure 28 (opposite). The directors of the Sun Mill (553), Chadderton, Oldham. The Sun Mill was built by a company which was established in 1858 by members of the Oldham Industrial Co-operative Society and which was financed as well as managed by working men. Here, fourteen proud directors and officers of the company are shown with a model of their mill which was displayed at the international exhibition of 1862 in London.

Figure 27. The Sun Mill (553), Chadderton, Oldham. This mill was designed by a local architect, J. Howard, and established new standards of construction. It was built (1860–2) to house 60,000 spindles, or more than threefold the average in local mills. Unlike the Gidlow Mill at Wigan, the Sun Mill established a pattern for imitation. It became a pioneer of the Oldham limiteds, which were established during the joint-stock boom of 1873–5. The Sun Mill increased its spindleage to 142,000 in 1875 and so became the largest mill in the Oldham district. It also provided the subject for one of the earliest of business histories, which was written in 1877 by the apostle of co-operation, William Marcroft (1822–94). The mill was destroyed by fire in 1985.

Figure 29. The Heron Mill (469) at Hollinwood, Oldham. A rare photograph of a mill under construction. The Heron Mill was built in 1905 and equipped with 104,400 mule spindles. The chimney to the rear bears the distinctive double roundel at the summit, which was a trademark of the architect P. S. Stott. The mill was acquired by the Lancashire Cotton Corporation in 1937 and became the northern headquarters for Courtaulds in the 1960s, undergoing an extension in 1977 (*The Magazine of Commerce*, February 1906, 103).

1886. Oldham became the leading mill town of the world with 12.4 per cent of the world's spindles at its zenith in 1890. It trebled its share of Lancashire's spindles from 9 per cent in 1866 to 30 per cent in 1916: its operative spinners in 1916–19 represented 42 per cent of the total membership of the Spinners' Amalgamation.

That ascent in status was achieved during the two great booms of 1873–5 and 1904–8 (Fig 29), the second of which added forty-two mills and 4,000,000 spindles to local capacity. Those spindles were predominantly mule spindles, manufactured by Platts. Oldham had indeed constructed the first purpose-built ring mill in Lancashire in the Palm Mill (514) in 1884 and had also built the largest ring mill in the world in the Nile Mill (507*). That mill was designed in 1898 to hold 90,000 spindles but began operations in 1900 with 53,000 spindles, rising to 74,200 in 1902, to 94,000 in 1907 and to 104,000 in 1915, after three extensions made in 1905, 1912 and 1914.[91]

Oldham businessmen also undertook from 1890 to rationalise the spinning industry on the Rochdale model by forming groups of mill companies under a common chairman. The most notable of those groups was that formed by the sharebroker John Bunting (1839–1923)[92] who by 1916 controlled from his terraced house at No. 110 Union Street some twenty mills. Those mills included two of the five largest spinning firms and mustered 1,800,000 spindles, or 8 per cent of the total in the Oldham, Rochdale and Middleton districts. Bunting had become a company promoter from 1889, a mill builder from 1898, and a 'company doctor' from 1911. The first mills he built in Oldham itself were the Bell Mill (409), in 1904, and the Iris Mill (474) (Fig 30), which was the first ring mill in his group and was built in the record time of four months (13 August–12 December 1907).[93] In 1906 he had planned to build Lancashire's largest mill in the Mammoth Mill of 250,000 spindles at Hathershaw behind the Bell Mill (409)[94] but he seems to have decided that Middleton rather than Oldham offered a more promising site. His distinctive financial technique was to employ a very high ratio of loan capital to ordinary (or equity)

Figure 30. Iris Mill (474), Oldham. A ring-spinning mill designed by Potts, Son and Hennings, the Iris Mill was one of the earliest purpose-built mills in the Bunting group. It was built in the record time of four months at a period when twelve months was regarded as speedy for the building of a mill. Such a record was possible because ring mills were smaller and more compact than mule mills. The Iris Mill housed 62,568 ring spindles in 1907 and proved a highly profitable member of the group, paying an average annual dividend of 86 per cent (1912–20).

capital, so enabling his mills to pay high dividends coupled with a low fixed interest to the loan holders. From 1912 all his mills regularly paid higher than average dividends because of their high proportion of loan capital. Thus the Bell Mill (409) paid an average annual dividend of 81 per cent for the ten years from 1910–11 to 1919–20 while the Iris Mill (474) paid on average 86 per cent for the eight years 1912–20.[95]

Oldham and Bolton reached their climacteric together in the year 1926. Between 1866 and 1886 they had together installed 96 per cent of the industry's net increment in spindles made during those twenty years. Their joint share of spinning capacity had doubled, from 17.5 per cent in 1866 (including 9 per cent in Oldham) to 36 per cent in 1886 (including 25 per cent in Oldham). Together the two great mill towns continued to expand their capacity after the other spinning towns reached their zenith at the close of 1911, so in effect expanding at the expense of the other centres. At the close of 1926 both towns reached their maximum capacity, with 7,800,000 spindles in Bolton and 17,700,000 in Oldham (see pp. 46–7). Together they had added 81 per cent of the industry's increment in spindleage since 1866 and together they controlled, in 1926, 44 per cent of its capacity.

Since the collapse of the firm of Radcliffe in 1892 Oldham's firms had never ranked amongst the largest business units in the industry as a whole. However in 1925 Lees and Wrigley, which had been founded at Greenbank Mills in 1816 and had been the largest local spinners since 1914, increased their spindles from 180,000 to 300,000 and so entered the ranks of the top ten spinning firms of Lancashire. Lees and Wrigley built their fifth mill in 1927–8 but never fully equipped it or brought it into operation.[96] After 1926 the history of Oldham and Bolton diverged as the relative position of Bolton improved progressively. The increase in their joint share of capacity to 48 per cent in 1962 reflected a significant shift in favour of Bolton, with 20 per cent of the total compared to Oldham's 28 per cent. The world's largest combine, the Lancashire

Figure 31. The Don Mill (636), Middleton. Middleton was one of the last townships to develop the staple trade of the county, symbolically building its Albany Mill (1883–1975) on the site of the original Middleton Hall. The Don Mill was the town's first modern joint-stock mill: it was built in 1899–1900 and began production in 1901 with 80,000 mule spindles (*Engineering*, 11 January 1907, 50).

Cotton Corporation, was formed in 1929 and included amongst its 109 constituent mills a limited contingent from Oldham, centre of the American section of the spinning trade, which numbered only twenty-seven mills and represented 12.7 per cent of Oldham's spindles and 12.5 per cent of the capacity of the new corporation. Thereafter the decline of Oldham proved to be rapid and irreversible, although it still remained until 1964 the largest single centre of cotton spinning.

During its heyday Oldham had extended its stimulating influence outwards into Royton, into Shaw and into Failsworth, which the local author Ben Brierley had christened Irkdale in 1881. Middleton may also be

Figure 32. The Times Mill (768), Middleton. Mill No. 1 to the left was built in 1875–9 as Dane Mill No. 4 of the Middleton and Tonge Cotton Mill Co Ltd (1860–1907). It was taken over in 1898 by John Bunting as the mortgagee. Bunting then went on to build the largest spinning mill in the world, the Times Mill No. 2, shown on the right of the picture. He placed with Platt Bros, machine makers of Oldham, on 10 October 1907, the largest single individual order ever received by that great firm, one for 128 mules with 174,496 spindles in the aggregate. The mill was built in 1908 and housed 160,000 spindles where Arkwright-type mills had held 1,000. The Times Mill No. 2 deserves the accolade of the largest single-unit mill ever built to a greater degree than such double mills as the Swan Lane Mills in Bolton or the Dunlop Mills in Rochdale. Together the two Times Mills employed 263,112 mule spindles on American cotton. The firm ranked from 1908 as one of the giants of the Lancashire cotton industry as well as the pride of the Bunting group: it proved to be the most financially successful firm in the industry. The mills were demolished in 1987.

ranked with Oldham as it was by both the local employers' and operatives' associations. Its history was, however, notably different. Middleton developed even later than Oldham and was converted, like Leigh, from handloom weaving to spinning as well as from silk to cotton, a tradition maintained, however, in the spinning of finer counts than its neighbours. Between 1883 and 1916 it expanded its capacity faster than any other town save for Farnworth and Radcliffe. In 1886 it lost its last combined spinning and weaving firm and became thereafter the most highly specialised of all cotton towns: its firms were either specialised spinners or specialised weavers. Only in 1899 did it participate in the mill-building boom, with the construction of the Don Mill (636) of 85,000 spindles (Fig 31). Thereafter Middleton became an important seat of joint-stock enterprise and the home of two of the largest spinning companies. The Times Mill (768) (Fig 32) was floated in 1898 by John Bunting,[97] who called up only 5 per cent of the company's ordinary capital and paid regular dividends of 40 per cent with the help of loan capital. Understandably the company proved an immediate success and built out of its profits a second mill in 1907–8 with 160,000 spindles.[98] The completion of that mill enabled Bunting to achieve his ambition of building the largest mill in the world. The Times Mill (768) thus increased its spindles to 264,000 and ascended in status to the fourth largest spinning firm in Lancashire. The Soudan Mill Ltd (749, 750) was registered in 1903 and built three mills in 1904, 1914 and 1921, trebling its spindleage from 85,000 in 1904 to 267,500 in 1921.

Middleton pioneered the use for spinning of the single-storeyed shed, built on the standard pattern used since 1830 of the weaving shed with a north-light roof truss and a saw-toothed profile, in the Cromer Mill (629) of 1903 with 60,000 ring spindles as well as a rope race (Figs 33 and 34).[99]

Figure 33. The Cromer Ring Mill (629), Middleton, in 1905. Here the ring mill assumed its ultimate form as a single-storeyed structure. It used the same type of building which had been developed since the 1830s for use as a powerloom-weaving shed, with north-light windows in the roof. The Cromer Mill even employed a horizontal rope race driven from the centrally sited engine house. The architect, P. S. Stott, also designed the two-storeyed Crest Ring Mill in Rochdale in 1906 (*The Textile Mercury*, 1905, 367).

Figure 34. Interior view of a ring-spinning room in the Cromer Mill (629). The photograph shows the frames with the attendant doffers, the internal tramway in the foreground for the easy carriage of skips, the overhead line shaft and the roof lights, increasing visibility to the maximum degree. Such single-storeyed buildings were less exposed to the risk of fire than multi-storeyed mills because they relied upon natural rather than artificial light. Thus they enjoyed lower insurance premiums and a longer life span. Indeed, specialised weaving firms rarely insured their sheds (*The Textile Mercury*, 1905, 123).

During the post-war boom its mills made national headlines when the Times Mill (768) paid the unprecedentedly high dividends of 400 per cent in 1919 and 600 per cent in 1920, so giving rise to questions in the House of Commons.[100] Middleton's spindles may have reached their maximum number in 1913 but its population increased faster in 1911–71 than that of any other town in the county. Its occupational structure, as that of a late developer, remained the most highly dependent upon the cotton industry and the most undiversified of all the boroughs of Greater Manchester.

## Bury and Rochdale, with Radcliffe and Heywood

Both Rochdale and Bury were old market towns and each became the centre of a dense web of manufacturing villages. Both carried on the woollen manufacture and both proved hospitable to small firms. Bury became the home of one of the county's oldest textile firms.[101] Such family firms developed the manufactures of both towns and converted them from woollen to cotton manufacture, using the water power of the Roch and Irwell. They grafted joint-stock enterprise on to their business more successfully than their peers in Bolton.

Bury had been endowed from 1773 with a new staple trade by the enterprise of the calico printing firm of Peel. It achieved notable technical innovations in handloom weaving, in mule spinning and in powerloom weaving.[102] Its population expanded faster (1775–1861) than that of any other cotton town save for Salford. After the Cotton Famine its rate of expansion was checked, however, by the competition of Oldham and sank below the Lancashire average to a level about half that of Rochdale during the years 1861–1911. During the decade 1882–92 Bury even suffered the loss of 12 per cent of its spindles. The town nevertheless preserved a

Figure 35. The Peel Mills (250), Bury. The company which built these mills took its name from the family which created the prosperity of Bury as an industrial town. Mill No. 1, built in 1885–7 and reduced in height by three storeys in 1963, may be seen to the left, with Mill No. 2 (1892) in the centre and Mill No. 3 (1913–15) to the right. Unusually these mills seem to have lacked any lodge but presumably made use of the nearby River Irwell. The company ceased cotton spinning in 1975, transformed itself into Peel Holdings in 1981 and entered upon a new career: by 1988 it had become the ninth-largest property company in the United Kingdom.

well-balanced economy, like Rochdale, and added joint-stock companies from 1885 to the ranks of its family firms. The Peel Spinning and Manufacturing Co Ltd (Fig 35) had its shares marketed in 1885 by John Bunting of Oldham: the completion of its six-storeyed mill in 1887 was rightly hailed as inaugurating a new era in the history of Bury.[103] The town acquired as high a proportion of ring spindles as Rochdale, or 39 per cent in 1927. It attained its peak loomage in 1915 and its peak spindleage in 1917. Thereafter its capacity declined almost as slowly as that of Rochdale, beneath the protection of modernised technology. Its rank in the hierarchy of spinning towns advanced but its relatively small size debarred it from admission to the ranks of the top ten spinning towns until 1960 (see pp. 46–7).

Amongst the many dependent townships of Bury two experienced different patterns of development. Ramsbottom registered its maximum spindleage in 1889 and retained in its waste trade until 1988 the last self-acting mule in Lancashire. Radcliffe enjoyed a late wave of expansion and attained its peak capacity only in 1914. Radcliffe has attracted the attention of industrial archaeologists[104] but has surfaced in textbooks only as the site of the first epidemic of 'factory fever' in the year 1784. A century later it attained new eminence by growing faster in spindleage between 1884 and 1917 than any other spinning town except for Farnworth. That growth was achieved by private employers since its first joint-stock limited, the Wilton Spinning Co, was not founded until 1907. Radcliffe also became a leading centre for the manufacture of coloured goods and added more powerlooms (1884–1914) than any other centre in south Lancashire apart from Bolton. It preserved a diversified economy and did not reduce its population but increased it between 1911 and 1971, like Bury and Heywood.[105]

Rochdale had built up since 1790 a flourishing cotton industry by the side of its flannel industry. It enjoyed a golden age during the Cotton Famine when woollens became once more price-competitive with cotton goods: its population increased by 66 per cent (1861–71), or by a higher proportion than any other cotton town in that decade. After the severe depression of 1877–8 Rochdale experienced a distinct revival with the conjuncture of three influences: the establishment from 1882 of limited spinning companies on the Oldham model, led by the Crawford Spinning Co (625),[106] the introduction from 1883 of a new trade in the manufacture of cotton flannelette and the establishment in Castleton in 1891 of Lancashire's last firm of textile engineers, Tweedale and Smalley, who specialised in the manufacture of ring frames.

Rochdale became not only a Mecca for co-operators but also the pioneer of a series of innovations in business organisation. First, it became the seat of the most successful producers' co-operative, in the Rochdale Co-operative Manufacturing Society (1854–1975), which was established by the Pioneers, built its mills at Mitchell Hey (700) in 1859–61 and paid an average annual dividend of 6.5 per cent (1854–1914).[107] Secondly, it created what became in the pre-Bunting era the most successful of joint-stock limiteds in the Lancashire cotton industry, the Rochdale Cotton Spinning Co Ltd,[108] which built its mill in Vavassour Street and paid an average annual dividend of 9.5 per cent (1886–1914), or almost double the general average. Above all, it developed in the early 1880s the informal organisation of companies into groups, first under the leadership of the Heaps, local flannel manufacturers.[109] Rochdale became the second largest centre of joint-stock enterprise in Lancashire after Oldham. Its new limiteds introduced the spinning of Oldham counts in 1882 and of Bolton counts in 1890. From 1892 those companies proved more successful financially than those of Oldham and they enjoyed a final decade of expansion between 1898 and 1907.

The Rochdale limiteds pioneered the local development of ring spinning[110] and so helped to make Tweedale and Smalley one of the most profitable engineering firms. Ring mills generated higher temperatures from their higher spindle speeds than mule mills and therefore required greater protection against the risk of fire. Rochdale accordingly adapted its modes of construction and acquired in 1906 the Crest Mill (626) at Castleton. That mill was unusual in so far as it had only two storeys, was built on the American slow-burning principle[111] and incorporated the labour-saving flow pattern whereby cotton moved from the cardroom on the upper floor down to the 66,240 ring spindles below.[112] The Dunlop Mills (640), built by the Dunlop Rubber Co in 1914–19 in twin blocks of seven storeys using 14,000,000 Accrington bricks and Trafford fireproof roofing tiles, were equipped with 191,520 ring spindles for the manufacture of special cord for car tyres and pioneered the resumption of night-shift working from 1920 (Fig 36).[113] Rochdale had been identified in 1915 as having the most polluted atmosphere in Lancashire and indeed in England.[114] Its mill-owners therefore adopted electric power extensively in a determined and pioneer bid to reduce the level of such pollution, so making the municipal electricity undertaking into the largest producer of power in Lancashire outside Manchester and Liverpool. Rochdale's spinning capacity declined more slowly in the 20th century than that of any town

Figure 36. The Dunlop Mills (640), Rochdale. These mills were described by their architect, P. S. Stott, as the largest cotton mills in the world. They were in fact a double mill built in 1914 and 1919 by the firm styled No. 2 D. R. Cotton Mills Ltd which renamed itself in 1927 Dunlop Cotton Mills Ltd. They housed 191,520 ring spindles for spinning special tyre yarns, which were woven into stout tyre canvas in the adjoining weaving sheds. In 1920 it was anticipated that these mills, working night and day, would consume one-third of Egypt's cotton crop. The ring rooms proved to be cleaner than mule rooms, employing women rather than men. The mills were demolished in 1977–9 after a serious fire but were then rebuilt (R. & T. Howard Ltd, Building and Public Works Contracts).

other than Wigan. As a result the borough rose in the hierarchy of spinning towns from the rank of sixth in 1884–99 to that of fourth in 1900 and to that of third in 1918–35, surpassing even Manchester in capacity (see pp. 46–7). Thus it could serve as the last refuge of the textile unions, when the Amalgamated Association of Textile Workers was established there in 1976.

Two of Rochdale's dependent townships experienced sharply contrasting patterns of development. Littleborough reached its peak spindleage in 1884 and was not rejuvenated by joint-stock enterprise. Heywood, however, attained its maximum capacity thirty years later in 1915, as the fifteenth largest centre of cotton spinning (see pp. 46–7). The township acquired its first limited companies in 1884, two years after the building of the Crawford Mills (625) in Rochdale. Those companies helped to maintain its spinning trade across the full spectrum of yarn production. They created specialist ring mills (in 1891 and 1907) and introduced the spinning of Bolton counts from 1892. The Mutual Spinning Co (704, 705), established in 1884, trebled its capacity between 1886 and 1914 to 246,000 spindles and became the largest firm in the town as well as much larger than any of the Rochdale limiteds. Capacity in Heywood was nevertheless reduced from the peak of 1915 at an unusually rapid rate. The speed of decline in Heywood was surpassed only in Glossop and contrasted sharply with the experience of Rochdale, Bury and Bolton, where the pace of decline was the slowest. During the last phase of the industry's history its mills became the object of serious study:[115] they acquired symbolic importance, they were numbered and they were even scheduled for preservation.[116] The first cotton mill in the region to be so distinguished was the Crimble Mill (627*), near Heywood, which was designated a Grade II listed building on 15 December 1967. Its site was characterised by continuity of industrial occupation and, above all, by the longevity of the firm rather than of the mill itself.[117]

**Table 1**

Spindleage of the major cotton spinning towns in the Lancashire region, 1883–1962 *

| | 1883 | | 1893 | | 1903 | | 1913 | | 1923 | | 1926 | | 1933 | | 1944 | | 1953 | | 1962 | | |
|---|---|---|---|---|---|---|---|---|---|---|---|---|---|---|---|---|---|---|---|---|---|
| Accrington | 590 | (18) | 438 | (23) | 467 | (22) | 660 | (21) | 691 | (21) | 718 | (20) | 469 | (20) | 287 | (19) | 152 | (22) | 92 | (16) | Accrington |
| Ashton | 1,574 | (8) | 1,731 | (7) | 1,781 | (6) | 2,001 | (8) | 1,955 | (8) | 1,898 | (8) | 1,144 | (9) | 644 | (11) | 633 | (10) | 182 | (9) | Ashton |
| Blackburn | 1,671 | (5) | 1,398 | (9) | 1,321 | (9) | 1,280 | (11) | 1,224 | (12) | 1,071 | (15) | 672 | (16) | 451 | (16) | 309 | (18) | 103 | (15) | Blackburn |
| Bolton | 4,086 | (2) | 4,770 | (2) | 5,457 | (2) | 6,797 | (2) | 7,371 | (2) | 7,842 | (2) | 7,507 | (2) | 6,204 | (2) | 4,886 | (2) | 1,772 | (2) | Bolton |
| Burnley | 1,126 | (11) | 734 | (19) | 667 | (18) | 563 | (22) | 538 | (22) | 507 | (22) | 240 | (23) | 182 | (24) | 144 | (23) | 14 | (31) | Burnley |
| Bury | 875 | (14) | 899 | (13) | 833 | (16) | 955 | (16) | 1,050 | (16) | 1,000 | (16) | 745 | (14) | 630 | (12) | 542 | (12) | 268 | (8) | Bury |
| Chorley | 552 | (20) | 527 | (20) | 541 | (20) | 856 | (18) | 838 | (17) | 837 | (18) | 739 | (15) | 491 | (14) | 397 | (15) | 122 | (13) | Chorley |
| Farnworth | 557 | (19) | 779 | (15) | 966 | (13) | 1,485 | (9) | 1,478 | (9) | 1,484 | (9) | 1,344 | (8) | 1,237 | (7) | 1,104 | (7) | 162 | (10) | Farnworth |
| Glossop | 1,106 | (12) | 1,158 | (11) | 968 | (12) | 882 | (16) | 821 | (18) | 839 | (17) | 524 | (18) | 204 | (23) | 154 | (21) | 10 | (33) | Glossop |
| Heywood | 660 | (16) | 887 | (14) | 836 | (15) | 1,070 | (15) | 1,100 | (15) | 1,096 | (14) | 864 | (12) | 545 | (13) | 533 | (13) | 68 | (20) | Heywood |
| Hyde | 590 | (17) | 499 | (19) | 533 | (20) | 741 | (20) | 793 | (20) | 696 | (21) | 475 | (19) | 366 | (17) | 337 | (16) | 58 | (21) | Hyde |
| Leigh | 1,337 | (9) | 1,514 | (8) | 1,679 | (7) | 2,445 | (5) | 2,761 | (5) | 2,925 | (5) | 2,891 | (5) | 2,615 | (4) | 2,336 | (3) | 548 | (4) | Leigh |
| Manchester | 2,445 | (3) | 2,353 | (3) | 2,225 | (4) | 3,703 | (3) | 3,307 | (4) | 3,439 | (4) | 3,417 | (4) | 2,974 | (3) | 1,934 | (5) | 271 | (7) | Manchester |
| Middleton | 498 | (22) | 494 | (21) | 645 | (19) | 1,278 | (12) | 1,268 | (11) | 1,252 | (11) | 1,041 | (10) | 1,193 | (8) | 923 | (9) | 161 | (11) | Middleton |
| Mossley | 1,153 | (10) | 1,217 | (10) | 1,033 | (10) | 1,288 | (10) | 1,297 | (10) | 1,289 | (10) | 371 | (21) | 264 | (20) | 256 | (19) | – | | Mossley |
| Oldham | 9,311 | (1) | 11,159 | (1) | 12,230 | (1) | 16,909 | (1) | 17,231 | (1) | 17,669 | (1) | 13,723 | (1) | 8,948 | (1) | 7,621 | (1) | 2,478 | (1) | Oldham |
| Preston | 2,146 | (4) | 1,883 | (4) | 2,074 | (5) | 2,161 | (7) | 1,997 | (7) | 1,965 | (7) | 1,592 | (7) | 1,146 | (9) | 1,024 | (8) | 278 | (6) | Preston |
| Rochdale | 1,627 | (6) | 1,835 | (5) | 2,422 | (3) | 3,645 | (4) | 3,749 | (3) | 3,793 | (3) | 3,539 | (3) | 2,459 | (5) | 1,936 | (4) | 983 | (3) | Rochdale |
| Stalybridge | 1,080 | (13) | 1,157 | (12) | 1,027 | (11) | 1,236 | (13) | 1,104 | (14) | 1,103 | (13) | 801 | (13) | 483 | (15) | 426 | (14) | 122 | (14) | Stalybridge |
| Stockport | 1,601 | (7) | 1,742 | (6) | 1,568 | (8) | 2,266 | (6) | 2,383 | (6) | 2,382 | (6) | 1,924 | (6) | 1,427 | (6) | 1,141 | (6) | 154 | (12) | Stockport |
| Wigan | 864 | (15) | 775 | (16) | 888 | (14) | 1,085 | (14) | 1,123 | (13) | 1,141 | (12) | 922 | (11) | 681 | (10) | 575 | (11) | 352 | (5) | Wigan |
| TOTAL | *39,075* | | *41,632* | | *43,568* | | *57,265* | | *57,425* | | *58,206* | | *47,183* | | *35,077* | | *28,686* | | *10,469* | | TOTAL |

\* in thousands of spindles

Source: Worrall 1884–1963; Farnie 1990*b*.

This table presents statistics of cotton-spinning spindleage for nine bench-mark years, plus the statistics for the summit year of 1926. The spindleages for twenty-one major towns (including six from outside Greater Manchester) are shown at each date in the table, together with the totals for the Lancashire region. Figures in brackets show the ranking of the towns within the cotton-spinning region. The statistics relate to the December of each year and have been drawn from the directory bearing the following year's date: the statistics for December 1883 have been compiled from the 1884 directory. For the first four years chosen, the spindleage has been recalculated in order to eliminate doubling spindles, using the average ratios of 1914–17, in order to confine the table to spinning spindles.

The townships included within each area are as follows:

| | |
|---|---|
| Ashton under Lyne | Bardsley, Guide Bridge, Hurst and Waterloo |
| Bolton | Ainsworth, Astley Bridge, Belmont, Blackrod, Bradley Fold, Breightmet, Bromley Cross, Chapeltown, Darcy Lever, Edgeworth, Egerton, Entwistle, Great Lever, Halliwell, Harwood, Horwich, Little Lever, Longworth, Lostock, Sharples, Tonge with Haulgh, Turton, Westhoughton |
| Bury | Blackford Bridge, Elton, Ewood Bridge, Gigg, Heap Bridge, Limefield, Pilsworth, Summerseat, Tottington, Walmersley, Walshaw, Woolfold |
| Farnworth | Kearsley, Little Hulton, Moses Gate, New Bury, Stoneclough, Walkden |
| Glossop | Broadbottom, Charlesworth, Dinting, Hadfield, Hollingworth, Mottram, Padfield |
| Heywood | Hopwood |
| Hyde | Denton, Gee Cross, Godley, Haughton, Newton Moor |
| Leigh | Astley, Atherton, Glazebury, Pennington, Tyldesley |
| Manchester | Central Manchester: Ancoats, Ardwick, Beswick, Bradford, Chorlton on Medlock, Cornbrook, Gaythorn, Gorton, Harpurhey, Hulme, Newton Heath, Miles Platting, Openshaw |
| Manchester suburbs: | Blackley, Boothstown, Clayton, Droylsden, Eccles, Failsworth, Fairfield, Flixton, Greengate, Islington, Monton, Ordsall, Patricroft, Pendlebury, Salford, Swinton, Weaste, Winton, Worsley |
| Middleton | Alkrington, Great Heaton, Tonge, Rhodes |
| Mossley | Brookbottom, Micklehurst, Roaches |
| Oldham | Chadderton, Crompton, Grotton, Hey, Hollinwood Lees, Royton, Shaw, Springhead, Thornham |
| Radcliffe | Besses o'th'Barn, Prestwich, Unsworth, Whitefield |
| Rochdale | Bagslate, Balderstone, Bamford, Buersil, Castleton, Cheesden, Facit, Greenbooth, Hamer, Milnrow, Newhey, Norden, Ogden, Shawforth, Smallbridge, Smithy Bridge, Spotland, Sudden, Wardle, Whitworth |
| Stalybridge | Copley, Millbrook, Staley |
| Stockport | Birch Vale, Cheadle Heath, Compstall, Furness Vale, Hayfield, Hazel Grove, Heaton Norris, Marple, Mellor, New Mills, Reddish, Romiley, Strines |
| Wigan | Aspull Moor, Hindley, Hindley Green, Ince, Orrell, Pemberton, Platt Bridge, Worthington. |

# 3

# Early mills, 1780–1825

THE period 1780 to 1825 saw a dramatic expansion of the cotton trade and the emergence of the multi-storeyed steam-powered cotton-spinning mill. Weaving continued to be organised by the established putting-out firms, each served by a network of handloom weavers, until the powerloom began to be introduced on a widespread basis after c.1820. During this early phase in the development of the factory, cotton-mill building started in a number of towns in the Greater Manchester area, and some of the most significant surviving structures date from this period.[1] Mill building was concentrated most heavily around Manchester itself, however, and this is where most of the surviving early mills are situated. Georgian Manchester became known internationally as a factory town, with more cotton firms, more factory workers, more mills and more steam power than any other town in the region. This necessarily brief discussion of early cotton mills therefore concentrates on Manchester and adjoining parts of Salford. Here the surviving mills can be seen as forerunners of the types of structure which later characterised the region's cotton industry. No typical example survives from Manchester's first generation of cotton-spinning mills, those built in the late 18th century, so a range of mills which do not survive are also described.

The absence of reliable statistics makes it difficult to ascertain exactly how many cotton mills were built in Manchester in this period. One source suggests there were forty-three in the township in 1815,[2] but contemporary rate books indicate that this might be an underestimate as they list thirty owner-occupied mills and up to thirty additional mills containing more than one firm.[3] The period included a mill-building boom in the early years of the 19th century, the number of cotton firms in Manchester more than doubling between 1799 and 1802 (see p. 19). Additional extensive mill building also took place immediately outside the township of Manchester from the late 1790s, notably in Salford and Chorlton on Medlock.

The lowland setting of the Manchester area was initially a disadvantage since water power was limited, but this was overcome by the common use

Figure 37. Loomshops were a type of early factory built in the Pennine areas for handloom weaving. This part of Dob Wheel Mill (635), built *c.*1800 near Rochdale, is one of the few possible examples in Greater Manchester.

of auxiliary steam engines to pump water up to a level where it could drive a waterwheel. The advantage of proximity to Manchester probably lay in the use of the town's commercial and transport infrastructure, which developed rapidly in the late 18th century. From the late 1790s Manchester became a hub of the regional canal system, with the Ashton and Rochdale Canals converging from the east, the earlier Bridgewater coming in from the west to its terminus at Castlefield and the Bolton and Bury Canal coming down from the north.

Early cotton mills occupied a specialised niche in the trade, supplying a huge demand for yarn from the cloth manufacturers. The putting-out firms of the cloth-manufacturing sector had expanded since the mid 18th century and formed a well-established system of production.[4] Thus between the construction of the first cotton mills in Manchester in the 1780s and the adoption of the powerloom by the mid 1820s the local cotton industry was characterised by two distinct levels of technology, with the factory-based spinning industry complementing the continued success of the extensively organised manufacturers. A similar business structure also developed in other parts of Greater Manchester, such as Bolton, albeit with fewer and smaller spinning mills.[5]

The intensive methods of the early spinning factories possessed a range of basic economic advantages over the extensive methods of the manufacturers. In particular, the widespread use of steam power[6] and of mules for spinning enabled the production of yarn in greater quantities and of better quality at a lower price. In addition, the dispersed nature of the putting-out firms involved a range of distribution and management problems[7] which were avoided by the centralised control of workers and production permitted by the factory system. In the Pennine woollen industry multistoreyed workshops were built for handlooms in this period, but no surviving examples have been found in Manchester (Fig 37). When the powerloom became economically viable in the 1820s it was mainly taken up locally by the spinning firms, who were already established in factory methods and had steam power readily available. Their success was matched by a slow decline of the putting-out firms.

Little is known about the designers and builders of early mills. Different aspects of mill construction were carried out by different firms, including builders, founders and millwrights. Some of the well-known cotton firms had partners who concentrated on the technical aspects of the business and played an important part in the design of the buildings.[8] Millwrights were concerned with the transmission of power to machinery, and their influence on mill design increased.[9] By the early 19th century Manchester-based firms dominated the millwrighting trade in Britain.[10]

## Eighteenth-century mills in Manchester

The oldest surviving mill in Manchester is Old Mill (362*), which was built in 1798 as part of Murray's Mills (358*). This was a large site in the new industrial suburb of Ancoats, but dozens of earlier mills, no longer extant, were built closer to the town centre. These mills included some important innovative buildings and many smaller mills occupied by more than one firm. The nature of 18th-century mill building in Manchester is discussed below with reference to some of the better-known examples. This is followed by a more detailed account of post-1800 mills based mainly on studies of the surviving buildings in the Manchester and Salford area.

Small-scale firms were a characteristic feature of Manchester's early cotton industry and because of the widespread sub-letting of factory space the number of firms greatly exceeded the number of mills. 'Room and power' mills, in which firms rented floorspace with powered line shafting, accommodated most of Manchester's cotton firms before the 1820s.[11]

The town's earliest powered textile mill may have been Garratt Mill (336), situated alongside the River Medlock. The firm of Gartside and Thackery was said to have built this mill *c*.1760, using a waterwheel to drive swivel looms for ribbon weaving, probably from silk.[12] This early experiment with powerlooms was not successful, however, and by 1784 the building was being used for cotton spinning and contained 2,000 spindles on water frames. In that year two atmospheric steam engines, manufactured by the Manchester engineer Joshua Wrigley, were installed to raise water for the waterwheels.[13] A number of innovative steam engines, all made locally, were added to Garratt Mill (336) in the 1780s and 1790s.[14] By the 1820s the site comprised two mills of three and four storeys, one with a wheelhouse, together with warehouses, workshops and a detached engine house, boilers and chimney.[15]

The first large purpose-built cotton-spinning mill was probably Shudehill Mill (374), built *c*.1782 by partners of Richard Arkwright and finally destroyed in the blitz of 1940. This was an extensive timber-floored mill, 60.9 metres long by 9.1 metres wide and of five storeys with an external wooden staircase.[16] It was an example of an early type of cotton mill built throughout England and Scotland to use Arkwright's patented machinery. These mills probably represent the first diffusion of the factory system in the cotton industry.[17] Shudehill Mill (374) was one of the largest of the Arkwright mills,[18] an indication of Manchester's significance as a commercial centre of the cotton trade by the 1780s. The water frame, the carding engine and other preparation machinery had all been developed by Arkwright for use in powered factories but their local adoption was limited by their expense and by patent restrictions. After Arkwright's patents lapsed in 1785, however, the use of powered preparation machinery became widespread in Manchester's early mills, but for spinning the water frame was largely ignored in favour of the cheaper and more adaptable mule.

Shudehill Mill (374) was possibly the first mill in the area to use a steam engine to raise water for the waterwheel, which in this case was 9.1 metres in diameter.[19] A distinctive feature of the site was Manchester's first mill chimney.[20] The engine may also have been made by Joshua Wrigley,[21] who had orders to install engines for use with waterwheels at thirteen Manchester mills by 1791.[22]

Some of the cotton industry's greatest firms were established in Manchester in this period and operated from room and power mills. The firm of McConnel and Kennedy, for example, which became the largest cotton-spinning firm in Manchester in the 19th century, in the 1790s was renting room and power in a number of small premises. These included Salvin's Factory (371), which the firm occupied in 1793 when John Kennedy is said to have first applied steam power to the mule for fine cotton spinning.[23] This mill was built across a small stream to the east of the town and was originally powered by a waterwheel, but a Wrigley steam engine was added by 1796.[24] In 1822 the site consisted of a six-storeyed mill standing partly across the stream with an external engine house and attached stair tower.[25]

The fact that the mule, unlike the water frame, could be hand-powered and was not restricted by patents encouraged its use by the smaller firms. It could also be used for the production of fine yarns for which there was a high demand. A number of firms actually started business as manufacturers of mules and other machines before concentrating on fine spinning themselves. The ability to improve the early mule has been cited as a key factor in the success of several notable early firms, including McConnel and Kennedy, Houldsworth's and Robert Owen.[26]

By the end of the 1780s owner-occupied mills were being built which were equipped entirely with mules and the associated preparation machinery. The best known was Piccadilly Mill (366), built by Peter Drinkwater, a successful fustian manufacturer and merchant.[27] This was originally a four-storeyed building which was under construction in 1789. Drinkwater was concerned with design features which were to remain significant in mill building throughout the 19th century. He was particularly interested to ensure that the windows should give adequate internal lighting and that the mill should have an external privy tower. From 1790 Piccadilly Mill (366) was the first mill in Manchester to be powered by a

Figure 38. The Ancoats mills, overlooking the Rochdale Canal, *c.*1830. In the centre is A. and G. Murray's Old Mill (362*), and Decker Mill (333*), built 1798 and 1802. In the background is McConnel and Kennedy's Old Mill (363), and Sedgwick Mill (372*), built 1798 and 1818–20 (Baines 1835, plate 17).

Boulton and Watt rotary beam engine, and was therefore fully independent of the site requirements of a water-power system.[28] The engine was initially only used to drive the preparation machinery, the 144-spindle mules being entirely hand operated. In 1822 the building was of five storeys with the engine and boilers attached mid-way along one side.[29] Up to 1794 Drinkwater employed the young Robert Owen to manage this mill and its 500 workers.[30]

Old Mill (362*), which forms the 1798 section of the Murray's Mills complex (358*), is Manchester's only surviving 18th-century mill. This site is atypical but nevertheless illustrates the limits reached by mill builders in this period. The mill was built in Ancoats outside the old town. The area was laid out in the early 1790s as part of a planned expansion of Manchester with new streets arranged in a grid pattern.[31] Murray's Mills (358*) overlooked the future line of the Rochdale Canal, not opened until 1804. The mill is shown with the slightly later Sedgwick Mill (372*) in an engraving of 1835 (Fig 38). Old Mill (362*) originally comprised an eight-storeyed building of eleven bays with plan dimensions of approximately 31 by 12 metres (Fig 190). External engine and boiler houses were attached at the east end. The Boulton and Watt rotary beam engine was typical of early mill engines in Manchester, having a timber beam, a timber trestle supporting the flywheel and timber supports for the beam (Fig 39).[32] It was of approximately ten horsepower with 'sun and planet' gearing, and was probably similar to those used at Drinkwater's Piccadilly Mill (366), and at McConnel and Kennedy's Old Mill (363). It was served by a single wagon-type boiler. In 1802 Old Mill (362*) was extended by the addition of the ten-bay Decker Mill (333*), and the original engine was replaced by one of about forty horsepower with a cast-iron beam.[33]

The building is now of seven storeys in Flemish-bond brickwork, with no original embellishment. The uniform segmental-headed windows are

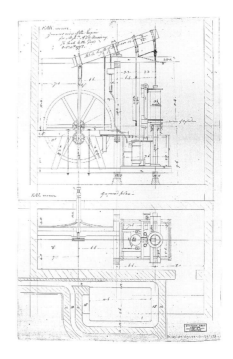

Figure 39. Murray's Old Mill, Manchester (362*), built in 1798, was powered by a Boulton and Watt beam engine with a timber framework and 'sun and planet' rotary motion. A similar engine was used at Piccadilly Mill (366) (Boulton and Watt Collection, Portfolio 167, Birmingham Library Services).

smaller than those in later mills but larger than those used in other types of contemporary building such as warehouses. The timber floors have been modified and the columns replaced, but it is likely that the mill originally had non-fireproof joisted floors supported by a single row of cruciform-section cast-iron columns. This floor construction can still be seen in the 1804 New Mill (359*), also part of Murray's Mills (358*). Cruciform-section cast-iron columns were generally superseded by the more familiar circular-section type in the first decades of the 19th century and are now rarely found *in situ*. The complex was probably built to contain partially powered mules made by Murray's themselves, although there is little surviving evidence of the original power transmission system.

## Early nineteenth-century mills in Manchester and Salford

Eleven cotton-spinning mills dating wholly or in part from 1800 to 1825 survive in Manchester and Salford.[34] These mills show a range of scale, layout and internal organisation, but nevertheless form a small and unrepresentative sample (less than 20 per cent) of Manchester's early cotton-spinning industry. The range of surviving mills is biased in favour of the larger owner-occupied mills built by the better-known firms, and includes the largest cotton mills to be built in the early period. Also represented, however, are mills built for sub-letting as 'room and power' for the smaller firms. Examples of a wide range of early methods of construction also survive, but the fireproof and fire-resistant types are now better represented than the non-fireproof types. No water-powered or water and steam-powered mills survive, nor any mills built for hand-powered machinery. All the extant mills were originally powered by rotary beam engines.

In comparison with other regions, Manchester was distinguished by the number and scale of its early cotton mills, its dependence on steam power, its use of mules for spinning and the emphatically urban setting of its mills. These 'town mills'[35] represented an important stage in the chain of development from the simple technology of the traditional corn and fulling mills to the massive steam-powered factories which became characteristic of Lancashire's industrial landscapes.

The siting of steam-powered cotton mills was conditioned by the availability of a water supply for boilers and engines. The banks of the major canal routes and a number of branch canals provided a high proportion of the mill-building sites in the early 19th century.[36] The use of canal water for steam plant obviated the need to construct reservoirs, enabling large mills to be built in distinctive, closely packed groups. In addition to providing water, the canal system was heavily used for the transportation of coal, raw cotton and finished textile products. Some mills were built alongside a canal with no special provision for the loading or unloading of boats, including Chepstow Street Mill, Manchester (322*), and Sedgwick Mill, Manchester (372*), but others had various types of private loading facilities. Beehive Mill, Manchester (306*), was built near the end of a branch canal and was served by a separate short basin running alongside the mill. The nearby Brownsfield Mill (315*) stood overlooking a junction of three canals; a wing of the mill alongside a canal branch incorporates an arched 'shipping hole' similar to those in contemporary canal warehouses, suggesting that boats may have entered the building itself. The incorporation of canal features in the design of a mill probably reached its ultimate development, however, with Murray's Mills, Manchester (358*), which when completed in 1806 comprised a quadrangle of large multi-storeyed buildings enclosing a central canal basin (Fig 190). The basin was entered by boats from the main Rochdale Canal via a tunnel passing beneath one side of the site and the surrounding streets. Rivers could also provide a water supply for steam-powered mills. The impressive group of factories in Chorlton on Medlock, just to the south of Manchester, were built from the late 1790s on farmland acquired for industrial development and took water for steam plant from the River Medlock (Fig 40).

Figure 40. The early to late 19th-century cotton mills at Chorlton on Medlock, Manchester, were not served by a canal but obtained water for steam plant from the River Medlock, now culverted beneath the mills.

## The size and layout of early mills

Surviving early spinning mills generally comprise large multi-storeyed buildings with attached wings, either original or added later, forming L or U-shaped site plans. The wings were sometimes used for warehousing or ancillary processes. These mills are wider than surviving late 18th-century mills in other areas but much narrower than cotton mills built later in the 19th century. Engine houses, boiler houses and chimneys were usually internal. Most sites included offices or counting houses, either in separate small buildings or incorporated into the warehouse.

Some aspects of the layout of early cotton mills suggest that security was an important consideration for the designers. Few had their main entrances in the front elevation facing the street, although in most cases doorways were inserted later. Most sites had an enclosed private yard from which the principal buildings were entered. In the larger sites the yard was completely surrounded by multi-storeyed buildings and was entered via a covered passage. Thus access to all parts of a large complex was controlled from the lodge at the entrance to the yard.

The overall form of surviving early 19th-century mills is distinctive. They are tall and narrow in proportion to their length, with more storeys than most later mills. They range from eleven to twenty bays in length, the main rooms measuring from around 25 metres long to the exceptional 56 metres of New Mill, Manchester (359*), added to Murray's site in 1804. Bay size, indicated by the longitudinal spacing of the main floor beams, was smaller than in later mills, at around 2.5 metres in non-fireproof mills and around 2.75 metres in fireproof mills. A few mills used a particularly heavy type of timber-floored construction without joists (see p. 62) and had slightly larger bays, those at Brownsfield Mill, Manchester (315*), for example, being of 3.38 metres. Internal width

Figure 41. Many early mills had basements. At some large complexes, such as Chorlton New Mill, Manchester (323*), communication between the different parts of the site was facilitated by tunnels under public roads.

ranged from 11.5 metres in Old Mill, Manchester (362*), to 15.3 metres in Brownsfield Mill (315*), built in 1825. All the surviving mills are wider than the 9 metres characteristic of the Arkwright-type mills of the late 18th century, but are narrower than most mid and late 19th-century mills. In height these early Manchester mills range from six to eight storeys, sometimes including basements and attics. Their great height was unusual and was probably related to increasing land values in the late 18th and early 19th centuries (see p. 19). Ceiling heights are around 3.3 metres in the bottom storeys and 2.7 metres above. Basements were found in some late 18th-century mills, such as Piccadilly Mill, Manchester (366), of 1790, and were also used in the early 19th century. Basements were usually lit by small windows, but when a mill was built on a sloping site it might only be possible to include windows along one side, as at Chepstow Street Mill, Manchester (322*). Chorlton New Mill, Manchester (323*), of 1813 was unusual in having two basements, the upper being linked with tunnels to the basements of surrounding mills owned by the same firm (Fig 41).

## External details

The external walls of all the early cotton-spinning mills in the Manchester area were probably of coarse handmade brick, the most readily available local building material. This red brick was fired from clay obtained in brick fields located around Manchester, or in some cases dug from the mill site itself.[37] In the Ancoats mills the walls facing the street were laid in Flemish bond, with burnt dark-blue headers creating a 'chequerboard' pattern. Elsewhere there was less concern for external appearance, bricks usually being laid in English bond. In other areas, such as the upland fringes of Greater Manchester, early textile mills were built in various types of stone, and in general the use of locally available walling materials for industrial buildings continued until the end of the 19th century. For the roofs of Manchester's town mills thin Welsh slate appears to have been used throughout the mill-building period, but in upland areas the smaller early mills were built with roofs of thick slate or flags.

The windows of early mills in the Manchester area are larger than those of contemporary domestic buildings or the earlier surviving mills in other areas, indicating that the provision of adequate internal lighting was already a factor in mill design. In this period windows occupied a far smaller proportion of the total wall area than in later mills, however, and since early mills were relatively narrow, windows were sometimes completely excluded from the end walls. Typical windows were of vertical rectangular shape, from about 1.4 to 1.8 metres high and from 0.9 to 1.1 metres wide. They reduced in height in the upper storeys but remained the same width. Windows in both timber-floored and fireproof mills usually had external brick segmental heads and stone sills. Flat stone lintels are also sometimes found and in the Manchester area usually indicate that the mill contains fireproof brick-vaulted ceilings (Fig 42). In this period most mill windows had sloping internal sills about 1 metre above the floor; some of the larger mills had 'step-in' bays with windows separated by piers of thicker brickwork. Glazing bars today are rarely original, but documentary sources indicate that early mill windows originally had many small panes with hinged sections opening for ventilation, sash-opening windows being rare.[38] Engine houses, both internal and external, were being built with characteristic round-headed windows by the early 19th century, although in a few cases ordinary segmental-headed windows were used. Mills with attics sometimes also feature large lunette windows in the gable end walls, for example at Beehive Mill, Manchester (306*), and Islington Mill, Salford (829*).

Most early mills have wide arched main entrances and a separate door to the offices. Warehouse blocks can also have taking-in doors to each storey with an external hoist beam. In some cases the large double gateway led via the yard to a doorway in the base of an external stair tower. Full-height stair towers are a characteristic feature of multi-storeyed textile mills of all periods. The surviving early mills have either attached or internal towers of square or circular plan, the latter type not being built in later periods. They contain stone steps and flagged landings in both fireproof and non-fireproof mills, and provided fireproof exit routes. Fire-fighting equipment was incorporated in staircase towers from the early 19th century; the 1802 stair tower at Murray's Mills, Manchester (358*), has a full-height central niche which still contains the original stand pipe with connections for hoses on each storey.[39] In some cases a circular staircase was wrapped around the attached or internal mill chimney, the stone steps adding structural support to the chimney breast (see pp. 67–8).

Full-height privy towers, slightly smaller in plan than stair towers, are normally attached to the sides of early spinning mills. They are square or rectangular, usually lacked windows and were originally equipped with

Figure 42. Flat-headed windows at the fireproof Sedgwick Mill, Manchester (372*), of 1818–20, and segmental-headed windows at the non-fireproof Old Mill of 1798 (362*).

only simple plumbing, an opening at the base of the tower being used for the removal of a bucket. Smaller still are the brick flues which are attached to some early mill buildings. These may have served small fireplaces in internal offices, but at Murray's Mills (358*) they probably formed part of a heating or ventilation system.[40]

Stylistic considerations appear to have played little or no role in early mill design in Manchester. Ornamentation in most early mills was restricted to the use of stone voussoirs at the arched main entrances (Fig 43).

Figure 46. The Bengal Street elevation at Murray's Mills, Manchester (358*), did not contain doorways but was enlivened by an identical arrangement of stone arches.

When other decoration is present it is found on the largest mills and is usually restrained; Sedgwick Mill, Manchester (372*), for example, the impressive fireproof building added to McConnel and Kennedy's site between 1818 and 1820, was distinguished only by the slightly projecting five central bays of the front elevation, highlighted by a plain stone parapet. The adjacent Murray's Mills (358*), the largest contemporary mill in Manchester, has more embellishment than any other early mill. The warehouse and office block on Murray Street has a symmetrical arrangement of voussoired doors and windows. This elevation includes unusual round-headed windows with sloping external sills, a feature which suggests that the openings originally functioned as taking-in doors (Fig 44). Above the central main entrance to the site are two distinctive three-light mullioned windows (Fig 45). On the rear elevation of the warehouse block, which overlooked the private canal basin, a pair of oriel office windows originally flanked the main entrance. The external elevation of the opposite side of the site, on Bengal Street, repeats the symmetry of the warehouse block with stone voussoirs around an identical but false arrangement of a central entrance and flanking doorways (Fig 46).

## Methods of construction

The internal construction of early 19th-century mills was of three broad types: non-fireproof timber floors, fireproof floors and heavy timber floors without joists. Roofs with timber trusses, slate-covered, were used with all three types of floor construction, although some of the more advanced fireproof and heavy timber-floored mills featured innovative roofs using cast and wrought-iron components.

Non-fireproof timber floors, similar to those used in non-industrial buildings, provided the cheapest method of constructing a mill. They probably continued to be the most widespread type of construction until the late 19th century.[41] In these mills transverse timber beams supported longitudinal joists on which the floorboards were laid. In some cases fire-resistance was improved by attaching a cladding to the beams or the underside of the joists, usually plaster or metal sheeting. A consequence of the many mill fires in the early 19th century is that mills of fireproof and fire-resistant construction, which were originally in the minority, account for most of the surviving buildings. Large non-fireproof early mills are now rarely found intact in Greater Manchester. The best examples in Manchester itself are Medlock Mill (354) and the much larger Murray's Mills complex (358*) (Fig 47).

By the early 19th century the width of cotton mills required the use of a central row of props or cast-iron columns to support the beams; in mills wider than about 10 metres the beams were often of two pieces joined together above the columns. The columns in the surviving buildings are of cast iron of either cylindrical or the earlier cruciform cross-section. Solid cruciform-type columns were first used in Shropshire and Derbyshire textile mills in the late 18th century, but in general were superseded

Figure 47 (above). Non-fireproof construction using joists and timber floors was used in the majority of early mills; this example is New Mill, Manchester (359*), an 1804 extension to Murray's Mills (358*). The building is of particular interest as a rare surviving example of the use of slender cruciform cast-iron columns.

Figure 48 (above right). Chorlton New Mill, Manchester (323*), has the typical cylindrical columns and cast-iron beams of an early fireproof mill. In this period beams have narrow, parallel-sided flanges, sometimes with wider sections for the attachment of line shafting.

by cylindrical types during the first decade of the 19th century. In the Manchester area cruciform columns are found in parts of Murray's Mills (358*) and may have been used in 18th-century mills which do not survive. A characteristic feature of Manchester's early 19th-century mills, however, appears to have been their early use of cylindrical columns. In this period these are distinguished from the columns in later mills by their thinner diameter, ranging from about 140mm in the bottom storey to about 100mm in the top storey, and by the absence of bolting faces for the attachment of line shafting. This was usually suspended from the ceiling in early mills (Fig 48).

In early fireproof mills the main beams were of cast iron instead of timber, usually supported by one or two rows of cylindrical cast-iron columns. The forerunners of iron-framed buildings were mills built at Ditherington in Shropshire and Belper in Derbyshire in the 1790s, and have been well documented.[42] The first fireproof mill in the Greater Manchester area was an extension to the Salford Twist Mill, Salford (849), built in 1802 for the firm of Phillips and Lee.[43] This innovative and expensive way of constructing multi-storeyed buildings was most commonly used for large mills built by the more successful firms, although a few relatively small fireproof mills were also built for sub-letting to small firms, such as Islington Mill, Salford (829*), built in 1823. Early fireproof mills were built at a time when the use of cast iron as a building material was not fully understood but was developing rapidly; close inspection of the surviving buildings suggests that engineers and builders frequently arrived at individual solutions to common structural problems.

There were two distinct types of early fireproof construction. In the most widely used type the main cast-iron beams were used to support brick ceiling vaults (Fig 49). These were covered with a layer of sand or ash on which was laid the flooring of flags, clay tiles or wooden boards. The beams and other components of brick-vaulted ceiling construction

Figure 49. The interior of Chorlton New Mill, Manchester (323*), built 1814, has typical brick-vaulted fireproof ceilings. Fireproof construction was not widespread in the early period but, significantly, accounts for a high proportion of the surviving mills. This mill was unusual for its date in having three rows of columns.

continued to be improved and this method of construction became common in new cotton-spinning mills by the second half of the 19th century. The second type was simpler, comprising a grid of interlocking cast-iron beams and joists of T or inverted T-section supporting a floor of stone flags. In Greater Manchester it was probably only used for smaller buildings, such as warehouses and other ancillary structures. This type of fireproof floor was certainly being constructed in the 1820s but its popularity was brief, lasting only a decade or two, and it had fallen out of use by the middle of the 19th century.

The columns and, in particular, the beams of early fireproof mills differ markedly from those used in later periods. Cruciform-section columns appear not to have been used in early fireproof mills in Greater Manchester, where the first fireproof mill, Salford Twist Mill (849), was also reputedly the first mill to have cylindrical columns.[44] The columns of this and later mills were slotted together one above the other, creating in effect a single column extending the full height of the building. Longitudinal wrought-iron tie-rods linked the columns together beneath the floors. These ran the full length of the mill and were secured in the end walls; they served both to keep the framework secure while the brick ceiling vaults were being built and to counter the horizontal thrust of the vaults. The main beams were joined together around the junctions with the columns, forming a self-supporting interior framework.

The design of cast-iron floor beams was critical and had to take into account the physical qualities of the material, which is strong in compression but brittle when subject to tension or bending. The basic form of the beams used in early mills with brick-vaulted ceilings was derived from those designed by Charles Bage for the world's first iron-framed mill, built at Ditherington, Shrewsbury, between 1796 and 1797.[45] In cross-section the beams are of inverted T-shape, with a narrow bottom flange but no top flange. The outer edges of the ceiling vaults rested on the surface of the bottom flange. Viewed from the side the bottom flange is flat but the top edge of the beam is convex. The method of joining beams around the columns usually involved clamping together projecting lugs on the ends of the beams with circular metal rings, which provided a limited amount of free movement in the joint. These 'shrink rings' are often visible near the column tops. The beams of each bay were linked by longitudinal tie-rods, similar to those used to link the columns, which are also sometimes partially exposed beneath the ceiling vaults.

Various details of this early form of cast-iron beam were modified by early mill builders, but a thorough understanding of cast-iron beam design was not obtained until the important series of experiments by Eaton Hodgkinson and William Fairbairn in Manchester in the late 1820s (see p. 80). The early design problems were exacerbated by an inadequate understanding of the casting process itself,[46] leading to a number of well-publicised and fatal collapses of fireproof mills in the first half of the 19th century. Several of these occurred in the Greater Manchester area, including that in 1824 of the newly built Islington Mill (829*), in Salford.

The second method of early fireproof construction, in which stone flag floors were laid on cast-iron beams, is best represented in Greater Manchester in the warehouse block of Beehive Mill (306*), built in Ancoats in 1824 (Fig 50). It is also found in the ceilings of entrance passages, in staircase landings and in some small early to mid 19th-century structures requiring a flat fireproof ceiling.[47] The beams are of T-shaped cross-section to provide a level surface on which to lay the floors. They are bolted around the column tops and in some cases, including Beehive Mill, have cast-in sockets enabling additional lighter joists to be slotted in place forming a grid pattern. Although the T-shaped cross-section and the simple method of joining the beams was later superseded, the

Figure 50. The unusual fireproof construction of the 1824 warehouse of Beehive Mill, Manchester (306*). The flag floors are supported by a complex grid of T-section cast-iron beams.

Figure 51. The interior of Brownsfield Mill, Manchester (315*), built 1825, showing the heavy timber floor construction of thick boards mounted directly on the beams without the use of joists.

sophisticated grid pattern of the floor beams at Beehive Mill (306*) was advanced. The use of floor beams in both a longitudinal and transverse direction is comparable to the use of primary, secondary and tertiary beams in the framing of much larger mills from the 1870s. This warehouse block is also distinguished by an advanced fireproof cast and wrought-iron roof (see pp. 62–5).

The main block of Beehive Mill (306*), built a few years before the fireproof warehouse, is a well-preserved example of the third type of early 19th-century mill construction, containing heavy timber floors without joists. Although apparently simple, the use of heavy timber floors in multi-storeyed mills may represent a significant conceptual development; it was widely emulated by mill builders in the United States of America, where the technique was known as 'slow-burning' construction. The only other known surviving example in a Manchester cotton mill is Brownsfield Mill (315*) of 1825.[48] In these mills, thick floorboards were laid directly on heavy transverse timber beams and the beams supported by cast-iron columns (Fig 51). This construction may have permitted higher floor loadings than joisted timber floors, which would have been an advantage in room and power mills, such as Beehive Mill (306*) and Brownsfield Mill (315*), enabling heavy machinery to be used by firms occupying the upper storeys. Another advantage was improved fire resistance, since the heavy beams and boards could be charred in a fire without being significantly weakened.[49] Recent research has claimed that the American system of slow-burning construction was originally copied from Manchester's heavy timber-floored mills of the 1820s. American mill builders developed the technique after it was described in a publication of 1826.[50] Ironically, heavy timber floors were not widely used in British mills, although at least one other example was built in Greater Manchester as late as the 1890s.[51]

Beehive Mill (306*) and Brownsfield Mill (315*) also show a number of other advanced details. Their columns incorporate bolting faces for the attachment of line shafting, a feature which was not commonplace until the mid 19th century. At Beehive Mill (306*) the timber beams were clamped between cast-iron 'compression plates' mounted on top of the columns, another feature which later became more widespread. The beams supported the weight of one floor only, the weight of the upper storeys being transmitted via the compression plates and columns directly into the foundations. Heavy timber may also have been a less restrictive building material than cast iron, since both mills are slightly wider than contemporary fireproof mills and have larger bays.

Most early mills had gabled roofs, although some double and triple-span designs were also built. Early roofs can be categorised according to their principal building materials. Timber roofs were used in combination with all three types of floor construction. Queen-strut roofs with collars were often used to create additional floorspace in the attic, such as at Brownsfield Mill (315*) (Fig 52). Islington Mill (829*) has a queen-post roof, while Chatham Mill, Manchester (320), has a modified queen-post roof with full-length dormer windows on one side, a feature also seen in the

Figure 52. Timber queen-strut trusses, such as these at Brownsfield Mill, Manchester (315*), were the most common type of roof construction in early mills.

Figure 53. In the main block of Beehive Mill, Manchester (306*), dating from the early 1820s, the trusses combine cast-iron and timber components in a design which provides a completely unobstructed attic floor.

early mills of other areas.[52] In mills where the roof space was not used as a working or storage area simple king-post roofs were used, as at Sedgwick Mill, Manchester (372*), and this type was also employed in smaller ancillary buildings such as external engine houses. Roof trusses made entirely of cast iron were used in mills throughout the 19th century, but were not particularly common. No example is known to survive from the early period in Greater Manchester. The main block of Beehive Mill (306*), however, has a spacious attic in which the trusses combine both cast-iron and timber components (Fig 53). The timber principal rafters are

Figure 54. The apex of a truss at Beehive Mill, Manchester (306*). The vertical square plates beneath the cast-iron ribs were mounting points for line shafts.

Figure 55. The 1824 warehouse at Beehive Mill, Manchester (306*), is an example of the most advanced type of early mill roof, utilising the different structural properties of cast and wrought iron.

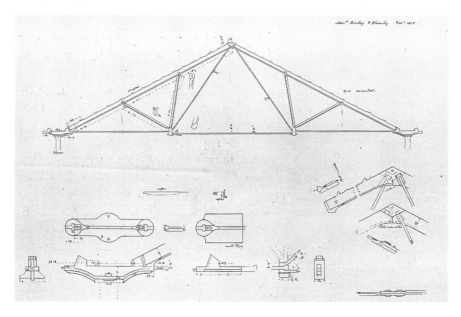

Figure 56. A cast and wrought-iron roof similar to that at Beehive Mill (306*) was designed for Chorlton New Mill, Manchester (323*), in 1815, but does not survive (Boulton and Watt Collection, Portfolio No. 449, Birmingham Library Services).

supported by slender curved cast-iron ribs. The ribs are of two pieces joined in the centre, where a short upright post supports the roof apex (Fig 54). The outer ends of both the ribs and the principals are supported on cast-iron brackets attached to the floor beams and the walls.

The most advanced early mill roofs used a combination of cast and wrought iron to create a relatively lightweight and fireproof spaceframe structure. Such roofs rely on the contrasting structural properties of the two types of iron, cast iron being used for the components in compression and wrought iron for those in tension. They were carefully designed and entirely prefabricated for assembly on the mill. The roof of the 1824 warehouse of Beehive Mill (306*) is the only known surviving example in Manchester. The principals, purlins and unusual combined queen struts and angled struts are all of cast iron (Fig 55). Vertical and horizontal wrought-iron tie-rods replace the king posts and horizontal tie-beams of a conventional timber truss. A more spectacular example survived at Chepstow Street Mill, Manchester (322*), until 1990. This seven-storeyed fireproof mill of *c*.1820 had a triple-span roof comprising cast-iron principals, angled struts and purlins, with wrought-iron vertical and horizontal tie-rods to each truss (Fig 187). Documentary evidence suggests that the nearby Chorlton New Mill (323*), built *c*.1814, originally had a very similar iron-framed roof (Fig 56).[53]

## Internal organisation

The internal arrangement of processes and machinery in cotton mills was more varied in the early 19th century than in later periods, although the larger firms began to adopt similar approaches to internal layout from an early stage. The variety was in part due to the significant technical improvements made in this period to machinery and power systems but was also a reflection of the continued presence in Manchester of many small firms, most renting part of a room and power mill. The mule was the dominant machine in Manchester's fine-spinning trade by the early 19th century, being used in most of the larger owner-occupied mills and also in room and power mills. Water frames and throstles were less significant in Manchester but may have been more commonly used by smaller firms in those surrounding towns such as Stockport which concentrated on the production of coarser yarns.[54]

A number of the more successful early cotton spinners made their own improvements to textile machinery. John Kennedy, for example, the first spinner to apply steam power to the mule, was also credited with making important detailed modifications to the mule.[55] With the construction of their first mill at the Ancoats site in 1798, later known as Old Mill, Manchester (363) (Fig 57), McConnel and Kennedy became the first cotton spinners to build a mill in which both mules and preparation machinery were steam powered. The firm's early inventories suggest that Old Mill (363) originally contained preparation machinery in the lower storeys with transversely located mules of between 250 and 350 spindles

each in the upper storeys.[56] The firm had recommended a similar internal layout to their customers for machinery from the mid-1790s.[57] The layout advocated by McConnel and Kennedy had several advantages and was used increasingly by other firms, significantly influencing the form of the Lancashire spinning mill by the late 19th century. The greater weight of the carding engines and the multiple line shafts required to drive them led to the preparation rooms being located in the lower storeys whenever possible, from where the prepared cotton was carried to the upper storeys for spinning. The initial processes of opening and scutching produced large quantities of cotton dust creating a serious fire hazard. For this reason they were confined to certain parts of the mill, sometimes in the basement or an attached wing, or were completely segregated in ancillary buildings. In spinning rooms with transversely located mules the fullest possible use was made of the available floorspace and daylight was spread as evenly as possible across the width of the mill.[58] In addition, the heaviest part of the mule could be located above the main floor beams.[59] As more new mills were built for mule spinning there developed a close relationship between the length of the mule and the width of the building, while the longitudinal spacing of the columns had to allow enough room for the draw of the mules.

Small room and power firms frequently occupied a single floor of a mill and so could not adopt the vertical separation of preparation and spinning used in the more progressive of the larger mills. In the late 18th century they had competed with the larger spinning firms but by the 1820s they were increasingly concerned with minor specialised branches of the

Figure 57. McConnel and Kennedy's early mills, built between 1798 and 1820 overlooking the Rochdale Canal in Ancoats. The firm made significant improvements to textile machinery and to the internal organisation of spinning mills (M'Connel 1906, 24).

textile trade. However, some surviving early room and power mills are of the more expensive fireproof and heavy timber-floored types of construction, suggesting that small firms were still perceived as a thriving sector of the local economy by speculative mill builders.[60] Room and power was also used by non-textile firms, such as machinery makers.

## Power systems

The power systems of Manchester's surviving early 19th-century mills generally comprised the steam-raising plant, engine and an upright shaft transmission system. Water power was insignificant in Manchester in comparison with its continued importance in other areas, and the transitional use of pumping engines in combination with waterwheels was decreasing. In addition to a steam-power system some of the larger mills had gas-lighting systems, using gas produced on the mill site.

Boilers were usually of the wagon type, which were smaller and produced steam at lower pressures than the later types (Fig 58). Documentary evidence suggests that at small sites they were often located outside the mill in lightly built sheds, either free-standing or attached to the mill. None of these sheds survives.[61] The boilers of larger mills were more frequently situated internally, either in the ground floor or the basement. Internal boiler houses are sometimes identifiable by the survival of a row of arched openings in an external wall, as at Sedgwick Mill, Manchester (372*). In some cases locating boilers internally was intended to help maintain high temperatures in the spinning rooms above.[62] Relatively few early mills had reservoirs to supply the boilers, a reflection of both the small size of the boilers and the availability of canal-side building sites.

A controllable flue and chimney were integral features of the steam-raising plant.[63] In the late 18th century Shudehill Mill, Manches-

Figure 58 (below). A wagon boiler similar to those used in early 19th-century mills (Bourne 1872, 217).

Figure 59 (centre). The combined chimney and stair tower of Brownsfield Mill, Manchester (315*), an early type of mill chimney in which the stone steps provide structural support to the chimney breast.

Figure 60 (far right). The interior of the combined chimney and stair tower at Brownsfield Mill, Manchester (315*).

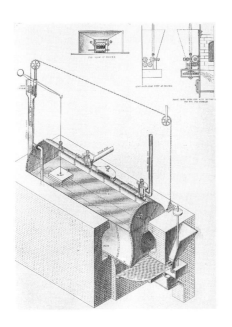

ter (374), and Garratt Mill, Manchester (336), had free-standing chimneys, but most early mills had attached or internal chimneys of square or rectangular section rising for a few metres above the mill roof or parapet. All have now been lowered.[64] A distinctive variation was provided by the cylindrical chimney, not tapered, which formed the centre of a spiral staircase (Fig 59). The stone steps were embedded in the chimney breast and in the outer wall of the staircase, giving structural support to most of the height of the stack (Fig 60). The exposed uppermost section of the stack extended for a few metres above the top of the staircase. The only fully intact example of a chimney and stair tower of this period is that of 1825 attached to Brownsfield Mill, Manchester (315*), now the oldest mill chimney in Manchester, although Islington Mill, Salford (829*), of 1823, originally had a very similar chimney. Chimney and stair towers were transitional features, allowing the chimney to be partially detached

Figure 61. A single-cylinder beam engine of the type used widely in early mills in Greater Manchester (Bourne 1872, 274).

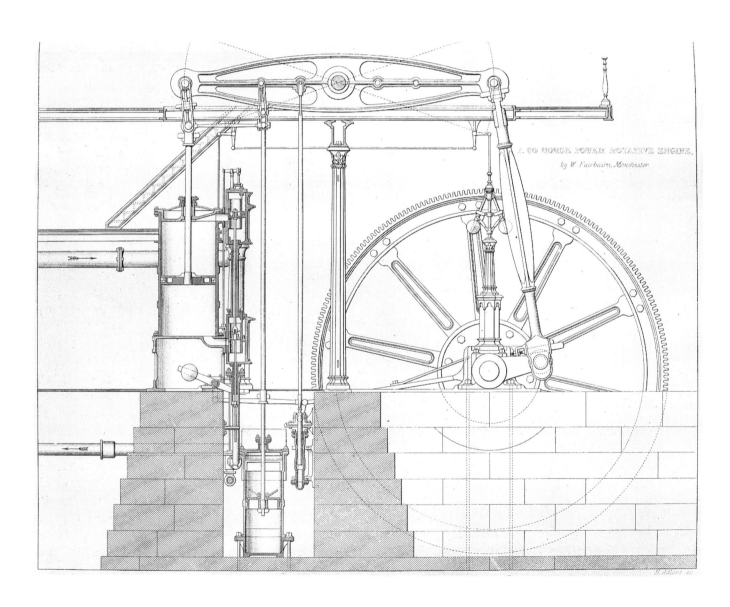

Figure 62. Most early steam-powered mills had upright-shaft transmission systems, although no example of an *in situ* early upright shaft is known. The former location of the upright shaft can sometimes be deduced from the survival of its cast-iron supports. This bracket supported the top of the upright shaft in Murray's New Mill, Manchester (359*). The water pipes are a later insertion.

from the mill before the development of free-standing stacks. Beehive Mill, Manchester (306*), retains an internal version, a combined chimney and staircase being situated between the side wall and the internal engine house.

The engines were typically single-cylinder condensing beam engines (Fig 61). Boulton and Watt of Birmingham supplied most of the larger examples, but there were also a number of local engineering firms concentrating on the smaller engines. The engines were usually integral with the engine house, or 'house built', with the main components attached to the walls or mounted on stone foundation blocks. Thus the proportions of the engine house and evidence of former attachments can be used to determine the approximate size and layout of the engine.[65] Engine houses were tall, often equivalent to two or three storeys of the mill, with a narrow rectangular floor plan. Most mills had an internal engine house situated transversely across one end, or in some cases a few bays in from the end. The engine's flywheel was located close to the centre line of the mill where the upright shaft was usually situated. During this period mills began to be built with a full-height internal cross-wall segregating the engine house from the main part of the building. This served as a fire barrier and provided a solid mounting for the gearing of the shaft transmission system, sometimes being referred to as the 'gearing wall'.[66] Fenestration is usually the best external indication of the site of the engine, for engine houses were lit by windows larger than those in the rest of the mill. Round-headed windows were used in the original detached engine houses of Murray's Mills, Manchester (358*), and from *c.*1820 tall windows extending the full height of an internal engine house were common. External engine houses were generally rare in early mills.

Little evidence of the power-transmission system usually survives in early mills. Power was transmitted from the engine to the machines via a cast-iron upright shaft which usually rose the full height of the mill. The upright shaft was turned by a horizontal shaft linked to the engine flywheel or spur wheel. Bevel gears on the upright shaft on each storey drove horizontal line shafting from which the machinery was driven by belts or ropes. In mills with a full-height gearing wall the upright shaft was either located in a slot in the face of the wall, as at Beehive Mill (306*), or enclosed in a duct within the wall, as at Chorlton New Mill, Manchester (323*). In mills without a full-height gearing wall the upright shaft was free-standing in the upper storeys, for example at Brownsfield Mill (315*). Murray's New Mill, Manchester (359*), of 1804 had a central upright shaft attached to the inside face of the side wall. The cast-iron bracket which supported the top of the upright shaft and the bevel gears for a top-floor line shaft is still *in situ* (Fig 62). The remains of traps in the floors may indicate the former position of the upright shaft. Extant mills often retain the large stone blocks which supported the base of the upright shaft. Similar stone blocks in the gearing wall, or less frequently the original cast-iron bearing boxes, show the position of and method for supporting the bevel gears driving the line shafting. The line

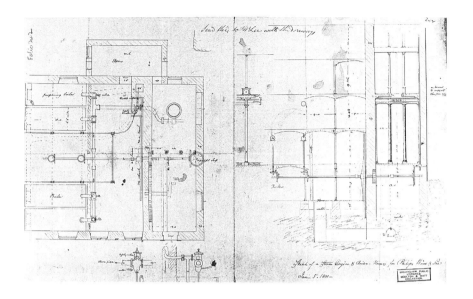

Figure 63. This 1801 plan and long section of part of the Salford Twist Mill, Salford (849), shows the engine house and the power transmission system, which used a combination of upright and horizontal main shafts (Boulton and Watt Collection, Portfolio 242, Birmingham Library Services).

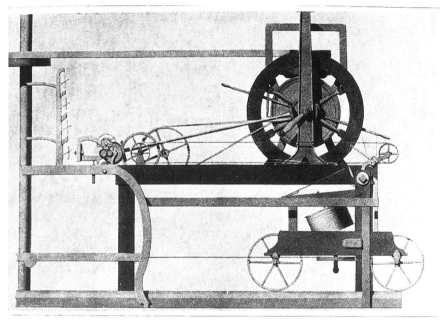

Figure 64. A cross-section of an early mule manufactured by McConnel and Kennedy, probably similar to the mules used in the firm's Ancoats mills. This example appears to be belt-driven from a vertical shaft on the left of the drawing (M'Connel 1906, 32).

shafts were usually supported by brackets hanging from the beams, although by the mid-1820s line shaft supports were increasingly attached to bolting faces cast on to the columns.

Significant improvements were made to the construction and gearing of line shafting in the early 19th century, partly as a result of the use of improved machinery in engineering works. In 1817 William Fairbairn, later to become the leading mill engineer of his day, received his first contract as a millwright involving the replacement of the line shafting in Murray's Mills (358*). The new line shafting he developed was a significant improvement on the heavy cast-iron or wooden shafting used in earlier mills. It was turned from wrought iron and was designed to work at higher

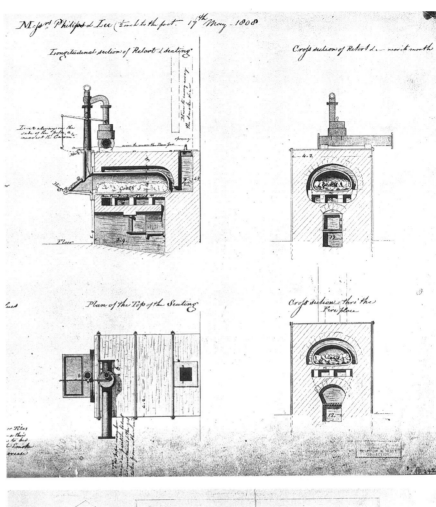

Figure 65. Gas retorts designed for use at Salford Twist Mill, Salford (849). This is thought to have been the first mill to be lit by gas, although a number of other early mills used similar gas-making plant (Boulton and Watt Collection, Portfolio 242, Birmingham Library Services).

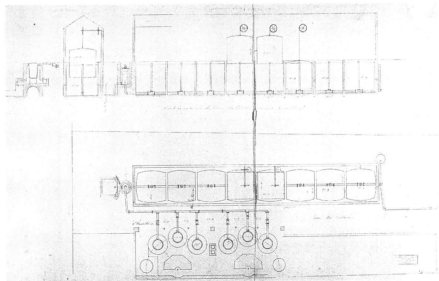

Figure 66. At Salford Twist Mill a row of eight small gas holders was located in a long building which was detached from the mill itself (Boulton and Watt, Portfolio No. 242, Birmingham Library Services).

speeds, thus reducing power losses due to friction. The modifications were successful and led to Fairbairn's next contract, the installation of the shafting in McConnel and Kennedy's fireproof Sedgwick Mill (372*), in 1818–20.[67]

Documentary evidence suggests that the greater variety of machinery layouts in early mills was matched by a variety of shafting layouts. Some early mills used a combination of horizontal and upright main shafts; an example of this arrangement in an unknown Manchester mill was described and sketched by the engineer Peter Ewart in 1791.[68] In this case the horizontal main shaft occupied the full length of the basement and drove a separate upright shaft in each of the mill's twelve bays. Eleven of the upright shafts rose through two storeys, but that in the bay adjacent to the engine house served a similar function to the upright main shafts in later mills, extending up to a third storey where it drove a single horizontal line shaft. The vertical arrangement of processes differed from that of later mills, with spinning in the lower storeys, powered by the upright shafts, and carding in the upper storey, powered by the horizontal line shaft. Original drawings of the 1802 extension to Salford Twist Mill, Salford (849), indicate that it contained a similar arrangement of upright and horizontal main shafts (Fig 63).[69] Further evidence of the use of

Figure 67. This plan of Chorlton New Mill, Manchester (323*), drawn in 1813, illustrates the original intention to locate the gas retorts and three gas holders in the basement alongside the engine and boilers. Gas was to be circulated around the mill using the hollow centres of the cast-iron columns (Boulton and Watt Collection, Portfolio 449, Birmingham Library Services).

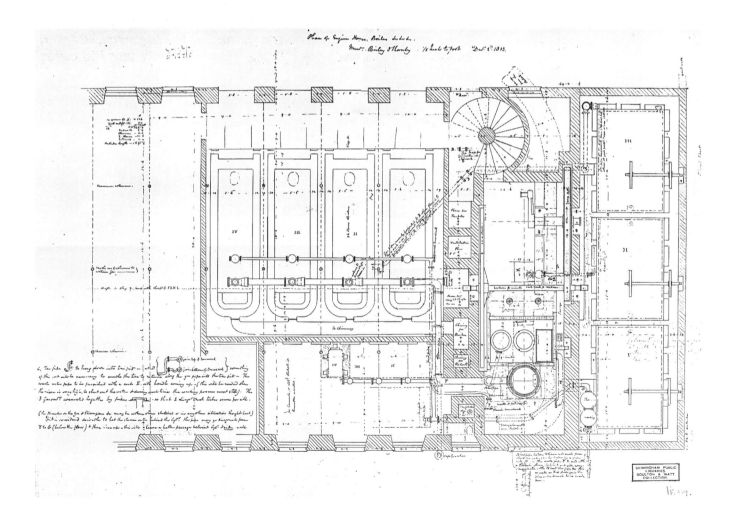

multiple upright shafts is provided by an illustration of an early mule manufactured by McConnel and Kennedy, which suggests that it too was powered from a belt drum on an upright shaft situated next to the machine (Fig 64). The firm's earliest surviving mill, however, Sedgwick Mill (372*), of 1818–20, contains no physical evidence of the use of vertical shafts to drive the mules, but there is good evidence that this type of power-transmission system was used in some later mills. At least one large mill of the 1830s used light vertical shafts to power the mule rooms (Fig 71).

Salford Twist Mill (849) was also reputed to be the first mill in the country to be built with a gas-lighting system.[70] The gas was produced on site in small retorts and stored in eight gas holders housed in a distinctive long narrow building (Figs 65 and 66). In the second decade of the century several other Manchester mills are known to have used gas-lighting systems, a further indication of the advanced nature of the cotton industry in this period. Some mills used the hollow centres of the cast-iron columns as conduits to circulate the gas around the building.[71] At Sedgwick Mill (372*), retorts were located in a long detached building in the yard, but the original drawings of Chorlton New Mill (323*) show the retorts in a segregated room in the basement. Another unusual feature of Chorlton New Mill (323*) was the internal location of the three gas holders, in a two-storeyed room next to the engine house (Fig 67). In general, however, intact evidence of early gas-lighting systems is rarely found in cotton mills.

# 4

# Mid nineteenth-century mills, 1825–1860

I N THE period 1825–60, significant improvements were made to textile machinery and, to a lesser extent, to power systems and methods of construction. The greatest technical development was the adoption of the powerloom for weaving. This led to the decline of the handloom, initially in Manchester and other early mill towns by the 1820s, later over a wider area. Weaving came to be organised in factories, first by the addition of powerlooms to spinning mills and later by the construction of purpose-built 'integrated' spinning and weaving mills. Specialised weaving mills were also being built by the 1850s. Manchester remained the largest mill town but did not experience any further mill-building booms on the scale of those between 1790 and 1825. In the surrounding areas, however, a gradual increase in mill building continued. Established firms in Manchester and the other early centres, such as Stockport, expanded by adding extensions to existing sites, but elsewhere a higher proportion of new mills was built. Consequently, mid 19th-century mill building is best illustrated with examples distributed around the whole of Greater Manchester.

## Size and layout

The internal width of new spinning mills increased slightly in the mid 19th century, reflecting improved methods of construction and in some cases the availability of larger machinery. Spotland Bridge New Mill (752*), for example, built near Rochdale in c.1833, is a non-fireproof structure with a length of 38 metres and an internal width of 18 metres, a fairly wide plan for this period (Fig 68). One of the largest mule-spinning mills was Brunswick Mill (316*), built outside Manchester in c.1840. This advanced fireproof structure utilised improved cast-iron floor beams giving an internal width of 16 metres, greater than earlier fireproof mills, to accommodate transverse self-acting mules of 400 to 500 spindles each.

Figure 68. Spotland Bridge New Mill, Rochdale (752*), illustrates the slightly wider plans of mid 19th-century spinning mills. The flat-roofed mill to the rear was added in the early 20th century.

The main block, of twenty-eight bays, was an unprecedented 92 metres long. It was equal to the tallest mid 19th-century mills, with seven storeys.

Brunswick Mill (316*) and Orrell's Mill (907), Stockport, of *c*.1834, demolished in 1975, illustrate a distinctive type of large mid 19th-century fireproof mill plan associated with the designs of William Fairbairn.[1] These mills comprise a long main block with forward-projecting wings at each end, forming a U-shaped plan (Fig 69). At Brunswick Mill (316*), the larger of the two, the wings were linked by a front block enclosing the central yard (Fig 70). Both the main block and the wings were relatively narrow in comparison with later spinning mills. By the early 20th century, mills of improved materials and construction were of similar length but much wider, occupying similar-sized sites with a single structure. Documentary evidence indicates that the original machinery in Brunswick Mill (316*) and Orrell's Mill (907) was laid out to make the best possible use

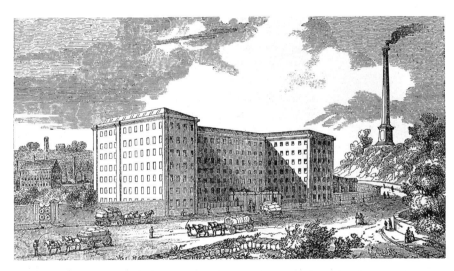

Figure 69. Orrell's Mill, Stockport (907), was built in 1834 with projecting wings at each end, a plan type used for the larger mid 19th-century mills (Ure 1835, frontispiece).

Figure 70. Brunswick Mill, Manchester (316*), of *c*.1840, one of the largest mid 19th-century mills, has a U-shaped plan with an additional front warehouse block linking the ends of the wings.

of the available floorspace, with transversely located mules occupying most of the width of the upper storeys and closely grouped preparation machinery below.[2] The link between the dimensions of cotton-spinning mills and the size and quantity of the machinery they were designed to contain is not clear, however. A general development of wider mills housing longer mules can be traced, but it is not clear which came first, the ability to build wider mills or the availability of longer mules.

Small weaving sheds were being added to spinning mills by about 1820. Their construction in Manchester increased during the 1820s, and by 1829 a particularly large shed containing 600 looms was added to Chorlton New Mill, Manchester (323*). Contemporary maps indicate that sheds adopted wider plan shapes than their adjoining spinning mills from an early date, presumably to minimise the length of the power transmission to the line shafts. The method of constructing sheds did not limit plan shape, but large sheds required extensive flat sites which were often not available in built-up areas.

The construction of large purpose-built integrated spinning and weaving mills began in the early 1830s. The first was reputed to be Compstall Mills (877) near Stockport, built by the Andrew family for spinning, weaving and cloth printing using water power, probably in combination with steam power.[3] Some of the four-storeyed spinning mills of this large complex survive intact, but the original weaving sheds were probably rebuilt later in the 19th century. The Andrews also built large reservoirs, a canal for transporting coal to the mill and a range of housing and community buildings for the workforce, most of which survive. This self-contained, paternalistic mill village illustrates the nature of industrialisation in rural areas, contrasting sharply with Manchester's closely grouped steam-powered town mills. Another large early integrated mill was Orrell's Mill, Stockport (907). This rapidly became well known for its layout, power system and internal organisation, and a detailed description was published in 1836.[4] The five-bay north-light weaving shed was attached to the side of the six-storeyed spinning block. Looms were situated throughout the shed and the ground floor of the spinning block, the window openings of which were left open on one side to give access into the shed (Fig 71).

Specialised weaving mills, in which the spun yarn was bought from a separate spinning mill, were more common by the middle of the 19th century, but soon became the characteristic type of mill in the cotton towns of north-east Lancashire. Martin's Mill, Rochdale (695*), built *c.*1850 and demolished in 1989 (Fig 72) was a typical example. Weaving mills comprised a shed with a steam-power system and attached ancillary buildings of two to four storeys. The latter were used mainly for warehousing, offices and for preparing the yarn for weaving.

Mid 19th-century cotton-waste mills were of similar proportions to but much smaller dimensions than full-sized spinning mills, and can be mistaken for spinning mills of an earlier date. They are typically from nine to eleven bays in length and of three or four storeys with an attic. Saint Helena Mill (129*), in Bolton is one of the best-preserved examples.

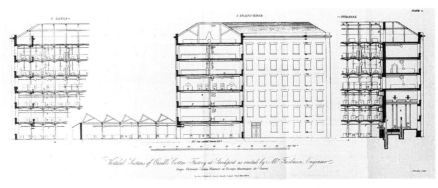

Figure 71. Orrell's Mill, Stockport (907), was built as an integrated factory with spinning machinery in the upper six floors of the multi-storeyed mill and powerlooms in the ground floor and the adjoining north-light shed (Ure 1836, plate 2).

Figure 72. Martin's Mill, Rochdale (695*), was a typical mid 19th-century steam-powered weaving mill. Adjoining the weaving shed are the engine house, boiler house and two-storeyed ancillary buildings.

## External details

Plain red brick remained the most widely used building material, although in the Pennine fringes of the county spinning mills such as Crown Mill (192*), near Bury, were of coursed stone or rubble (Fig 73). Functional external features generally differed little from those of the early 19th century. From the 1830s, however, spinning mills gave greater emphasis to architectural adornment. The most widely used ornamentation was the pilaster with a stone cornice, usually applied to the main corners of the mill and in some cases to the ancillary buildings. The cornice might be continued around the whole of the mill. The front elevations of some of the larger mills also had stone parapets. Rusticated voussoirs or stone gate piers continued to be used to highlight the main entrance, for example at Brunswick Mill, Manchester (316*) (Fig 74). Windows were slightly

Figure 73. Stone remained the most widely used mill-building material in the upland fringes of Greater Manchester. Crown Mill (192*), for example, to the north of Bury, was built in the mid 19th century, probably for cotton-waste spinning.

Figure 74 (far left). The main entrance to Brunswick Mill, Manchester (316*). The voussoired through-passage with flanking doorways is similar to the entrances of some earlier mills, but the double pilasters to either side are more characteristic of the mid 19th century.

Figure 75. The top of one of the unusual stair towers at Brunswick Mill, Manchester (316*).

larger, usually with lower sills, but remained of similar proportions. They were glazed with twenty or more small panes, usually with a hinged or swinging central panel for ventilation. Most had wooden glazing bars although cast iron was also used. Original glazing bars are rarely found. Stair and privy towers were attached to most spinning mills. They were usually square or circular in plan. Brunswick Mill (316*) has internal semi-circular stair towers in both wings, each having a half-domed ceiling in the top storey (Fig 75). Some half-octagonal towers were also built in this period, for example at Oxford Mills (1010), near Dukinfield, and Great Bridgewater Street Mills, Manchester (339).

The origins of specialist mill architecture can be seen in the construction of the larger fireproof mills. In the 1820s the design and appearance of the typical cotton mill was derived from the combined work of millwrights, engineers and builders, and in general no individual took sole responsibility for the design of the mill. In the mid 19th century, however, it seems that textile mills were increasingly built by specialist building firms. An important Manchester firm specialising in industrial structures was that of David Bellhouse, whose mills included the fireproof Islington Mill, Salford (829*), in 1823 and Brunswick Mill (316*) in *c.*1840.[5] This firm appears to have combined the range of trades involved with fireproof mill construction, occupying a foundry and a timber yard and being referred to as 'architects' from the early 1820s.[6]

Another important Manchester firm was that of the eminent millwright and engineer William Fairbairn and his partners. Fairbairn later boldly claimed to have improved the embellishment of textile mills, having produced 'designs for a new mill of a different class' in around 1827.[7] He reputedly designed the technically advanced Orrell's Mill, Stockport (907),[8] which was also an early example of typical 19th-century mill embellishment. At other mills, however, Fairbairn co-operated with established architects, his own involvement being restricted to the design of the ironwork.[9]

By the late 1850s a greater quantity and variety of ornamentation was beginning to be used in the larger mills, for example in the entrance and engine house of Gilnow Mill, Bolton (71*), which was built in 1858 (Fig 76). Features such as double pilasters, stone mouldings, dentilated cornices and round-headed windows were applied selectively to emphasise the most important parts of the mill. The use of these kinds of Italianate details was continued by specialist mill architects in the late 19th century (see p. 100).

Figure 76. Gilnow Mill, Bolton (71*), is a fine example of mid 19th-century embellishment. The main functional features are distinguished by a selective use of round-headed windows, double pilasters, string courses, a dentilated cornice and various other Italianate details.

# Methods of construction

The widespread adoption of fireproof construction was held up by a number of well-publicised collapses of fireproof mills in the first half of the 19th century, such as that mentioned above at Islington Mill, Salford (829*), in 1824 (p. 61). These collapses were caused by failures of cast-iron beams and columns. Casting techniques and beam design were still fallible, reflecting a lack of scientific information regarding the material's properties. In response to these continuing problems an investigation into the physical properties of cast iron and the optimum design of floor beams was carried out in Manchester in the 1820s by Eaton Hodgkinson, partly at the Ancoats foundry of William Fairbairn. In the early 1830s Fairbairn started to produce a greatly improved type of beam based on the results of Hodgkinson's experiments. These beams were of I-shaped cross-section with a wider bottom flange, the sides of which formed a convex parabolic curve when viewed from below. The narrower top flange, which was hidden within the thickness of the floor, followed a similar convex curve, as did the upper edge of the beam when viewed from the side. It was claimed that these beams were lighter and could safely be made longer than the earlier inverted T-section beams. Official concern about the collapses of fireproof mills eventually resulted in a Parliamentary investigation led by Fairbairn in 1845, which not surprisingly stressed the great importance of efficient floor-beam design.[10] Other types of cast-iron beam, with parallel-sided flanges, continued to be used after Fairbairn's introduction of the 'Hodgkinson' beam, however, and the impact of the new technology on mill building may have been limited by the comparatively slow expansion of the cotton industry in this period. Following the publication of the results of Hodgkinson's work in 1831,[11] it is likely that other engineering firms produced alternative improved beams.

The most spectacular application of Hodgkinson beams can be seen in some of the largest spinning mills built in the mid 19th century. They were used in an extension to Wear Mill, Stockport (934*), in c.1840 (Fig 77), at Orrell's Mill, Stockport (907), in 1834 and at Brunswick Mill, Manchester (316*), in c.1840. Another example of c.1840 is the cotton mill added to Great Bridgewater Street Mills (339), in Manchester, while one of the smallest was Fireproof Mill, Manchester (335*), an 1842 addition to Murray's Mills (358*). A contemporary fireproof structure which does not have Hodgkinson beams is an 1845 extension to Chorlton New Mill, Manchester (323*), in which the beams have parallel-sided bottom flanges.

Other components of fireproof construction remained relatively unaltered. Thicker cast-iron columns were used, frequently equipped with cast-on bolting faces or embossed rings for the attachment of line-shaft brackets. Transverse brick ceiling vaults with an ash infill supporting floors of clay tiles or wooden boards remained the most widespread construction. The bay size, indicated by the longitudinal spacing of the columns, changed little from that of the larger early 19th-century mills.

Figure 77. Brick-vaulted ceilings supported by cast-iron beams and columns continued to be the most widespread type of fireproof construction in the mid 19th century. Improved types of cast-iron floor beams were introduced, however, and are found in mills from the mid 1830s. This example is part of Wear Mill, Stockport (934*), dating from c.1840.

Brick-vaulted ceilings were not used exclusively, however. At least one more example of a multi-storeyed building with flat fireproof ceilings of stone flags laid on cast-iron beams was built, namely the wing of the cotton mill at the Great Bridgewater Street Mills complex (339). The wing probably dates from c.1840. The cast-iron beams are of inverted T-section and may be a development of the T-section beams used in 1824 at Beehive Mill, Manchester (306*). Other contrasts with the earlier example are the absence of cast-iron columns and the less complex layout of the beams. A similar though much smaller ceiling was used in about 1830 for the internal boiler house of Saint Helena Mill (129*), in Bolton.

Non-fireproof joisted timber floors probably continued to account for the majority of spinning mills built until the late 19th century.[12] Some of the surviving examples, such as Spotland Bridge New Mill, Rochdale (752*), are of greater width and have greater spacing between the columns than contemporary fireproof mills (Fig 78). Joisted floors were also used for cotton-waste mills (Fig 79). Thicker columns with bolting faces or embossed rings were used in non-fireproof mills of all sizes by the 1850s (Fig 80). The use of cast-iron compression plates on the column tops, to avoid stressing the timber floor beams, became more widespread even in relatively small mills, such as Field Mill, Ramsbottom (205*), of c.1850. The only known example of heavy timber-floored construction, without joists, in a mid 19th-century mill is in the Great Bridgewater Street Mills complex in Manchester (339). Here, the lower three storeys of the seven-storeyed Silk Mill and all seven storeys of its attached wing had heavy timber floors, both structures dating from the late 1820s.

Figure 78. Non-fireproof construction with joisted timber floors continued to be used in the majority of new mills. This view shows the interior of Spotland Bridge New Mill, Rochdale (752*).

Figure 79. Joisted wooden floors were also commonplace in the smaller cotton-waste mills, such as Saint Helena Mill (129*) in Bolton.

Roof construction also showed little development in comparison with the early 19th century. The use of multi-ridge roofs became more common as the width of spinning mills increased in the second half of the century. Orrell's Mill (907) had an unusual mansard roof (Fig 71). Timber roof trusses were still widely used, especially queen-post and queen-strut

Figure 80 (above). The use of flat bolting faces in the sides of cast-iron columns became widespread in the mid 19th century, providing attachment points for line shafting.

Figure 81 (above right). Timber queen-strut trusses were used in many multi-storeyed mills, such as Spotland Bridge New Mill, Rochdale (752*).

Figure 82. For weaving-shed roofs the asymmetrical north-light profile was adopted from the early 1830s. Mid 19th-century shed roofs were predominantly of timber, as here at Wear Mill, Stockport (934*).

types. These enabled the attic to be used either for storage, as at Wear Mill (934*), or, when combined with skylights, for powered processes, such as at Spotland Bridge New Mill (752*) (Fig 81). Cast-iron roof trusses remained relatively uncommon; the best surviving example is probably that of the *c*.1831 fireproof Wellington Mill, Stockport (937).

Surviving examples of pre-1850 weaving sheds are rare. The asymmetrical saw-tooth or north-light roof later became common but its first known documented use was not until 1834 at Orrell's Mill (907). Shed roofs used timber trusses. Horizontal tie-beams supported the rafters and the valley gutters which ran across the roof, such as at Wear Mill (934*) (Fig 82). Cast-iron columns stood beneath the intersection of the tie-beams and the valley gutters and supported most of the weight of the roof, so the walls were lightly built. The columns might include bolting faces or embossed rings for the brackets of the many line shafts which powered a shed. The characteristic feature of the north-light weaving shed was its use of glazing only on the steeper, north-facing side of the ridge. A consequence of the use of skylights is that shed walls rarely have windows. Sheds were usually floored with stone flags.

## Internal organisation

Large mills built for mule spinning followed the type of internal organisation used earlier at McConnel and Kennedy's Ancoats mills, Manchester, such as Old Mill (363) and Sedgwick Mill (372*), with transversely oriented mules in the upper storeys and preparation machinery mainly on the ground floor. At Brunswick Mill, Manchester (316*), however, documentary evidence indicates that the ground floor was probably originally used for storage, a feature which became more common in the late 19th century, with preparation and carding in the second storey and self-acting mules in the five upper storeys.[13] Throstles were more compact than mules but were also often located transversely across a mill. In mills

Figure 83. Mount Pleasant Mill (241) and its workers' village were built in an isolated upland site to the north of Bury. The complex originated in *c*.1820 as the centre of an extensive network of handloom weavers, but later developed into a steam-powered spinning and weaving mill.

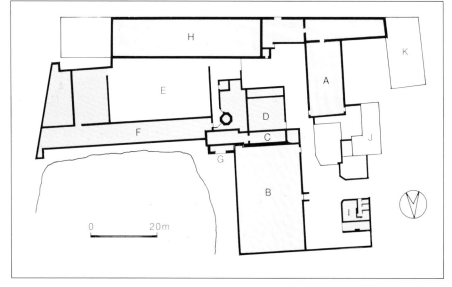

Figure 84. Mount Pleasant Mill.
A:  original unpowered mill
B:  steam-powered spinning mill
C:  engine house
D:  boiler house
E:  site of powerloom-weaving shed
F:  ancillary building to shed
G:  later engine house
H:  housing converted to second
     weaving shed
I:  offices
J:  stable
K:  manager's house

of sufficient internal width the machines were arranged side by side forming two rows along the floor with each row powered from a separate line shaft, as at Orrell's Mill, Stockport (907) (Fig 71). Some of the larger fine-spinning firms extended their premises to accommodate yarn-doubling machinery, first to supply the lace-making industry but increasingly to meet the growing demand for sewing cotton. In Manchester Murray's added Doubling Mill (334*), in 1842, powered by an internal steam engine and used exclusively for doubling yarn spun in the firm's earlier mills.

Sheds were used for weaving because of the considerable weight and vibration of the powerlooms, and because the north-light design permitted even internal lighting. The powerlooms in weaving sheds were arranged in rows between the columns. They were oriented to face the north lights, so avoiding casting shadows on to the cloth. Although handloom weaving and the putting-out system were in decline by the 1830s significant numbers of handloom weavers remained active throughout the mid 19th century, increasingly concentrating on the demand for specialised fabrics. A successful firm which developed an extensive network of handloom weavers in addition to an integrated mill was that of John Hall at Mount Pleasant Mill (241), north of Bury. This firm specialised in the production of high-quality quilted fabrics, and by the 1830s controlled over a thousand handloom weavers scattered up to a dozen miles from Mount Pleasant.[14] The mill itself was located in an isolated upland site and by the 1830s included terraced housing to accommodate the workforce (Figs 83 and 84).

In integrated mills the spinning and weaving areas were usually interconnected, but spinning was still organised vertically on successive floors of a multi-storeyed block and with weaving at ground level in an adjoining shed. When a shed was attached to a spinning mill the ground-floor bays of the intervening wall were often left open to allow free access between the two buildings. The extent to which production was integrated sometimes included processes in addition to spinning and weaving. Compstall Mills (877) near Stockport, for example, began as a cloth-printing works in the 1820s; when spinning and weaving were added the full range of processes from raw cotton to finished cloth were carried out at the site. At Orrell's Mill (907), two floors of the spinning block contained throstles to produce the weft and two contained mules producing warp. The internal organisation of this mill was also unusual in that the preparation processes were situated in the middle storey, with the mule rooms above and the throstles below (Fig 71). At Mount Pleasant Mill (241), a steam-powered spinning mill was added to earlier buildings containing handlooms. Powerloom sheds were added later.

In cotton-waste mills the waste was obtained from the larger mills spinning raw cotton and was used for the production of low-grade cloths, such as flannels. The limited supply of waste restricted both the extent of the cotton-waste trade and the size of the individual mills. The initial processes of cleaning and blending differed from those used for raw cotton, but thereafter the carding, spinning and weaving were carried out on machinery similar to that used in larger mills. Mules were used for spinning cotton waste at Saint Helena Mill, Bolton (129*), for example, from the mid 1830s.

## Power systems

In Greater Manchester the importance of water power and hand power declined further in the mid 19th century as steam became the predominant source of power in textile mills. The demand for more powerful engines resulted in improvements to boilers and an increase in the size of boiler houses. The most important technical development was the introduction of the double-flue 'Lancashire' boiler, patented by William Fairbairn and John Hetherington in 1844, which was to become the standard boiler design used in cotton mills. It was larger than the earlier wagon boilers, being typically 9.1 metres long (Fig 85). Its use led to the increased construction of external boiler houses by the middle of the 19th century. These were single-storeyed rectangular buildings usually situated close to the engine house and the chimney. Their size was determined by the number of boilers they contained; in a common arrangement two boilers were housed longitudinally beneath either side of a wide-gabled roof. The front end wall contained one or more large openings, sometimes arched, giving access to the 'firing floor' at the front of the boilers (Fig 86). The roof frequently had a louvred apex vent. Internal boiler houses became less common but in larger mills are identifiable by a row of wide-arched openings similar to those seen in some early mills. The construction of reservoirs to supply steam plant was still relatively uncommon, the

Figure 87 (right). The economic efficiency of boilers was greatly improved with the introduction of the Green's economiser. The hot gases in the chimney flue were used to pre-heat the water entering the boiler (Nasmith and Nasmith 1909, figure 114).

Figure 88 (far right). Square chimneys continued to be built in the mid 19th century at smaller mills such as Saint Helena Mill, Bolton (129*).

Figure 85 (left). 'Lancashire' boilers replaced earlier types from the mid 1840s. These surviving Lancashire boilers at Chorlton New Mill, Manchester (323*), probably date from the late 19th century.

Figure 86 (below). With the introduction of larger boilers, external boiler houses became more common. This typical mid 19th-century boiler house for three Lancashire boilers was added to Dob Wheel Mill near Rochdale (635) in 1854.

majority of steam-powered mills being built alongside natural water-courses or canals.

The efficiency of steam boilers was greatly improved by the invention of the economiser by E. Green of Wakefield in 1845 (Fig 87). This consisted of a nest of cast-iron pipes mounted in the flue between the boiler and the chimney. Water entering the boiler was first passed through the pipes and was heated by up to 200 degrees Fahrenheit by the exhaust gases in the flue, significantly cutting fuel costs.[15] Economisers were

contained within a rectangular brick box at the rear of a boiler house or sometimes in a small shed or brick structure between the boiler house and the chimney. No surviving mid 19th-century examples are known, although they became more widespread in Greater Manchester mills in the second half of the 19th century.

Chimneys gradually developed from the attached or internal types to tapered free-standing types of octagonal cross-section. Small mills, such as Saint Helena Mill, Bolton (129*), continued to be built with attached square-section chimneys similar to those used in the early 19th century (Fig 88). A transitional type was the octagonal chimney mounted on a tall square plinth, the plinth being attached to the wall of the mill. An example can be seen at Good Hope Mill (979*), in Ashton under Lyne, where the stack itself was probably replaced later (Fig 89). The largest mills, in which the size of the steam plant required a particularly strong draught, were given tall free-standing chimneys from the early 1830s. These received a similar level of architectural embellishment to the mill itself. The chimney of Orrell's Mill, Stockport (907), was a particularly fine example standing on a hill overlooking the site. The octagonal stack was topped by a prominent corbelled crown and was mounted on a square plinth, which had recessed panels to each face and a cornice (Fig 69).

Figure 89. Many mid 19th-century mills had octagonal chimneys mounted on tall square plinths, as at Good Hope Mill, Ashton under Lyne (979*). Most were built with corbelled crowns at the top but these rarely survive intact. Taller, free-standing chimneys were only built for the largest mid 19th-century mills.

House-built beam engines remained the most widely used type of steam engine in cotton mills, but other types were occasionally used. The 1829 weaving shed added to Chorlton New Mill, Manchester (323*), for example, was powered by a Boulton and Watt marine-type engine, with the beam mounted on the side.[16] This engine was installed in the former gasometer room in the north end of the mill, which had insufficient ceiling height for a normal beam engine. Engine technology did not develop as rapidly as in the early 19th century or in later periods, so the requirements for more power were initially met by simply adding an extra cylinder to the familiar beam-engine design. By the mid 1830s double-beam engines, with two side-by-side cylinders working a single flywheel, were increasingly used. Spotland Bridge New Mill, Rochdale (752*), and Orrell's Mill

(907) both had this type of engine. The most common evidence for such engines is the plan of their engine houses, wider than those built for single-cylinder beam engines, and the frequent use of a pair of tall arched windows instead of a single window in the end wall. In some cases the distinctive engine beds also survive. The largest mills could still accommodate the bulk of a double-beam engine internally, but in more typical mills external engine houses were being built by the 1850s.

The most significant technical development related to steam engines was linked to the higher steam pressures generated by Lancashire boilers. The power of an engine could be increased by adding an extra high-pressure cylinder, an alteration known as 'compounding'. The most common system for compounding an engine was patented by William McNaught of Bury in 1845; in this arrangement an upright high-pressure cylinder was installed beneath the beam in line with the main cylinder. This was known as 'McNaughting' an engine.[17] In other cases a horizontal high-pressure cylinder was added, for example at Martin's Mill, Rochdale (695*). Such modifications might be carried out when the mill was extended or the machinery replaced, and were often accompanied by the installation of a new boiler. By the middle of the 19th century the use of ready-built compound engines was becoming more common in cotton mills (Fig 90). One effect of the improvement of single-cylinder beam engines was that narrow engine houses continued to be built. By the 1840s, however, double-compounded beam engines needing wider engine houses were being installed in some of the larger mills, for example at Chorlton New Mill (323*), in 1845.

Water power was still widely used in rural areas in the mid 19th century and significant technical advances were made in the design of water-wheels. Mid 19th-century maps show numerous small water-powered textile mills situated in the northern and eastern fringes of Greater Manchester but few representative examples, if any, survive intact. Two extant sites illustrate the larger-scale application of water power, although the waterwheels of both were eventually replaced by steam power. These sites were not typical of water-powered mills in Greater Manchester but are similar to the scale of mid 19th-century installations in other regions. Crimble Mill (627*), near Heywood, was built *c*.1829 and was powered by a pair of wooden-framed wheels located in the centre of the basement. The wheels, which had iron buckets, were fed from a large reservoir dammed against the back wall of the mill.[18] In other respects this mill was of similar scale and appearance to contemporary steam-powered spinning mills in urban areas. Steam power was added in the 1850s when a tall external beam-engine house was attached to one end. At the large integrated mill complex at Compstall, a spectacular iron waterwheel by Fairbairn and Lillie was installed in 1838, measuring 15 metres in diameter and over 5 metres wide.[19] It was replaced by water turbines in 1881 and by steam power in 1906.

Throughout the mid 19th century, upright shafts were used to transmit power to line shafts in spinning mills. Only one intact example of an upright shaft is known to survive in Greater Manchester, in the cotton mill

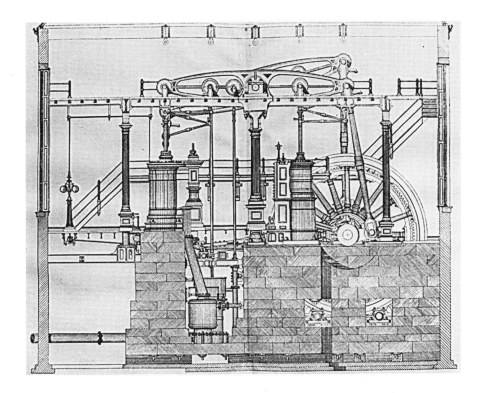

Figure 90. A double McNaughted beam engine, typical of those used in the larger mid 19th-century mills (*The Textile Manufacturer*, 1877, 228).

of the Great Bridgewater Street Mills complex, Manchester (339), dating from *c.*1840. Mule-spinning mills, such as Brunswick Mill, Manchester (316*), used a similar machinery layout to that used earlier at McConnel and Kennedy's mills and may have required a similar arrangement of line shafting. Brunswick Mill (316*) does not contain evidence of the use of short vertical shafts passing between the floors, so the machinery may have been powered directly from belt drums on the line shafts, as was common in the late 19th century. Mills built for spinning on throstles, which required more power, might have two line shafts in spinning rooms wide enough to contain two rows of machines. One line shaft powered each row, as was probably the case at Spotland Bridge New Mill (752*). At Orrell's Mill (907) both types of spinning machine were used, requiring a different arrangement of line shafting in different floors of the building (Fig 71). Each of the throstle rooms contained two line shafts. The mules, however, were driven by light vertical shafts passing through the floor in alternate bays, a similar arrangement to that used in some large late 18th and early 19th-century mills (see pp. 70–2). The vertical shafts were powered from a single line shaft in the uppermost spinning room, driving the mules on that floor and in the storey below.

Weaving sheds contained a similar arrangement of multiple line-shafting to that used in the preparation rooms of spinning mills. The line shafts, one to each row of looms, were usually fixed to the columns and driven by a horizontal main shaft attached to a side or end wall. When the weaving shed was a later addition to a spinning mill it was often powered by a new engine, as occurred at Chorlton New Mill (323*) in 1829. In purpose-built integrated mills the whole site might be powered from a single large engine house, the weaving shed's main shaft driven from the engine or from the base of the upright shaft in the spinning mill, as for example at Orrell's Mill (907) and Gilnow Mill, Bolton (71*).

# 5

# Late nineteenth-century mills, 1860–1900

THE resurgence of the cotton industry in Greater Manchester in the late 19th century accounted for a high proportion of the mills surviving today. Most of these new mills were built in the areas surrounding Manchester during a series of economic boom periods (see Chapter 2). Mill building in Manchester itself decreased slowly from the 1850s as the city developed into a commercial centre serving the international cotton trade. In the surrounding towns, the size of new mills increased, while their form and detailed design saw considerable development under the influence of specialist architects. The increased competition within the industry prompted a greater emphasis on the achievement of an efficient internal layout of processes. The development of machinery and power systems thus continued to be a major influence on the form of cotton mills.

The expansion of the industry in some parts of the county, particularly in Oldham, was partly a consequence of legislation which allowed the formation of large numbers of 'limited' firms. As the number of mills increased, however, competition between firms led to other changes in the nature and distribution of mill building. In particular, the proportion of integrated spinning and weaving firms decreased as specialised production became the more economically viable option. In spinning, Oldham's mills concentrated on coarse counts of yarn and Bolton's on medium to fine counts, while Manchester's firms continued to specialise in the finest yarns. Regional specialisation also developed further, with a greater emphasis on weaving in the expanding towns of north-east Lancashire and on spinning in south-east Lancashire, now Greater Manchester.

## Size and layout

The size, shape and layout of spinning mills saw considerable development in the late 19th century, reflecting parallel developments in methods of construction, textile machinery and power systems. By the late 19th century new mills were typically both longer and wider than most earlier mills. Anchor Mill, Oldham (400*) (Fig 91), with eighteen bays, is a relatively small example built in 1881, while Prince of Wales Mill (524*)

Figure 91. Anchor Mill, Oldham (400*), illustrates the typical proportions of a cotton-spinning mill of the 1880s. The greater width of late 19th-century mills enabled larger mules to be accommodated efficiently in a transverse layout and was made possible by improved methods of construction.

Figure 92. Prince of Wales Mill, Oldham (524*), is a much larger mule-spinning mill than Anchor Mill, Oldham (400*), but has a similar wide plan.

Figure 93. The width of mills designed for mule spinning increased throughout the late 19th century. The multi-storeyed block of Barnfield Mills, Tyldesley (1060*), built in 1894 and designed by Bradshaw and Gass, had an internal width of 40 metres.

(Fig 92), of 1875, also in Oldham, was particularly large with twenty-six bays. Still larger mills were built later, but improved methods of construction frequently led to an increase in the size of each bay, so that the total number of bays actually decreased. The tendency for the width of new mule-spinning mills to increase, which can be detected in the mid 19th century, became much more pronounced. The average internal width for a mule-spinning mill in the 1870s was 30.5 to 33.5 metres, which would accommodate mules of 800 to 1,200 spindles each.[1] The width of the larger mule mills ranged from about 35 metres at Houldsworth's Mill, Reddish (899*) in 1865 to about 40 metres at Barnfield Mills, Tyldesley (1060*) (Fig 93) in 1894. By the 1880s the width of new mills designed to contain mules was usually greater than half their length. Mills built for spinning on throstles or the newly developed ring frames appeared in greater numbers abroad but remained in the minority in Britain. They were usually distinctive, however, with narrower plans and in some cases fewer storeys. There was no notable change to the typical number of storeys in spinning mills, most still having from four to six floors, although improved methods of construction often resulted in higher ceilings.

Changes also occurred to the internal layout of late 19th-century spinning mills, partly in response to their greater width. Internal engine houses remained commonplace until the 1880s, usually related to a full-height cross-wall or gearing-wall segregating one end of the mill.[2] The cross-wall was a substantial feature, sometimes containing the power transmission system, ventilation system, a hoist or staircase and the standpipes of the sprinkler system. It was also used to separate the main preparation and

Figure 94. The preparation machines in the ground floors of late 19th-century spinning mills often required a greater floor area than the spinning machines in the upper floors. As a result the ground floor had to be extended beyond the sides of the spinning rooms. The extension itself often contained carding engines. Lateral extensions to ground-floor preparation rooms can be seen in the Atlas Mills complex, Bolton.

Figure 95. At Anchor Mill, Oldham (400*), the preparation room was extended beyond the end wall.

spinning rooms from processes with a higher fire risk. External engine houses with rope-drive systems became more widespread in the 1880s, however, and thereafter fewer mills were built with cross-walls.

A distinctive feature which became widespread in the late 19th century was the extension of the ground floor beyond the walls of the upper storeys, giving the mill a stepped profile. This provided the additional space for carding and other preparation processes, which had become necessary with the use of larger and more efficient spinning machines. Such extensions often had saw-tooth roofs and can be mistaken for weaving sheds. Examples can be seen at the Atlas Mills complex, Bolton (Fig 94), and Anchor Mill, Oldham (400*) (Fig 95), of 1881.

An important variation of the typical spinning mill, the 'double mill', comprised two spinning mills of similar size built end-to-end and powered from a central engine house. The two mills might be built at the same time, but it was not unusual for one to be built some years after the mill first became operational. In some cases they were detached, but double mills also sometimes share a single large roof, for example at Ivy Mill, Failsworth (475) (Fig 96). The huge scale of the double mills was

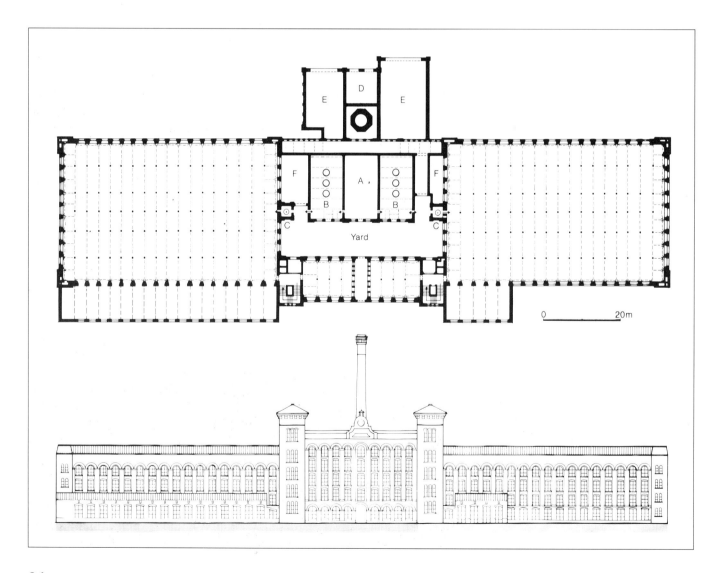

Figure 96 (opposite, top). Double mills became more widespread in the late 19th century. In this layout a pair of spinning mills was driven from a central power system. Ivy Mill (475), built in Failsworth in 1881, is an example of a double mill in which the spinning mills and the power system are attached with a continuous roof.

Figure 97 (opposite, below). At Houldsworth's Mill, Reddish (899*), the functional symmetry of a double mill is matched by the architectural symmetry of the front elevation. In this case the spinning mills are separated and linked by a narrower front block containing the entrance and the stair towers.
A: original engine house
B: original boiler house
C: shaft towers
D: pump house
E: later boiler houses
F: later engine houses

Figure 98 and 99. Offices were built with most large 19th-century mills, and were often distinguished by a greater use of embellishment and etched or stained glass. The two-storeyed offices of Atlas No. 6 Mill, Bolton (17*), are attached to the main block. The contrasting single-storeyed offices of Barnfield Mills, Tyldesley (1060*), are detached and overlook the site entrance.

impressive but the layout itself was not entirely innovative. Their origins can be seen in large 18th-century water-powered textile mills with central waterwheels and in a number of large early 19th-century steam-powered mills, such as Murray's Mills, Manchester (358*). Double mills were, however, the largest type of textile mill to be built and their construction was a viable proposition for only the most successful firms. One of the best-preserved examples is Houldsworth's Mill (899*) (Fig 97), built in 1865. In this case two spinning mills of eighteen bays each are separated by a narrower eleven-bay central block containing warehousing and offices. Behind the central block are the engine house, boiler house and chimney. The front elevation has an overall length of approximately 160 metres.

Late 19th-century spinning mills were often built with a full range of ancillary buildings including a prominent stair tower, an office block, the engine house, boiler house, chimney and perhaps a warehouse. The site might be enclosed by a wall or railings with an impressive main gateway. Offices typically comprised a small block of one or two storeys and three to five bays. They were either attached to the mill, often at the base of the stair tower as at Atlas No. 6 Mill, Bolton (17*) (Fig 98), or built to one side of the site entrance, for example at Barnfield Mills (1060*) (Fig 99). Internally they often included one larger office, the boardroom, distinguished by wooden panelling. The use of etched or stained-glass office windows was another common feature, the design usually including the name of the mill. When all the ancillary structures were contemporary they often featured similar materials and embellishment. Some notable examples of complete assemblages of mid and late 19th-century mill buildings still survive, for example at Gilnow Mill, Bolton (71*), but fully intact sites are increasingly rare. A marked trend in this period was for architects to concentrate the principal elements of a mill at one end or one corner, usually behind the main gate.

Figure 100. Some of the larger early 19th-century mills in town centre areas, where building land was restricted, were either rebuilt or extended in the late 19th century to create complex multi-period sites. An example is Wear Mill (934*), Stockport, at which a five-storeyed mill was rebuilt and a two-storeyed mill added.

Figure 101. Fewer integrated mills were built in the late 19th century. Gidlow Works, Wigan (1078), of 1865, illustrates the large size of later integrated complexes.

The late 19th-century growth of the cotton trade also prompted the extension of mills dating from earlier periods, either with the addition of a new wing or the building of a complete new mill. Extensions were most common in large town-centre sites where there was insufficient space for the construction of new mills. These sometimes contained new processes. Sedgwick New Mill, Manchester (373*), for example, was added to McConnel and Kennedy's Ancoats site for the doubling of cotton yarn. The engine house and boiler house were often extended or rebuilt when the mill was extended, as occurred at Copley Mill (970*), near Staly-bridge, in 1873. In this case an internal engine house containing a beam engine with an upright shaft transmission system was replaced by an external engine house containing a horizontal engine with a rope-drive system. A result of these extensions to earlier mills was the development of a number of large and complex multi-phase town-centre sites, for example Wear Mill, Stockport (934*) (Fig 100).

Few integrated mills were built in this period and those which remained in use were often exceptionally large sites, such as the Ashtons' mills in Hyde, principally Carrfield Mill (961) and Bayley Field Mill (952) (Fig 19), and John Rylands' Gidlow Works in Wigan (1078) (Fig 101). Specialised weaving mills continued to be built in Greater Manchester and invariably adopted a single-storeyed layout. The maximum size of sheds varied considerably, but the majority of weaving firms remained relatively small.[3] By the 1880s the newer, larger weaving mills were composed entirely of single-storeyed sheds, with fewer examples of the multi-storeyed ancillary buildings seen attached to sheds in the 1850s and 1860s. An example of the later type of shed was Carrs Mill, Ashton under Lyne (963*) (Fig 102), of 1884. The advantages of using single-storeyed sheds as opposed to multi-storeyed mills for spinning were extolled by a number of architects throughout the late 19th and the early 20th centuries, but the idea was not widely adopted and north-light sheds continued to be most commonly used for weaving.[4]

Figure 102. Specialised weaving mills began to be built without the attached multi-storeyed buildings seen at earlier sites. At Carrs Mill, Ashton under Lyne (963*), a large weaving mill of 1884, ancillary processes were located in a single-storeyed extension to the end of the main weaving shed.

The late 19th-century economic boom meant that cotton-waste mills continued to be built, especially in town-centre areas, but they remained of similar small scale to those built in the mid 19th century. A number began integrated working with the addition of attached north-light sheds for weaving, such as at Field Mill, Ramsbottom (205\*), and Saint Helena Mill, Bolton (129\*).

## The influence of the specialist mill architect

Mill design required a good understanding of production methods, including the optimum organisation of processes, machinery layouts and power systems, and of the latest methods of constructing large multi-storeyed buildings.[5] Cotton-mill architecture was thus a specialised field which in the late 19th century was dominated by a handful of locally based firms.[6] Competition for mill commissions led different architects to develop a variety of new methods of fireproof construction and encouraged the creative use of ornamentation. The most prolific architects were probably members of the Stott family of Oldham. Abraham H. Stott (1822–1904) and his brother Joseph (1837–94) established rival firms which accounted for a significant proportion of new mill building in Oldham and the surrounding towns. Abraham Stott, for example, designed the spectacular Houldsworth's Mill, Reddish (899\*), built in 1865, while Joseph's work focused on more typical late 19th-century mills, which in Oldham included Anchor Mill (400\*) of 1881 and Lees Brook Mill (483) of 1884. Abraham's son, P. S. Stott (1858–1937), later Sir Sidney, continued the family business as Stotts and Sons of Manchester and eventually designed eighty new mills in Lancashire.[7] Joseph's son George (1876–1936) was also active during the Edwardian mill-building boom. In the west of the county many new mills were built by architects based in Bolton. One of the most successful was George Woodhouse (1827–83), whose commissions included two large and architecturally distinctive mills at Gidlow Works (1078), the 1865 Wigan mill of John Rylands (Figs 25 and 26), and Victoria Mill, Miles Platting (383), of *c.*1869.[8] Another important Bolton firm was the partnership of Jonas Bradshaw (1837–1912) and John Gass (1855–1939). Their work included a number of large mill complexes and can be identified by the careful use of Italianate details.[9] Other successful mill architects in the Greater Manchester area included Edward Potts (1839–1909), who worked for a while in partnership with Woodhouse and pioneered the use of concrete floor construction,[10] and F. W. Dixon (1854–1935), whose mills can be identified by the use of brick pilasters between each bay and by their distinctive towers.[11]

## External details

Factory-made red brick replaced the handmade brick which was used in early 19th-century mills and can be distinguished by its finer texture and more regular size. Hard red Accrington brick was not used until the late 1890s. From about 1860 blue brick and yellow or cream brick was used, at first mainly for decoration around openings or cornices. At about the same time moulded brick and terracotta were introduced as ornamentation and were increasingly used thereafter. Up to the 1880s, however, yellow sandstone was probably the most widely used material for mill embellishment.

Most external functional features differed from those found on earlier cotton mills. In multi-storeyed mills the stair tower, for example, was now usually attached externally and was a prominent feature, extending high above the roof of the mill. From the 1870s the top of the stair tower usually contained a large iron water tank to supply the mill's sprinkler system.[12] Privies were less frequently located in the small external towers used up to the mid 19th century. They were built either into the corners of the mill, sometimes disguised as pilasters, or incorporated into the stair tower. The main entrance was at the base of the stair tower, while the end walls often contained taking-in doors to each storey, those in the upper floors probably used for the installation of machinery. The external features of the power system also differed from those of earlier mills and were increasingly distinguished by embellishment. External engine houses were more common and the larger shaft-driven mills might have an attached tower containing the upright shaft. With the introduction of rope drive from the mid 1870s external rope races became more widespread. From the 1860s almost all mills had external or detached boiler houses and free-standing chimneys.

Windows were generally larger than in earlier mills, the proportion of glass to wall area continuing to increase throughout the late 19th century. Increasing the size of windows was a general aim of mill designers,

Figure 103 (below). Architects increasingly concentrated the principal features of a mill near the entrance, where they were further distinguished by a greater use of embellishment. At Anchor Mill, Oldham (400*), of 1881, by J. Stott, the stair tower, offices, engine house window and even the anchor emblem on the chimney all faced the site entrance.

Figure 104 (below, right). Stair towers had a variety of roof forms. Copper-domed roofs, such as that at Barnfield Mills, Tyldesley (1060*), were used from the 1890s.

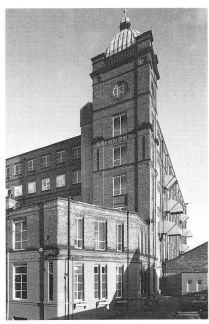

Figure 105. At some of the larger mills a greater concern for architectural quality can be seen in all parts of the building, not just at the entrance. A good example is Houldsworth's Mill, Reddish (899*), where extensive use was made of Italianate details by the architect A. H. Stott.

necessitated by the need to build wider mills, and was made possible by the introduction of improved methods of construction. Up to the 1880s most brick-built mills had large segmental-headed windows of vertical-rectangular or square shape. Flat-headed windows were more common in stone-built mills. By the 1890s mills with steel-and-concrete floor construction were distinguished by very large horizontal-rectangular windows with flat heads and sometimes a central cast-iron mullion, as at Barnfield Mills, Tyldesley (1060*).

The greater and more creative use of embellishment was a hallmark of the late 19th-century cotton mill and was indicative of the increasing influence of specialist architects on the growth of the industry. The most widely used style may be loosely referred to as 'Italianate', contrasting with the Gothic which dominated national architectural fashions in the high Victorian period. Italianate architecture was strongly associated with commerce and the ideals of free trade, and was more widespread in industrial regions. In the north-west it was perhaps best epitomised in the 'palazzo' textile warehouses of Manchester's commercial districts, many of which were built by millowning firms.[13] Similar Italianate details were used in cotton mills, but embellishment was usually carefully restrained to create a dignified appearance without detracting from the intrinsic architectural qualities of the textile mill.

There were two broad approaches to the embellishment of cotton mills. In the first and most common approach ornamentation similar to that used in the mid 19th century was employed but in greater quantity and with stronger emphasis given to the main façade of the mill. Corner pilasters with sandstone capitals, a feature of mid 19th-century mills, continued to be employed as a decorative feature in the late 19th century, but a new concern for the massing of offices, towers and other prominent features at the front of the mill and more abundant use of sandstone, brick or terracotta gave them a markedly changed aspect (Fig 103). Stair towers received particular attention, with embellishment in a range of individual styles. Some towers had ornate parapets or stone balustrades, while tower roofs could be pyramidal, of mansard form or, from the 1890s, capped by copper domes (Fig 104). The second approach is seen only in mills built by the most prosperous firms, for example the large double mills such as Victoria Mill, Miles Platting (383), and Houldsworth's Mill, Reddish (899*) (Fig 105). Throughout these buildings more lavish use was made of such new materials as polychromatic brick, and of such Italianate details as pyramidal tower roofs or rustication. The front or the entrance was still given emphasis, but the impression is of a building or complex in which architectural quality was a major consideration in the design of the whole site rather than simply of the main elevation.

## Methods of construction

The growth of the cotton industry, the demand for larger mills and the emergence of specialist architects led to renewed innovation in mill construction. New materials were introduced and significant improvements made to the structural framing of multi-storeyed mills. The result was the development of new types of fireproof floor construction. Large non-fireproof mills with joisted timber floors were still being built in the 1860s but by the 1870s almost all new cotton-spinning mills were fireproof. Weaving sheds showed little structural development and continued to be built with north-light roofs. Cast-iron trusses were being used by the 1880s, for example at Carrs Mill, Ashton under Lyne (963*), in 1884 (Fig 106), and by the 1890s the use of rolled-iron or steel tie-beams permitted a significantly wider spacing between the columns (Fig 107).[14]

A late example of timber-floor construction occurs at Atlas No. 2 Mill, Bolton (13*), built in the late 1860s. In this case, one end of the mill was

Figure 106. Cast-iron roof trusses began to be used in weaving-shed construction in the late 19th century. The one-piece cast-iron trusses at Carrs Mill, Ashton under Lyne (963*), of 1884, are of sufficient rigidity to preclude the need for the longitudinal tie-beams seen in earlier sheds.

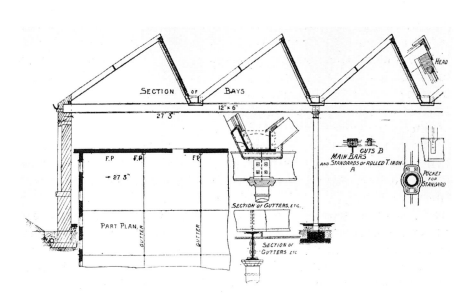

Figure 107. In other sheds the use of stronger rolled-iron or steel tie-beams permitted a reduction in the number of columns (Nasmith and Nasmith 1909, 70).

**101**

Figure 108. Mills of heavy timber-floored or slow-burning construction remained uncommon in Greater Manchester. A late example was the two-storeyed Crest Mill (626), near Rochdale, in which both the upper floor and the roof were slow burning.

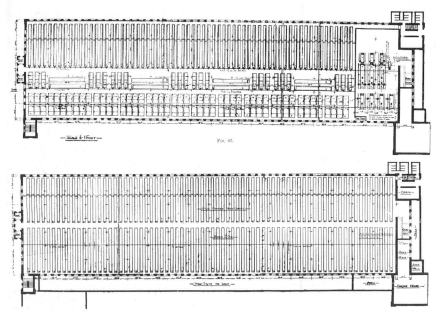

Figure 109. The machinery layout of Crest Mill (626). This mill was unusual in that preparation machines were in the upper floor above the ring frames, but the building illustrates the narrow plan typical of ring mills (Nasmith and Nasmith 1909, 174).

segregated by a cross-wall and was of brick-vaulted fireproof construction. The timber-floored main rooms occupied about three-quarters of the length of the building. The joists were not exposed but were protected by fire-resistant sheeting. Towards the end of the 19th century there was some renewed interest in slow-burning construction, which had been widely used in the United States of America and was promoted by a number of architects.[15] Only one late example is known in Greater Manchester, Crest Mill (626), near Rochdale (Figs 108 and 109), an unusual two-storeyed mill built for ring spinning.[16]

Figure 110. Brick-vaulted ceilings remained the most common form of fireproof construction. Sedgwick New Mill, Manchester (373*), of 1868, for example, has similar transverse vaults to those used in earlier fireproof mills. New types of vaulting were introduced during the 1870s.

Figure 111. Atlas No. 4 Mill, Bolton (15*) was also built with standard transverse brick vaults. In the late 19th century, mills with this type of vaulting often contained short longitudinal vaults in the end bays.

Improvements in the methods of framing spinning mills were perhaps the mill architect's most significant step forward in the late 19th century, since these enabled the construction of wider and better-lit structures of great rigidity. Rolled-iron or steel beams were now widely, but not invariably, used in place of cast iron. Cast-iron beams were thought to provide a more rigid floor, and in some mills cast iron was used for the cardroom floor with rolled-iron or steel beams above.[17] In the new approach to framing, longitudinal and transverse primary beams were joined together in a grid pattern supporting each floor. The outer ends of these beams were supported by the walls and their intersections by cast-iron columns.[18] Different designs utilised various combinations of additional lighter beams within the basic grid pattern as a means to strengthen the floors further. The result was largely to eliminate any horizontal thrust into the walls generated by the weight of the floors, which was a particular problem in mills with brick-vaulted ceilings. A high proportion of the weight of the floors was thus transmitted through the columns directly to the foundations. The walls supported only the outermost parts of the floors. They were of 'pier and panel' construction, with thicker brick piers to support the ends of the beams separated in turn by thinner panels containing the windows.

The majority of mill architects continued to use brick-vaulted ceiling construction, although the traditional type of vaulting was superseded in the 1870s by a number of new techniques using longitudinal vaulting or multiple transverse vaulting in each bay. Conventional transverse vaulting was used by A. H. Stott in 1865 for Houldsworth's Mill, Reddish (899*), and was also used at Sedgwick New Mill, Manchester (373*), in 1868 (Fig 110) and Atlas No. 4 Mill, Bolton (15*) (Fig 111), in *c*.1885. Such late examples of transverse vaulting often had short lengths of longitudinal vaulting in the end bays, probably to reduce horizontal thrust

Figure 112. At Anchor Mill, Oldham (400*), the use of both longitudinal and transverse primary beams permitted wider spacing of the columns and two transverse vaults per bay.

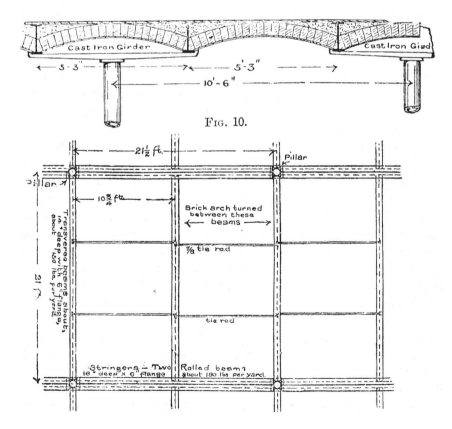

Figure 113. The upper drawing shows a type of construction similar to that patented by A. H. Stott in 1871, in which a wider spacing of the columns is made possible by mounting the iron beams at the ends of horizontal brackets. The lower drawing illustrates the type of construction used at Anchor Mill, Oldham (400*) (see Figure 112) (*The Textile Manufacturer*, 1891, 230).

Figure 114. The 1884 addition to Wear Mill, Stockport (934*), has a distinctive type of construction associated with the architects Edward Potts and George Woodhouse. Narrow longitudinal vaults spring from light beams which are supported by unusually heavy transverse cast-iron beams.

to the end walls.[19] Another development in mule-spinning mills was to place the rows of columns near the centre of the floors closer together, as can be seen at Houldsworth's Mill (899*) (Fig 97). This strengthened the floors beneath the heavy mule headstocks and the central line shaft suspended from the ceiling.[20] Joseph Stott used heavy longitudinal and transverse beams with two transverse vaults in each bay, for example at Anchor Mill, Oldham (400*). This permitted greater longitudinal spacing of the columns and therefore larger windows (Fig 112). P. S. Stott made widespread use of triple vaulting, with column spacing of 6.7 metres.[21] The main benefit of wider column spacing was that it allowed the two mules operated by a spinner to be located in a single bay, as for example at the Bolton Textile Mill, Farnworth (25), designed by P. S. Stott in 1894.[22] A new approach to brick vaulting, patented by A. H. Stott in 1871, used transverse vaults supported by rolled-iron beams carried on brackets attached to the sides of the columns (Fig 113).[23] Another novel form of vaulting can be seen in mills by George Woodhouse and Edward Potts, who for a time worked in partnership. These mills have unusually narrow longitudinal vaults springing from light iron joists. The joists are mounted on brackets cast into the sides of heavy transverse cast-iron beams. The thrust of the arches is not transmitted to the walls but is taken up by the transverse beams.[24] Examples include Prince of Wales Mill, Oldham (524*), designed by Potts in 1875, and part of Wear Mill, Stockport (934*) (Fig 114), built in 1884.

In addition to the development of new types of brick-vaulted construction, some earlier cast-iron framed mills were modified in the late 19th century to accommodate new machinery. At Sedgwick Mill, Manchester (372*), for example, one of the two rows of columns in the upper six storeys was moved outwards by about a metre to give clearance for the

Figure 115. The structural ironwork of some earlier mills was modified in the late 19th century when new machinery was installed. At Sedgwick Mill, Manchester (372*), the right-hand row of columns is a replacement of *c.*1860, giving sufficient clearance for the installation of new mules.

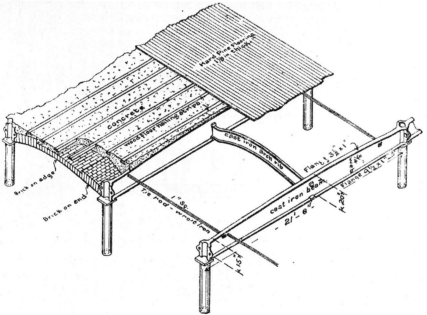

Figure 116. Concrete was first used in mill construction in combination with brick ceiling vaults (*The Textile Manufacturer*, 1891, 178).

installation of new longer mules. The new columns included wide brackets to support the original joint in the floor beams (Fig 115).

Concrete was being used to strengthen the floors of mills with brick-vaulted ceilings by the 1860s,[25] and a type of concrete-vaulted ceiling,

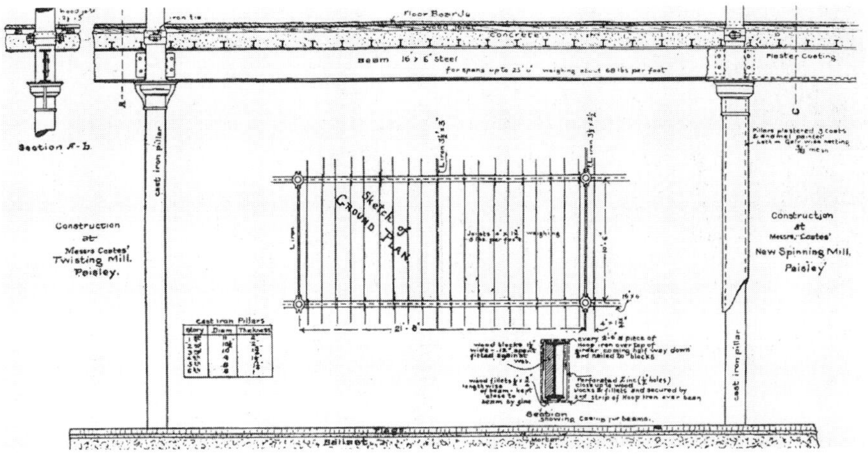

Figure 117. In early examples of reinforced-concrete floor construction the rolled-steel beams were exposed beneath the flat ceilings (*The Textile Manufacturer*, 1891, 230).

Figure 118. Reinforced-concrete floor construction with exposed steel beams in Atlas No. 6 Mill, Bolton (17*), of 1888.

Figure 119. An early improvement to concrete-floored mills was to encase the steel beams in plaster or concrete, as at Barnfield Mill, Tyldesley (1060*), of 1894.

Figures 120 and 121. Most late 19th-century spinning mills had roofs of multiple slate ridges. In some cases, such as Brunswick Mill, Mossley (959), the roof incorporated full-length skylights along each side to create a well-lit attic.

known as the Dennett system, was used in a large Yorkshire mill in the 1870s.[26] In Greater Manchester, concrete infill was widely used with various types of brick-vaulted ceilings by the 1880s (Fig 116).[27] Flat floors of reinforced concrete supported by rolled-steel beams began to be used in the 1880s, one of the earliest examples being Palm Mill, Oldham (514), designed in 1884 by Potts, Pickup and Dixon.[28] The concrete was cast *in situ* around iron joists and formed a floor about 180mm thick (Fig 117). In early concrete-floored mills the H-section rolled-steel beams were exposed beneath the ceilings, for example at Atlas No. 6 Mill, Bolton (17*), of 1888 (Fig 118). This was considered to be a fire risk, however, and by the mid 1890s the steel beams were themselves encased in concrete or plaster, as at Barnfield Mills, Tyldesley (1060*) (Fig 119).[29] In some mills the cast-iron columns were themselves protected from fire with a layer of plaster. With concrete floors the loadbearing function of the walls was reduced still further; consequently these mills can usually be identified by their unusually large flat-headed windows.

The roofs of late 19th-century spinning mills normally comprised multiple slate-covered ridges supported by light timber trusses. The ridges typically ran longitudinally, but transverse ridges were sometimes used on particularly wide mills. There were few examples of the cast and wrought-iron roof trusses used in early 19th-century fireproof mills. In Manchester, however, part of the Chorlton Old Mill (325) site was rebuilt in 1866 with a triple-span attic roof of cast-iron trusses. Some large mills, including Houldsworth's Mill (899*) and Brunswick Mill, Mossley (959), had a type of well-lit attic of mansard cross-section with inclined full-length glazed panels forming the sides (Figs 120 and 121). One of the earliest spinning mills to have a flat roof was Abbey Mill, Oldham (391), of 1876.[30] A later example can be seen at Milton Mills (1004), north of Mossley, built in 1894 (Fig 122). In this case the roof was utilised as a

Figure 122. Flat roofs became more common as concrete was adopted as a building material. Milton Mills (1004), north of Mossley, of 1894, is one example where the flat roof was utilised as a reservoir.

rainwater reservoir to supply the sprinkler tank in the stair tower. Flat roofs were not particularly common until the early 20th century, however, when they were a feature of spinning mills with both reinforced concrete and brick-vaulted floor construction.

## Internal organisation

By the late 19th century the importance of achieving the most cost-effective layout of processes and machinery was well understood by spinning-mill designers. This, together with the general need to build larger mills containing larger machines, led to the introduction of 'certain methodological rules' regarding the layout of machinery.[31] Thus the majority of spinning firms adopted a fairly standard approach to internal organisation, which was eventually reflected in the similar range of functional features found in the later mills. Available evidence suggests that the internal organisation of the later spinning mills was a development of the approach used in the larger early 19th-century mills, such as McConnel and Kennedy's Sedgwick Mill, Ancoats (372*).

Before the 1880s the cross-wall supporting the power transmission was used to separate processes with a high fire risk, such as scutching, from the main production areas. Throughout the late 19th century there was also a strong emphasis on efficient inter-communication between different parts of the mill. The larger mills might have two or more hoists powered from the line shafting, while metal tracks attached to the floors assisted the movement of the raw material around the mill in wheeled trolleys.

Figure 123. Processes with a high fire risk were contained in the small rooms behind the internal cross-walls of late 19th-century mills. At some larger mills the cross-wall incorporated a staircase with fireproof iron doors, as at Atlas No. 6 Mill, Bolton (17*).

The greater width of the typical spinning mill was determined by the length of the mules or ring frames to be installed, and in general mule mills were wider than ring mills.[32] When late 19th-century spinning machines were installed into earlier mills they had to be located longitudinally because of the narrow plan of the buildings, as occurred at Sedgwick Mill (372*) around 1860. The need to make a profit in a competitive industry largely determined the minimum number of spindles per machine and the total number of machines in the mill. The spinning machines were arranged transversely in the upper storeys, as occurred in earlier mills, and depending on the spacing of the columns there might be one or two mules per bay (Fig 2). Ring frames were shorter than mules and were often arranged side-by-side across the mill, giving either two or four machines per bay. The quantity of carding engines and other preparation machines, usually sited in the lower storeys, was itself determined by the number of spindles on the spinning machines. As a general guideline it was thought that three mule-spinning storeys would require an equal-sized storey for carding and preparation.[33] When four or more storeys were used for spinning the ground floor would need to be extended beyond the area of the spinning rooms to contain a sufficient number of machines. Since most late 19th-century mills were of four or more storeys, lateral extensions to ground-floor carding and preparation rooms became a common feature.

Inside the cardroom the arrangement of machines, typically carding engines, drawing frames and doubling frames, was more varied, being influenced by such factors as the need for good lighting, the requirements of the supervisors and the practical experience of the designers. It became normal, however, to arrange the carding engines along one or both side walls, possibly continuing into the shed extension. The other machines were then located either along the opposite side wall or in the middle of the room.[34] Contemporary plans of the machinery layouts in cardrooms illustrate how fully the available floorspace was used (Fig 2).

The smaller rooms beyond the cross-wall might be of fireproof construction even when the main rooms were not. In some cases the rooms on adjoining floors were connected by fireproof staircases attached to or contained within the cross-wall. Such staircases were equipped with iron fire doors as an extra precaution, for example in the Atlas Mills complex, Bolton (13*, 15*, 17*) (Fig 123). The opening and mixing of the raw cotton was usually done on the first floor, with scutching or willowing on the ground floor from whence the cotton could be carried directly into the adjoining cardroom.

In the late 19th century the basements of spinning mills were increasingly used for the storage of cotton yarn. They often included a conditioning cellar, with controlled high humidity, and a separate warehouse where the yarn was stored prior to being sold (Fig 124). Humidity was sometimes achieved by flooding the floor of the conditioning cellar.[35]

Late 19th-century mills also illustrate a greater concern for efficient dust extraction and ventilation. Flues were often built into the cross-wall to extract cotton dust from the adjoining opening and scutching rooms,

Figure 124. Cotton yarn was stored in humid conditions in the basement, known as the conditioning cellar, to improve its handling qualities before it left the mill. This is the conditioning cellar of Anchor Mill, Oldham (400*).

for example at Anchor Mill, Oldham (400*). From the 1890s, rope-driven mills often had the dust flue incorporated into the rope race, as at Barnfield Mills, Tyldesley (1060*) (Fig 125). Combined humidification and ventilation systems were included in some 1890s mills. The Bolton Textile Mill, Bolton (25), of 1894, for example, was to be equipped with the 'Droposphore' system, in which 115 machines would produce a fine mist of water throughout the mill and air moisteners in the windows would admit about 200,000 cubic feet of fresh air per hour.[36]

There were some notable variations to the typical internal layout, however, one example being Crest Mill (626), near Rochdale. This two-storeyed mill of slow-burning construction had a narrow plan typical of ring-spinning mills. The carding and preparation room was on the upper floor, apparently to assist the transfer of prepared cotton down to the ring frames in the ground floor (Fig 109).[37]

## Power systems

The double-flue Lancashire boiler continued to be the standard type used in Greater Manchester mills in the late 19th century. The basic design was gradually improved, resulting in a number of derivative types and higher steam pressures.[38] The latter enabled the widespread use of more powerful compound engines. Green's economisers were more widely used to reduce fuel costs. The number of boilers was related to the size and type of engine, the majority of spinning mills having from two to four. Steam from the boilers was also used for the heating and humidification of cotton mills.

Figure 125. Greater emphasis was given to ventilation and dust-extraction systems in late 19th-century mills. Some mills had external dust flues, often incorporated into a stair tower, or, as in this Italianate dust flue at Barnfield Mills, Tyldesley (1060*), the rope race.

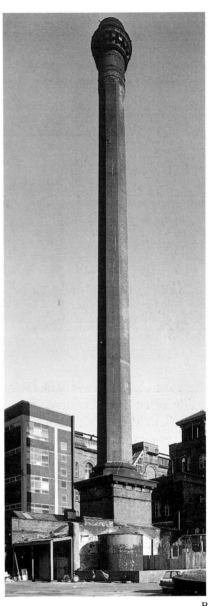

A

B

Figure 126. A. Most late 19th-century mills had large detached octagonal chimneys with a prominent corbelled crown, few of which survive intact. The chimney of Atlas No. 4 Mill, Bolton (15*), is typical of the period.
B. The chimney at Houldsworth's Mill, Reddish (899*), of 1865, is a more elaborate example mounted on a plinth.

The number of boilers largely determined the height of the chimney. After 1860 most chimneys were detached from the mill and of octagonal shape, as at Atlas No. 4 Mill, Bolton (15*) (Fig 126a). In the 1860s the larger stacks were often mounted on a square plinth but by the end of the century plinths were less common. The corbelled crown or oversailer, which assisted the dispersal of the smoke,[39] was frequently highly embellished, as for example at Houldsworth's Mill, Reddish (899*), of 1865 (Fig 126b). Few mill chimneys still survive to their original height, however. In smaller mills, such as weaving sheds, circular chimneys were being built by the 1860s.[40] A distinctive type of large circular chimney can be seen at Victoria Mill, Miles Platting (383), and Cavendish Mill, Ashton

**113**

under Lyne (965). In this case the stack protrudes from the main stair tower, which is octagonal in plan, a similar arrangement to the chimney and stair towers of some early 19th-century mills, notably Brownsfield Mill, Ancoats (315*).

As mills were more frequently built away from canals and more powerful engines were installed a higher proportion of sites were equipped with reservoirs. The reservoir, or lodge, was designed to ensure a constant supply of sufficiently cold water for the engine's condenser. Its surface area and volume was determined by the horsepower of the engine. It was usually situated at a higher level than the boilers, enclosed by a rubble embankment or a low wall and lined with clay or concrete. Many mills had two connecting reservoirs, one receiving the hot condensate from the engine and the other supplying the cooled water. By the 1890s some reservoirs were subdivided into several sections by brick partition walls, the hot water being cooled as it passed from section to section. Other means used to cool the condensate included channelling it along an open cast-iron trough or over a cascade on its way back to the reservoir.[41]

The power requirements of the larger mills were met by the introduction of a variety of more efficient types of engine, which in turn led to changes in the form of engine houses. Stationary steam engines were the subject of development throughout the late 19th century, with many innovations in Britain and abroad. The result was a considerable increase in the horsepower available for use in textile mills. The increase in engine power in even a short period is illustrated by Abbey Mill, Oldham (391), built in 1876 as a large mule-spinning mill driven by engines of 700 horsepower,[42] and by Nile Mill, Chadderton (507*), constructed only twenty-three years later as a large ring-spinning mill and requiring a massive 2,500 horsepower.[43]

From the 1870s compound engines with horizontal cylinders became more common in new mills than beam engines.[44] Horizontal engines were either of the tandem type, with the low and high-pressure cylinders in line, or of the cross-compound type, with the cylinders side by side (Fig 127). Cross-compound engines were also produced in tandem form, with two

Figure 127. More powerful engines with horizontal cylinders began to replace beam engines from the 1870s. This horizontal cross-compound engine, with separate high and low-pressure cylinders, is typical of the period. The flywheel is shown with the ropes of a rope-drive system (*The Textile Manufacturer*, 1887, 430).

Figure 128. Compound engines with inverted cylinders were used in some of the larger later mills, and could be accommodated in a more compact engine house (*The Textile Manufacturer*, 1898, 260).

rows of cylinders, and were probably the most commonly used type.[45] One of the largest was that of 1,700 horsepower installed in 1892 at Ellenroad Mill (644) near Milnrow.[46] By the 1880s compound engines with inverted-vertical cylinders were introduced. These were more compact than horizontal engines and could be accommodated in smaller, roughly square engine houses (Fig 128). In the 1890s boilers producing steam pressures in excess of 160 pounds per square inch were available, enabling the introduction of more complex triple-expansion and quadruple-

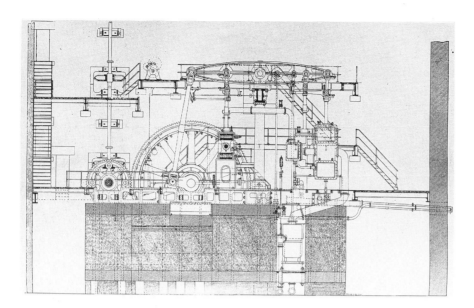

Figure 129. Improvements to boilers led to the introduction of even more powerful triple-expansion engines in the 1890s. This unusual triple-expansion double-beam engine was installed at Nile Mill, Chadderton (507*), in 1898. The upright shaft is shown on the left (*The Textile Manufacturer*, 1898, 422).

Figure 130. McNaughted beam engines were still installed in mills up to the 1870s. Their engine houses were of similar proportions to those of early 19th-century mills, but much larger. This view shows the engine house at Atlas No. 2 Mill, Bolton (13*).

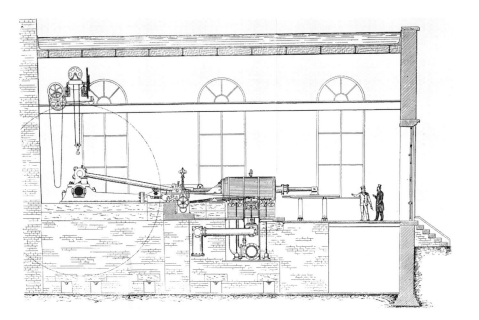

Figure 131 (above). The size and proportions of engines with horizontal cylinders meant they could not be accommodated easily inside the mill and were usually located in external engine houses (*The Textile Manufacturer*, 1887, 5).

Figure 132 (above right). Some mills retain evidence of more than one type of engine. At Brunswick Mill, Mossley (959), the narrow beam-engine house to the left of the chimney was replaced by the wider engine house to the right. The new engine house was probably designed for a large inverted engine.

expansion engines. The engine at Nile Mill (507*), for example, was possibly the last beam engine to be installed in a cotton mill but was an unusual design, with six cylinders working on the triple-expansion principle (Fig 129).

The dimensions of the engine influenced the shape and location of the engine house. Some mills of the 1860s and 1870s had large McNaughted beam engines in internal engine houses. These engine houses are of similar proportions and have similar features to those of earlier periods but are much larger, for example at Atlas No. 2 Mill, Bolton (13*) (Fig

Figure 133. Upright shaft transmission systems were installed throughout the late 19th century, but were gradually superseded by rope drives. Surviving bearing boxes, such as this one at Prince of Wales Mill, Oldham (524*), indicate that upright shafts and gearing were more heavily constructed than those in early 19th-century mills.

130). In this period internal engine houses were located longitudinally in one corner of the mill, unlike the transverse internal engine houses of the narrower early 19th-century mills, such as those in Manchester. Horizontal tandem engines required only a narrow engine house, of similar width to those used for beam engines but longer and of lower ceiling height. Cross-compound engines were wider and were usually sited in large external engine houses (Fig 131). Mills which have been extended or rebuilt sometimes retain two or more engine houses of different types. At Brunswick Mill, Mossley (959), for example, a narrow beam-engine house with an attached chimney, probably dating from the mid 19th century, stands alongside a wider engine house of *c.*1890 (Fig 132). The proportions of the latter suggest that it contained an inverted compound engine; it was added when the mid 19th-century mill was rebuilt.

Power-transmission systems were developed to suit the larger mills, and also influenced the layout of the power system. Upright shaft drive had been used in most mills up to the 1860s and continued to be installed throughout the late 19th century. No upright shaft system is known to survive intact from this period, but *in situ* bearings and shaft boxes indicate that the shafts and gearing were much more substantial than those used in the early 19th century (Fig 133). The upright shaft was usually located close to the centre-line of the mill, either attached to the face of the cross-wall or housed in an external tower attached to the end wall. When attached to a cross-wall its base was driven from the engine by a horizontal shaft, known as the second-motion shaft. Examples of mills with upright shaft drive include Houldsworth's Mill, Reddish (899*), of 1865, Prince of Wales Mill, Oldham (524*), of 1875, and Anchor Mill, Oldham (400*), of 1881, while its last use was reputedly at Nile Mill (507*) in 1899 (Fig 129).

From the 1870s, alternatives to the upright shaft were developed. Belt drive, the normal means of driving mills in the United States of America, was introduced to Britain in the 1860s but never became widespread.[47] Drums mounted on the ends of the line shafts were driven from the engine's flywheel by a system of leather belts. The belts were located in a duct which extended the full height of the mill. A notable early example in Greater Manchester was Abbey Mill (391), of 1876.[48] Rope-drive systems were introduced about the same time and used a similar layout, with pulleys on the ends of the line shafts driven by heavy cotton ropes. The engine's flywheel was grooved to take the ropes; the duct containing the line shaft pulleys was known as the rope race and sometimes occupied a full bay of the building. It was often incorporated into the end wall, where it is identifiable as a narrow full-height projection, usually without windows and open to the engine house at the base. Rope drive was cheaper to install than belt drive and easier to maintain and quieter in use than shaft drive.[49] A major advantage was that a broken rope would only affect the drive to one line shaft; a broken upright shaft resulted in the whole mill stopping work. It was much preferred for the larger spinning mills, such as Atlas No. 6 Mill, Bolton (17*) (Figs 134 and 135), and was probably used for all steam-powered early 20th-century spinning mills.

Figures 134 and 135. Most of the larger mills had external engine houses and rope-drive systems by the 1890s. Atlas No. 6 Mill, Bolton (17*), of 1888, for example, was powered from a huge external engine house. The end wall was open to the mill's internal rope race.

Figure 136. Weaving sheds might be either shaft or rope driven. These heavy cast-iron brackets supported the horizontal main shaft at Carrs Mill, Ashton under Lyne (963*).

In weaving sheds shaft-drive systems were common, although rope drive was also used. At the 1884 Carrs Mill, Ashton under Lyne (963*), for example, the horizontal main shaft was gear-driven from the engine and mounted on heavy bearings in a shaft alley which ran across the full width of the shed (Fig 136). Line shafting was attached to each row of columns in the shed and driven by bevel gears on the horizontal shaft. At large integrated sites the spinning mill and weaving shed might be powered by separate engines with independent transmission systems. At Gilnow Mill, Bolton (71*), however, which began working as an integrated mill, a single large engine drove both the base of the upright shaft in the spinning mill and a long horizontal shaft which passed into the adjoining weaving shed.

Electric lighting was introduced into textile mills during the late 19th century, but electricity was not widely used as a source of motive power until after 1900. A system of electric lighting was in use in French factories by 1877. It was thought preferable to gas lighting both for economic reasons and because of the quality of the light obtained.[50] An early example of electric lighting in Greater Manchester's cotton mills was at Atlas No. 3 Mill, Bolton (14), where a small American-made steam engine was installed to drive an electric lighting generator in 1877.[51] By the 1890s the use of electric lighting in the larger mills was widespread.

# 6

# Early twentieth-century mills, 1900–1926

THE final stage in the development of the cotton mill in Greater Manchester was distinguished by the construction of dozens of large spinning mills by established architects from Oldham or Bolton. Many of these mills were built outside the existing urban areas, but others replaced 19th-century town mills. Groupings of these mills became a characteristic feature of the county's landscape (Fig 137). Most embodied principles of structure and design which had been developed earlier, and they may therefore be regarded as less progressive than the mills of the late 19th century. They do, however, represent the culmination of a tradition of industrial building which had begun over a century before. In comparison with earlier periods these mills are easily distinguished by their massive scale, many being built to contain over 100,000 spindles, and by their often flamboyant use of red brick and terracotta ornament, reflecting both Edwardian architectural fashions and the prosperity of the industry. Among the most significant new technical developments was the gradual introduction of electric power for driving textile machinery. Some new types of concrete construction were introduced, including the use of prefabricated floors.

## Size and layout

In general the range of buildings at a mill site remained similar to that described for the late 19th century, with offices, stair towers and the components of the power system either attached or close to the main block. In most cases, prominent features were still concentrated around the entrance at the front of the mill, where they were distinguished by a higher level of embellishment. The vast size of the largest early 20th-century sites meant this was difficult to achieve, however, and the offices at the main gate to the site were sometimes a considerable distance from the mill itself.

120

Figure 137. Early 20th-century cotton-spinning mills dominate the landscape in many parts of Greater Manchester. This view shows Waterhead near Oldham.

The majority of new mills were still built for spinning on mules. Their scale is illustrated by Kent Mill, Chadderton (478*) (Fig 138), a typical example built in 1908 to contain around 90,000 mule spindles. The five-storeyed main block includes a basement and is twelve bays in length. In common with most new mills the size of the individual bays, indicated by the longitudinal spacing of the columns, was more than double that of the typical fireproof mill of the mid 19th century. The main rooms consist of eleven bays measuring approximately 84.6 metres by 43.9 metres.

The greater size of spinning mills was seen in the dimensions of individual buildings and in the increased construction of double mills. The high level of confidence within the industry resulted in mills being laid out with a view to simplifying their later extension into double mills. Thus the external engine house and rope race were situated at one end, to which a second mill could be attached at a later date and the power system extended, for example at Ram Mill, Chadderton (525) (Fig 139). A significant proportion of new mills were of this 'planned double' type but relatively few were actually extended into double mills.

The only surviving double mill of this period in Greater Manchester is the six-storeyed Swan Lane No. 1 and No. 2 Mills, Bolton (138*). This huge structure, built in 1902 and 1905, was designed to contain 210,000 mule spindles under a single roof (Fig 140). The largest double mill to be

Figure 139. Planned double mills were designed to facilitate their extension into double mills at a later date. Ram Mill, Chadderton (525), was built in 1907 leaving empty space for an extension.

Figure 138 (left). Kent Mill (478*), built in Chadderton in 1908, illustrates the typical proportions of an Edwardian mule-spinning mill.

planned was Pear New Mill, Bredbury (909). The first mill, completed in 1912 for 137,000 spindles, is of eleven bays with an overall length of 90.5 metres, but its twin was never in fact constructed.[1] Most mule mills were of between four and six storeys, although the tallest was probably the eight-storeyed Swan Lane No. 3 Mill, Bolton (139), of 1915 (Fig 141). Ring-spinning machines were smaller and heavier but exceeded the yarn

Figure 140. The Swan Lane Mills complex, Bolton. The No. 1 and No. 2 Mills (138*), on the right, were built in 1902 and 1905 as a double mill. On the left is No. 3 Mill (139) of 1915.

Figure 141. Swan Lane No. 3 Mill, Bolton (139), was distinguished by its flamboyant embellishment and, with eight storeys, its unusual height.

output of mules, so ring mills continued to be built with narrower plans and fewer storeys.[2]

Ground-floor extensions to house the necessary quantity of preparation machinery were more commonplace and were often more extensive than those used in the late 19th century, for example at Swan Lane No. 3 Mill (139). In some of the larger mills the extensions were of two storeys, the lower floor containing preparation machinery and the upper an extension to the first spinning room, as at Pear New Mill (909).[3]

## External details

Early 20th-century spinning mills differ from earlier mills in having more external towers, typically a full-height stair tower at each end with separate smaller towers connecting particular floors, such as the basement and the cardroom. The stair towers normally also contained hoists for the movement of cotton. External engine houses were larger than those of earlier mills, their plan reflecting the type of engine they contained (see pp. 131–5). Rope races were usually integral to an end wall and were distinguished externally by pilasters and sometimes a separate parapet or a hipped roof. The dust flue, of square or rectangular shape, was often built into the rope race but might also take the form of an external tower, sometimes added to an earlier mill and distinguishable from the other towers by the absence of windows. Taking-in doors are often found in the end walls of the mill with others giving access to the yarn store in the basement. Most mills now had two or three windows per bay in the side walls. Wide flat-headed windows usually still indicated reinforced-

Figure 142. Reinforced-concrete floor construction became more widespread in this period. The windows of these mills could be either flat-headed or segmental-headed, such as those at Paragon Mill (364*), left, and Royal Mill (370*), Manchester.

concrete floor construction, but some architects preferred to use large segmental-headed windows, as for example at Paragon Mill, Manchester (364*), and Royal Mill, Manchester (370*) (Fig 142).

The most widely used new external material was red Accrington brick, also known as 'Nori' brick.[4] Yellow brick was extensively used for embellishment by some Oldham architects. Sandstone continued to be used, but moulded terracotta was the most popular material for decoration. Embellishment was more generally used throughout the mill than was the case in the 19th century. The company name was often proudly displayed on the stair tower and in some cases on the chimney in white

Figure 143. Manor Mill (495) and Kent Mill (478*), in Chadderton, both designed by George Stott, are externally similar except for the contrasting tower roofs.

Figures 144, 145 and 146. At the more lavishly embellished Edwardian mills the company emblem provided an ornamental theme which recurs in different parts of the building. At Swan Lane No. 3 Mill, Bolton (139), for example, terracotta swans adorn the main entrance and the parapets.

brick. Some features of 19th-century design continued to be used, notably the pilaster, employed at the corners of the main mill, towers, offices, engine house, boiler house and rope race of most Edwardian sites. The façades of mills by the architect F. W. Dixon were relieved by the use of pilasters between each bay extending up to the parapet,[5] as at Fox Mill, Oldham (452), and Rutland Mill, Shaw (539). The parapet might feature brick corbelling, moulded tiles or dentilation. At Swan Lane No. 1 and 2 Mills, Bolton (138*), the parapets of the stair towers and the corner pilasters were highlighted with stone balustrades. George Stott enlivened flat window heads with stepped oversailers, for example at Kent Mill, Chadderton (478*).

Less restrained application of ornament, reflecting contemporary architectural fashions, was usually restricted to the more prominent features at the front of the site. Copper domes were more widely used to highlight the principal stair tower, allowing some highly unusual roofs, Pear New Mill, Bredbury (909), for example, taking its name from the shape of the tower roof. Mansard tower roofs, which were relatively conservative Italianate features, continued to be used, in some cases with ornate cast-iron balustrades, as at Kent Mill (478*). The domed tower of Manor Mill, Chadderton (495), adjacent to Kent Mill (478*) and also by George Stott, suggests a Baroque influence (Fig 143). The fluted forms in the towers of

**125**

Figure 147. Croal Mill, Bolton (48), by the Bolton architects Bradshaw, Gass and Hope.

Broadstone Mill, Reddish (871), and Butts Mill, Leigh (1067), both by Stott and Sons, are distinctly Byzantine. The architectural theme used in the tower of a mill was often continued in the offices and the engine house. Some of the more lavishly embellished mills featured appropriate sculptured ornaments. At Swan Lane No. 3 Mill, Bolton (139), for example, the swan theme is used above the main entrance and terracotta swans look down from the parapets (Figs 144, 145 and 146). Pear New Mill (909) has terracotta pears adorning the corner turrets, chimney plinth and engine house.

Most spinning mills were designed by specialist architects who had become well established in the 19th century, sometimes in new partnerships. The Stotts of Oldham, particularly A. H. and P. S. Stott, accounted for the highest number, building mills in all parts of Greater Manchester as well as abroad.[6] In Bolton the partnership of Bradshaw and Gass was joined by Arthur Hope and continued to build large local mills in plain brick with distinctive external detailing. A notable example is Croal Mill, Bolton (48), of 1907 (Fig 147).[7] The last steam-powered Lancashire cotton mill, Elk Mill, Oldham (443), of 1926, was designed by the Oldham firm of Arthur Turner and his son Percy.[8] This firm remained active during the mid 20th century as architects of mill extensions.

## Methods of construction

In general, early 20th-century spinning mills used techniques of floor construction which were refined versions of the tried and tested methods used for the slightly smaller mills in the late 19th century. Although reinforced-concrete floor construction had been introduced by the early 1880s and its advantages were well known, brick-vaulted types of construction remained widespread during the first decade of the 20th century. The early use of rolled-steel beams was similarly limited,[9] while unprotected cast-iron columns continued to be used as floor supports in almost all mills. Walls remained loadbearing, although their loadbearing function was greatly reduced, and in spite of the preference for multi-storeyed buildings no steel-framed cotton mills were ever built. This conservatism on the part of mill architects occurred at a time when new methods for the construction of large buildings were being developed and promoted. It may have been a reflection of a need to restrict unnecessary expenditure by mill-building firms.[10] The continued influence of established architects and their contractors may itself have discouraged the introduction of new materials and methods of construction. Another factor was probably the conservatism of the cotton-spinning firms themselves. The structural and organisational advantages of single-storeyed shed mills, for example, had been known since the 1860s but very few were actually built.

At Swan Lane No. 2 Mill, Bolton (138*), Stott and Sons used longitudinal primary beams with lighter transverse beams supporting three brick vaults per bay, the size of each bay being sufficient to accommodate two mules (Fig 148). Apart from the use of heavier primary beams, probably of rolled steel, this construction was little different from that seen in mills of the 1880s. It permitted the use of three large segmental-headed windows per bay, one to each ceiling vault. For Kent Mill, Chadderton (478*), George Stott employed another method in which both longitudinal and transverse primary beams are exposed in the ceilings (Fig 149). Longitudinal brick vaults are used beneath the central parts of the floors and short transverse vaults along the side walls, giving three flat-headed windows to each bay. Above the brick vaults was a layer of coke breeze, upon which the wooden flooring was laid.

Reinforced-concrete floor construction became increasingly widespread and probably accounted for most spinning mills built after about 1908.

Figure 148. Brick-vaulted ceilings were still used in large mills during the first decade of the 20th century. The internal framework of Swan Lane No. 2 Mill, Bolton (138*), has similar transverse brick vaults to those seen in earlier mills, but the use of three vaults per bay allowed wider spacing of the columns.

Figure 149. Kent Mill, Chadderton (478*), uses narrower longitudinal vaults with short transverse vaults adjacent to the side walls.

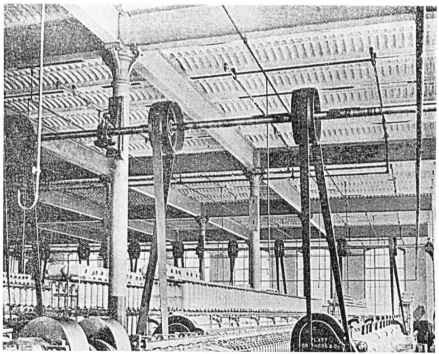

Figure 150. Reinforced-concrete floor construction became more common after *c*.1908. By this time the steel beams of most concrete-floored mills were encased in plaster or concrete, as at Royal Mill, Manchester (370*).

Figure 151. Floors constructed of prefabricated concrete blocks were rarely used in mills. This is one example, the 'Fram' system, at Brook Mills, Oldham (417) (*The Textile Mercury*, 1903, 202).

The main development was to encase the rolled-steel beams in plaster or concrete, which was first seen in the 1890s. It was known that leaving the beams and columns exposed might result in structural failure in the event of a serious fire.[11] Falcon Mill, Bolton (66), of 1904–8 was apparently the first mill to have concrete floors and concrete joists.[12] Other concrete-floored mills included Kearsley Mill, Kearsley (89*), of *c*.1906, Royal

Figure 152. The floors of some earlier mills were reinforced when new machinery was installed. At Brunswick Mill, Manchester (316*), the original Hodgkinson-type floor beams were strengthened by the addition of trussed wrought-iron tie-rods, probably when the mules were replaced by heavier ring frames.

Mill, Manchester (370*), of 1912 (Fig 150) and Pear New Mill, Bredbury (909), also of 1912. The column spacing in these mills was similar to that achieved with the advanced forms of brick-vaulted construction, allowing two mules per bay.

The majority of spinning mills were now built with flat roofs, normally formed of concrete with a layer of bitumen. The roof was completely enclosed by the parapet and was allowed to flood with rainwater. This provided a ready supply of water for the sprinkler tank at the top of the stair tower.

Prefabricated floor construction received favourable publicity but was never widely used.[13] Pre-cast concrete blocks of various specially designed shapes were laid on rolled-steel joists and covered with a layer of concrete. One example is the *c*.1903 two-storeyed extension to Brook Mills, Oldham (417) (Fig 151), built with the 'Fram' system.[14]

The installation of new machinery, especially of ring frames in a mill built for mules, often necessitated the strengthening of the structural framework. This might involve the insertion of extra beams or additional columns beneath the beams. At Brunswick Mill, Manchester (316*), of *c*.1840, when ring frames were installed the cast-iron floor beams were strengthened by a system of trussed tie-rods mounted beneath the beams on short vertical brackets (Fig 152).

## Internal organisation

The self-acting mule continued to be the most widely used spinning machine, albeit in greatly improved form with over 1,300 spindles per mule. Ring frames were much more common abroad, however, especially in the United States of America, and their use in English cotton mills gradually increased in the mid 20th century. The dimensions of these two machines, installed transversely, continued to determine the width of most spinning mills. Similar principles of internal organisation to those seen in the late 19th century were adhered to, but the room layout of spinning mills was simplified by the exclusion of the cross-walls used in late 19th-century mills. The floors of most Edwardian spinning mills were thus open from end to end. This led to even greater emphasis on separating the main stages of production into adjacent storeys, rather than in adjoining rooms of the same storey. One effect of this was to increase the quantity of machinery in the ground-floor preparation areas, and hence the size of ground-floor extensions (Fig 153). The blowing room, for example, which was previously in the ground floor adjoining the card-room, was now often located in a segregated room in the cellar, as at Kent Mill, Chadderton (478*).

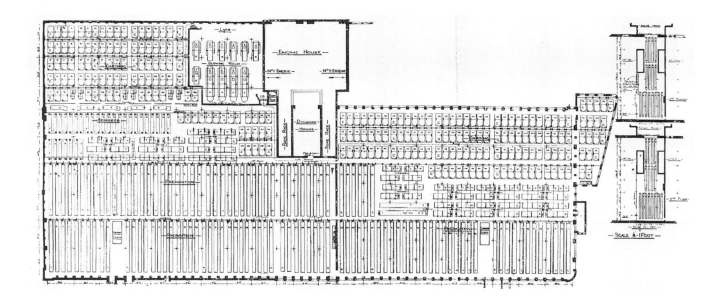

Architects showed greater concern for the efficient movement of cotton through the various stages of production. External hoist and stair towers were sited to assist transportation of cotton between particular processes. Kent Mill (478*) was a typical example, where an external two-storeyed hoist tower was used to take cotton laps from the blowing room in the cellar to the carding engines along the north side of the ground-floor preparation room. After carding the cotton was passed through successive groups of machines arranged in the centre and along the south side of the preparation room. The prepared rovings were then taken up to the mule-spinning rooms in the three upper floors in hoist towers attached to each end of the south side.

The features of the ventilation or dust-extraction system were more conspicuous in early 20th-century mills. At the base of the dust flue was the dust chamber, a small room containing banks of filters. Air from the mill laden with cotton dust was carried along ducting into the chamber, passing through the filters and out through the flue. The greatest quantity of cotton dust was released in the blowing room, which was thus usually

Figure 153. In the early 20th century designers gave greater emphasis to the vertical segregation of processes in spinning mills, and to the concentration of the preparation machinery on the ground floor. This is the ground-floor machinery layout of Swan Lane No. 1 and No. 2 Mills, Bolton (138*), where the upper four floors were used for mule spinning (Nasmith and Nasmith 1909, 166).

sited next to the dust chamber. At Kent Mill (478*), ducting for dust extraction was originally located beneath the floor of the blowing room. At earlier mills larger dust flues and dust chambers were frequently added in this period, for example at Atlas No. 4 Mill, Bolton (15*). In such cases the dust chamber might be inserted into one of the upper storeys. At Brunswick Mill, Manchester (316*), however, a large external dust flue was added with the dust chamber at its base inserted into the former boiler house.

The construction of specially designed shed mills for spinning was promoted by some architectural writers but seems to have been largely ignored by the mill-building industry.[15] Part of the reason for this may have been the continued influence of architects and contractors who had become established by building traditional but more expensive multi-storeyed mills. Plans showing a proposed layout for a shed mill were published in 1892, comprising three mule-spinning rooms and a preparation room located to either side of a central engine house and rope drive.[16] The design incorporated all the main features provided on different levels by a multi-storeyed mill. A shed mill along similar lines, the Cromer Mill, Chadderton (629), was built to contain 60,000 ring spindles.[17] A surviving, smaller example, Spur Mill (919), at Reddish, was built for doubling cotton yarn.[18]

## Power systems

Lancashire boilers with economisers remained the standard form of steam plant in cotton mills. The largest mills required extensive boiler installations. Swan Lane Mills, Bolton (138* and 139), for example, had a set of ten boilers with economisers and superheaters.[19] Superheated steam was often used with the larger and more advanced engines, and was produced

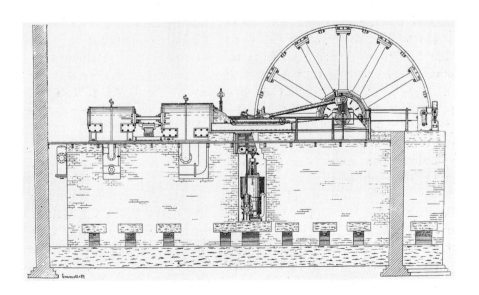

Figure 154. Large horizontal triple-expansion engines in external engine houses were the most widely used source of power in early 20th-century mills (*The Textile Manufacturer*, 1891, 292).

Figure 155. A 1,500-horsepower triple-expansion engine and rope drive in a Stockport mill of 1897. The photograph shows an engine house layout which remained typical in the early 20th century (*The Textile Mercury*, 1897, 291).

by passing ordinary steam through pipes heated by the flue at the rear of the boiler. Chimneys were now usually circular and were taller to provide sufficient draught; many chimneys have since been lowered. At the larger or more highly ornamented mills circular chimneys were mounted on plinths, for example at Pear New Mill, Bredbury (909), and Butts Mill, Leigh (1067). Reservoirs of sufficient size to supply the boilers and cool the engine condensate were built when there was no alternative water supply, but a greater number of mills were now built outside urban areas adjacent to natural watercourses.

Three basic types of advanced steam engine were used.[20] Large horizontal cross-compound engines were the most common type, usually working on the triple-expansion or quadruple-expansion principles (Fig 154). Their engine houses tend to be rectangular in plan with sufficient roof height to clear the flywheel and the ropes entering the rope race (Fig 155). Inverted marine-type compound engines were more powerful and became more widespread as the average size of new mills increased. Their engine houses were square in plan and of taller proportions than those for horizontal engines, for example at Swan Lane No. 3 Mill (139) (Fig 156). The third type, 'Manhattan' engines, comprised both vertical and horizontal cylinders. They included some of the largest and most powerful mill engines ever built, the one installed at Pear New Mill (909), for example, being rated at 3,500 horsepower.[21]

Most new spinning mills had rope transmission systems, although there were some examples of steel-belt drive.[22] The width of the engine flywheel was determined by the number of rope grooves needed. The Kent Mill, Chadderton (478*), flywheel was 7.9 metres in diameter and drove twenty-eight ropes.[23] The flywheel with the widest rim was said to have been that at Pear New Mill (909), which was over 4 metres wide with grooves for seventy-three ropes.[24] Rope races were sometimes lit by side

Figure 156 (above). Swan Lane No. 3 Mill, Bolton (139), has an external engine house of taller proportions for an inverted compound engine.

Figure 157 (top right). The rope race of Kent Mill, Chadderton (478*), still retains some of the line shaft pulleys. The engine house is in the background.

Figure 158. This external engine house containing an inverted compound engine was added to Atlas No. 4 Mill, Bolton (15*), in 1907. The mill was earlier powered from an internal engine house.

windows and a roof skylight. They usually contained a series of cast-iron platforms level with each storey of the mill to allow maintenance of the line shaft pulleys (Fig 157). Line shaft layouts remained similar to those in use in the late 19th century, with multiple shafting in preparation rooms and a single central line shaft in spinning rooms containing mules. Ring frames could be driven either from a single line shaft or by separate line shafts above each row of machines. Line shafts in the spinning rooms were usually attached to bolting faces on the columns. A result of the greater spacing between the columns in most new mills, however, was that the multiple line shafting used in preparation rooms was more frequently mounted on hanging brackets attached to the beams.

Some of the larger 19th-century mills were re-equipped with modern engines and rope-drive systems to replace the earlier shaft drives. At Houldsworth's Mill, Reddish (899*), of 1865, for example, external engine houses and rope races were added to each of the two multi-storeyed blocks on either side of the original central engine house. The

Figure 159. The first electrically powered mills generated their own electricity on site, but mills were soon built to use the mains supply. Little Mill (351*), part of Murray's Mills, Manchester, was rebuilt in *c.*1908 to use mains electric power. The tower which housed the electric motors is on the left.

new engines were of the inverted compound type.[25] A similar modification took place at Victoria Mill, Miles Platting (383), another double mill.[26] Very large marine-type engines with rope drives were added to Atlas No. 3 and No. 4 Mills, Bolton (14 and 15*) (Fig 158).[27]

The first mills to use electricity for driving machinery generated their own power on site. The first examples were Falcon Mill, Bolton (66), of 1904–8, Kearsley Mill, Kearsley (89*), of 1906 and Welkin Ring Mill (935), originally named Ark Mill, near Bredbury, also of *c.*1906. Such mills had similar boiler houses and chimneys to steam-powered mills. The generators were driven by steam-turbine engines in a power house attached or close to the mill. At Kearsley Mill (89*), the generator building has arched windows similar to those in contemporary engine houses. Group-drive electric motors were sited on each floor, and because they were thought to be a fire risk they were sited in external towers, one motor driving each line shaft. The use of large motors to drive groups of machines declined in the mid 20th century, when smaller motors were used to power machines individually.

The construction of mills designed to utilise mains electricity began at about the same time, but was initially restricted by the extent of the mains supply. The first was probably Acme Mills, Pendlebury (807), of 1904. This 80,000 spindle mill was equipped with an equal number of ring and mule spindles and used current from the district power station at Radcliffe, over three miles from the site.[28] A number of advanced electrically powered mills were added to the oldest Manchester mills a few years later. In *c.*1908 Little Mill (351*) was rebuilt at the Murray's Mills complex in Manchester, and used mains electricity to power group-drive motors for

Figures 160 and 161. Brunswick Mill, Manchester (316*), was one of the first steam-powered mills to be converted to mains electric drive. The photographs show electric motors coupled to the ends of the earlier line shafts to drive carding engines and draw frames (*The Textile Mercury*, 1910, 144).

mule spinning (Fig 159). In 1912, two larger mule-spinning mills with a similar electric-power system, Royal Mill (370*) and Paragon Mill (364*), were added to the nearby McConnel and Kennedy site.

Steam-powered mills began to be converted for electric drive in the same period. The first in Manchester was probably Brunswick Mill (316*) in 1908 (Figs 160, 161). A small transformer house was added to the mill and the motors were coupled to the existing line shafting. The motors were housed externally in two glass and steel towers.[29] Atlas No.

4 Mill (15*) appears to have been converted for electric drive at about the same time as the new engine and rope drive were added. The combination of steam and electric drive may have permitted greater flexibility in the use of the individual floors of this very large mill.

# Epilogue

For 150 years the textile industry and mill building developed together. The rapid decline of the industry after 1930, however, brought the evolution of mill architecture to an effective halt. The cotton branch suffered from competition from the Far East, and the Greater Manchester region developed a specialism in man-made fibres, capitalising on the area's strong base in the chemical industry. As a result, very few significant additions were made after 1930 to the county's cotton mills. Today, the textile industry continues in Greater Manchester, but at a much reduced level of activity. The county's landscape and economy have changed in consequence. As new industries grow, so new types of factory are developed to suit their requirements, and buildings designed for the textile industry are turned to new uses at best, or demolished or left empty to decay. The use of Manchester's great Cotton Exchange as a theatre, the silence of the mills of Ancoats and other industrial districts, and the gaps in both urban and rural landscapes where mills have been demolished, all testify to the passing of the era of King Cotton.

# Inventory of selected mills

THE Inventory comprises thirty-nine studies of mills recorded in detail during the survey. These mills formed the basis of the interpretation of mill development covered in Chapters 3 to 6. Where appropriate the Inventory is cross-referenced to figures used in earlier chapters. The monument numbers identifying each mill are taken from the Gazetteer, where locational details are given in the form of national grid references.

## The Atlas Mills Complex, Bolton

In the late 19th century Musgraves was the largest cotton-spinning firm in Bolton, building the huge Atlas Mills complex between 1864 and 1888 (Fig 94). By the 1890s they operated eight mills in Bolton, including at least one for weaving, and were the fourth largest cotton-spinning firm in the world.[1] Other members of the family established a successful engineering business in Bolton which supplied both steam engines and the structural ironwork for the mills. The three decades during which the mill complex was built saw many new developments in mill design and construction, so the Atlas Mills include a range of construction types, power systems and architectural features.

### (13)   Atlas No. 2 Mill

Atlas No. 2 Mill, built in 1868, is of similar size and plan to other late 19th-century mills but its construction and power system are more typical of the mid 19th century. The mill is of twenty-one bays and four storeys, with each floor supported by five rows of columns (Fig 162). A two-storeyed extension of nine bays was added to the west end and ground-floor shed extensions to the north side before the end of the 19th century. A full-height cross-wall segregates the internal engine house from the main rooms. The cross-wall also supported the main upright shaft and incorporated a dust flue. The main rooms have timber floors but the

Figure 162. Atlas No. 2 Mill, Bolton, notable for its large internal engine house. Attached to the left end are the later dust flue and electric motor tower.

Figure 163. The offices of Atlas No. 2 Mill, Bolton.

smaller rooms next to the engine house are of fireproof construction, with transverse brick-vaulted ceilings and flag floors. The fireproof area includes a basement, which was probably used as a conditioning cellar. The engine house is oriented longitudinally in one corner, a typical arrangement in this period which contrasts with the transverse internal engine houses of earlier mills.

Preparation processes were located in the ground floor of the mill and transversely located mules in the three upper floors. Opening and scutching the raw cotton were undertaken in the smaller fireproof rooms beyond the cross-wall. A two-storeyed external office block is attached to the side wall opposite the engine house (Fig 163). The offices include the main entrance leading to the fireproof staircase. The stairs enclose a central hoist, which was powered from the line shafting in the mill.

The engine house is unusually well preserved with the original tall-arched external windows, the engine beds and the bearing boxes *in situ* (Fig 130). It contained a large compound beam engine manufactured by

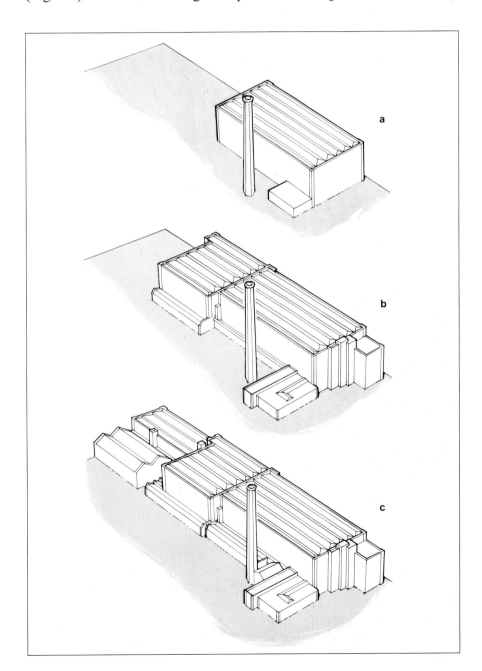

Figure 164. The original Atlas No. 4 Mill, Bolton, was more than doubled in size and given a more powerful engine and rope-drive system.
A: original mill *c*.1875
B: full-height extension and warehouse added to left, external engine house and rope race to the right, *c*.1910
C: second warehouse added and shed extensions replaced, mid 20th century

Musgraves.[2] The original boiler house is attached to the side of the engine house. A system of large reservoirs located immediately to the west was used by this and the later Atlas Mills. The shaft transmission system was similar to that of earlier cotton-spinning mills except that the engine was separated from the main upright shaft. The latter was attached to the cross-wall close to the centre-line of the mill and was driven by a horizontal shaft geared to the engine's flywheel. Several ground-floor line shafts were also driven by the horizontal shaft, while the upright shaft drove a single central line shaft in each of the mule-spinning rooms in the upper floors.

Atlas No. 2 was modified in the early 20th century along with the other Atlas Mills after Musgraves had been amalgamated into the Fine Cotton Spinners and Doublers Association. In 1906 an electric motor tower was added to one end. A single motor was coupled to the line shaft on each of the upper storeys.[3] The ventilation system was also modified, with the addition of a larger external dust flue and an internal dust chamber in one of the upper storeys.

### (15)   Atlas No. 4 Mill

Atlas No. 4 Mill was built in *c.*1875 as a five-storeyed fireproof block of twenty-three bays with dimensions comparable to other large mills of the 1870s (A in Fig 164). Its internal layout and power system were similar to those at the earlier Atlas No. 2 Mill (13*). Later additions to Atlas No. 4 Mill have created an unusually large mill illustrating the development of cotton-mill design in the late 19th and early 20th centuries (B and C). In the decade after 1875 a full-height extension of twelve bays was added, to which was attached a further warehouse extension (Fig 165).

The mill is of 'traditional' fireproof construction, with transverse brick-vaulted ceilings (Fig 111), contrasting with the newly developed methods of fireproof construction used in other large contemporary mills. It

Figure 165. Atlas No. 4 Mill, Bolton. The original mill with an internal engine house is on the right.

contained transversely located mules in the upper storeys with preparation on the ground floor.

Early 20th-century modifications included the addition of an external dust flue to replace the original flue in the cross-wall, a similar modification to that at Atlas No. 2 Mill (13*). An external engine house was added to the north end of the main mill in Accrington brick and contained an advanced 2,200 horsepower inverted compound engine (Fig 158). The external rope race incorporated mounts for electric motors in the upper storeys indicating that the mule-spinning rooms could be driven by either steam or electric power.[4] The original internal engine house was converted into an additional boiler house supplementing an external boiler house attached to the east side. The continued use of the mill for cotton spinning into the mid 20th century resulted in the addition of a second detached warehouse and shed extensions to the ground-floor preparation areas of the spinning blocks (C). See also Fig 126a.

## (17)   Atlas No. 6 Mill

Atlas No. 6 Mill was added in *c.*1888 and featured some of the latest developments in cotton-mill design and construction. It was the largest single phase of building in the Atlas complex, being of four storeys with a basement at one end and twenty-nine bays long. The overall internal dimensions are approximately 92.7 metres long by 38.8 metres wide. The mill was used for fine spinning on mules, and the ground-floor preparation area was extended into sheds along both sides of the mill (Fig 166).

Atlas No. 6 is an early concrete-floored mill, the concrete cast around iron joists supported by exposed transverse steel beams (Fig 118). This permitted large flat-headed windows occupying a high proportion of the external wall area. The mill did not have the flat roof which was

Figure 166. Atlas No. 6 Mill, Bolton, of *c.*1888 was the largest mill in the Atlas complex. The main block has stair towers at each end and lateral extensions to the ground-floor preparation room.

Figure 167. The external engine house and boiler house of Atlas No. 6 Mill, Bolton.

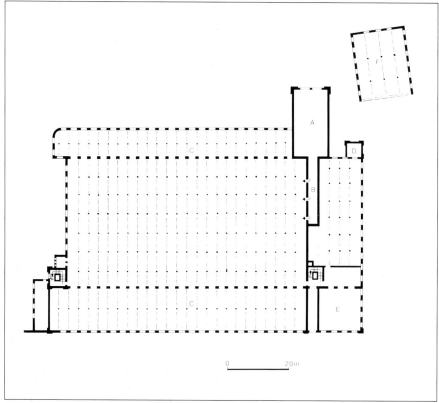

Figure 168. Atlas No. 6 Mill, ground-floor plan.
A: engine house
B: rope race
C: shed extensions
D: dust flue
E: offices
F: boiler house

characteristic of later concrete-floored mills: instead its roof is of slate with multiple longitudinal ridges.

Power was provided by a large horizontal tandem cross-compound engine of 1,750 horsepower in an external engine house with a rope transmission system (Figs 134, 167; A and B in Fig 168). The engine later also powered the nearby Atlas No. 7 Mill (18) via a long horizontal main shaft which was supported on piers above the reservoir between the two mills.[5] Atlas No. 6 continued to be steam driven until the mid 1960s. The rope race (Fig 135) is located near one end and thus served a similar function to the cross-walls of earlier shaft-driven mills, creating a segregated area at one end of the mill for processes involving a high fire risk. The basement was probably used as a conditioning cellar. Later rope-driven mills had their rope races built into an end wall, with the main floors uninterrupted by a cross-wall. See also Figs 98, 123.

## (71)   Gilnow Mill, Bolton

Gilnow Mill was built as an integrated cotton-spinning and weaving mill in the late 1850s by P. R. Arrowsmith, a former Mayor of Bolton.[6] Following a fire in 1868 the site was acquired by the firm of Crosses and Winkworth and the multi-storeyed spinning mill was probably rebuilt. Crosses and Winkworth expanded to become one of Boltons largest fine-cotton-spinning firms, occupying over twenty mills.[7] Cotton-mill design and construction was developing rapidly in this period and the two principal phases of Gilnow Mill feature contrasting methods of fireproof construction. The overall layout of the site probably remained unaltered, however, and still illustrates the organisation of a large mid 19th-century integrated cotton mill (Fig 169).

The mill comprises a spinning mill, weaving shed, warehouse and power plant. The entrance to the mill itself is through the long warehouse block of the late 1850s, twenty-seven bays long and of two storeys with a half basement. The spinning mill and weaving shed are attached to the rear. The west end of the warehouse is of mid 19th-century fireproof construction, with transverse brick ceiling vaults, and includes the engine

Figure 169. An aerial view of Gilnow Mill, Bolton, from the south east, showing the layout of the site with mill, weaving shed, warehouse and engine house. Originally an integrated site with a multi-storeyed spinning mill and attached weaving shed, this mill later specialised in spinning.

**143**

house attached to the south end of the spinning mill. The east section of the warehouse is of non-fireproof construction and contains the offices. The four-storeyed spinning mill of *c.*1870 is of sixteen bays with a multi-ridge roof. It was designed to contain preparation and carding machinery on the ground floor and transverse mules in the three upper storeys. It is notably wider in proportion to its length than earlier spinning mills, reflecting both the greater length of the mules in use by *c.*1870 and the use of a new type of fireproof construction. The latter comprises five rows of columns supporting a grid of deep transverse cast-iron primary beams and lighter longitudinal cast-iron secondary beams. Narrow longitudinal brick ceiling vaults spring from the secondary beams.

The attached weaving shed is directly accessible from the spinning mill, the east side wall of which is open on the ground floor and supported by massive cast-iron columns. The absence of joints between the shed and the warehouse suggests the shed is contemporary with the other original buildings. The timber-framed north-light roof is supported by cast-iron columns with decorated capitals.

The engine house contained a double-beam engine by J. Musgraves and Son of Bolton, installed during the initial construction of the mill in 1856.[8] The spinning mill was driven by an upright main shaft and the weaving shed by a horizontal shaft, both of which were geared to the single flywheel. The modified detached boiler house retains its wide-arched front openings. The octagonal chimney stands to the west of the mill but has been lowered.

The whole site is well preserved with an extensive yard at the front enclosed by wrought-iron railings. In comparison with earlier mills greater emphasis is given to embellishment in brick and stone (Fig 76). Typical Italianate details, including double pilasters and sandstone mouldings, are used throughout the site. The parapets of the earlier buildings are adorned with moulded antefixae, while those of the later spinning mill are highlighted with a band of yellow brick. An external fireproof stair tower with a pyramidal roof is attached to the south end. It was entered from the main doorway in the front of the warehouse block.

## (89)   Kearsley Mill, Kearsley, Bolton

The majority of Lancashire cotton-spinning mills built in the early 20th century were designed for steam power, characterised by large external engine houses, boiler houses, chimneys and rope transmission systems. The technical and economic advantages of electric power were known in this period but far fewer electric mills were built in Lancashire, for example, than in the United States of America. A small number of early electric mills were built before the availability of a mains supply and were therefore still dependent on steam engines to generate electricity on site. These mills had both steam and electric power features and could be readily converted to mains electricity when it became available.

Kearsley Mill, built by the Kearsley Spinning Company in 1906, is of six storeys and twenty-four bays and has typical dimensions and propor-

Figure 170. Kearsley Mill, Kearsley, was built for electric power before the availability of a mains supply. Current was generated by a steam turbine in the power house attached to the end of the mill. The adjoining tower contained the electric motors.

tions for an Edwardian mule-spinning mill (Fig 170). It was distinguished by its use of steam-turbine generators in place of a conventional engine, with electric motors housed in a projecting tower. The motors were segregated from the spinning and preparation areas to protect them from cotton dust. The mill is of similar internal construction to Barnfield Mills, Tyldesley (1060*), with concrete floors supported by steel beams and cast-iron columns. Preparation was concentrated in the ground floor, which included a wide flat-roofed extension along the north side. The upper storeys each contained twenty-four transversely located mules of around 1,350 spindles each, giving a total of 117,888 spindles. The line-shafting layout was also typical, with multiple line shafts in the ground floor and the extension and single line shafts in the mule-spinning rooms. The turbine generators were housed in an attached power house adjoining the base of the motor tower which had arched windows similar to those seen in contemporary engine houses. Three motors located in the power house itself were directly coupled to the ground-floor line shafts while the motor tower was positioned so that the motors for the mule-spinning rooms above could be coupled directly to the single line shafts. Kearsley Mill thus used a group-drive system, each motor driving a group of machines via a line shaft. In later mills separate motors powered individual machines. Steam for the turbines was supplied by four Lancashire boilers in a boiler house attached to the power house.[9]

**145**

## (129)   Saint Helena Mill, Bolton

Saint Helena Mill is of interest as one of Bolton's oldest mills and contrasts in its size, materials and the scale of its power system with the larger early mills in Manchester. The eleven-bay steam-powered mill was built in the late 1820s with four storeys and an attic (Fig 171). It stands partly on the site of an earlier water-powered mill.[10] It may have originally been used for fine cotton spinning, but from the 1830s was occupied by Robert Walker and Company for cotton-waste spinning, probably on mules.[11] Its continued use as a cotton-waste mill probably explains the survival of the building; it is of similar dimensions to purpose-built cotton-waste mills of later date. The site also includes a small attached north-light shed and three other mills added in the late 19th and early 20th centuries, and therefore spans all the main stages in the development of the cotton-waste mill (Fig 172).

The walls are of rubble stone with small flat-headed windows. There are rows of taking-in doors to the south end and the east side. The north end wall is of brick and may be a later rebuilding. It includes a projecting square-section brick chimney (Fig 88). The joisted timber floors are supported by a single row of columns to which line shafts were attached (Fig 79). Other line shafts were supported from the beams. The gabled attic has queen-strut trusses and was also used for powered processes.

Figure 171 (below). The oldest extant building at Saint Helena Mill, Bolton, was probably built in the late 1820s for cotton-waste spinning. It stands close to the site of an earlier water-powered mill.

Figure 172. Late 19th and early 20th-century mills were added to Saint Helena Mill, Bolton, which was used for cotton-waste spinning for over a century.

The mill was entered through a small door giving access to a fireproof internal staircase by the east side wall. Both the engine and the boilers were probably located internally. The boiler room is in the north end bay: it has a wide entrance in the west side wall and a ceiling of stone flags laid on cast-iron beams. The beams are of T-shaped cross-section but with a narrow bottom flange, and as such are a development of the plain T-shaped beams used in earlier examples of this type of construction, such as Beehive Mill, Manchester (306*), of 1824 (see pp. 61, 151). The two-storeyed engine house, probably for a small beam engine, is situated in the next bay to the north.

## (138)   Swan Lane No. 1 and No. 2 Mills, Bolton

The expansion of the Lancashire cotton industry in the early 20th century was characterised by the construction of very large spinning mills throughout the Greater Manchester area, normally containing over 100,000 spindles. A small number of firms built double mills of gigantic proportions, although many 'planned double mills' survive where the second half of the site was never built. Swan Lane No. 1 and No. 2 Mills were completed in two phases (1902, 1905) as a 210,000-spindle double mill with a central power system (Fig 173). It was claimed to be the largest spinning mill in the world under a single roof.[12] This title was probably lost by 1907 when the Broadstone Spinning Company (871) completed another double mill with 262,000 spindles at Reddish near Stockport, although in 1914 Swan Lane No. 3 Mill (139) was added with a further 120,000 mule spindles (Fig 174).

Swan Lane No. 1 and No. 2, designed by Stott and Sons, are of six storeys including a basement and twenty-one bays long. The two halves

Figure 173. Swan Lane No. 1 and No. 2 Mills, Bolton, built as a double mill in 1902 and 1905, was claimed to be the largest cotton-spinning mill in the world under one roof, with 210,000 mule spindles. The two halves of the building were organised as separate mills producing different counts of yarn.

Figure 174. Swan Lane No. 3 Mill,
Bolton, was completed in 1914, adding
a further 120,000 spindles to the site.

of the mill were powered independently and were organised internally as
separate mills.[13] No. 1 Mill concentrated on spinning fine counts from Sea
Island cotton and No. 2 on medium counts from Egyptian cotton. Both
mills contained mules for spinning in the upper storeys. The sequence of
preparation processes prior to spinning differed, however, the cotton used
for fine spinning being combed. Internal construction was similar
throughout, with longitudinal and transverse steel beams supporting three
transverse brick vaults in each bay (Fig 148). The building has a flat roof.
A shed extension to the ground floor of No. 1 Mill contained carding
engines and the segregated blowing room with its own dust flue. The
power features are on a scale commensurate with the rest of the site. The
huge external engine house contained two tandem cross-compound engines located side by side with two rope races, between which was the
dynamo room. The engines were separated by a row of thick cast-iron
columns with ornate capitals. The adjoining boiler house served Nos. 1
and 2 and also the later No. 3 Mill. It contained ten Lancashire boilers with
superheaters and economisers, one of the largest boiler installations to be
used at a cotton mill.[14] See also Figs 140, 141, 144–6, 153, 156.

## (192)  Crown Mill, Hawkshaw, Bury

This small mid 19th-century stone-built mill was added to the end of an
earlier row of cottages and used for the production of towelling, probably
from cotton waste (Figs 73, 175). The end cottage was converted to form
the entrance and staircase for the mill. It functioned as a small steam-

Figure 175. Crown Mill, near Bury, was built in the 1830s and an external engine house was added later to the right end. By the 1880s it was used as an integrated cotton-waste mill.

powered integrated factory, containing 1,100 spindles and forty looms by the 1880s. By the 1890s, however, it was used entirely for weaving.[15] Some of the details of the building are similar to earlier mills elsewhere. The flat-headed windows are notably small and there are taking-in doors to the east end and the south side. The floors and the roof trusses are of non-fireproof timber construction. An engine house and boiler house are attached to the east end, both probably added shortly after the original date of construction. A small concrete-and-steel shed was added to the north side in the 1950s to contain electrically powered looms and the site continued to be used for the cotton trade up to the late 20th century.

## (205)   Field Mill, Ramsbottom, Bury

The Field Mill site consists of a small stone-built spinning mill dating from the middle of the 19th century with an adjoining weaving shed of similar date and a variety of attached ancillary buildings (Fig 176a). Its scale and construction suggest that it was probably built as a cotton-waste mill. The spinning mill is of three storeys and an attic, and nine bays in length. It is non-fireproof, with joisted timber floors supported by a single row of columns. It was originally powered by a steam engine in a small external engine house attached to the north end. The main upright shaft was attached to the inside of the end wall. The north-light weaving shed to the south was built to a square plan of ten bays. The shed was originally powered from the engine house, but both it and the spinning mill were converted to electric power in the early 20th century.

A

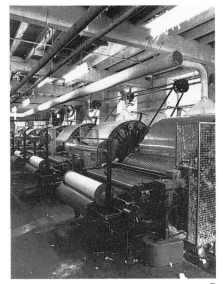

B

C

D

At the time of recording in 1988 the site was still in use as a cotton-waste mill. The weaving shed contained modern looms with individual electric motors. The spinning mill, however, contained machinery more typical of the late 19th century. The line shafting was rope driven from two large electric motors in a group-drive system. The motors themselves were of early 20th-century date. Carding engines were located at ground level with two pairs of mules arranged longitudinally in the first and second floors (Figs 176b and 176c). The carding engines were belt-driven from

Figure 176 (opposite). Field Mill, Ramsbottom.

A: the small steam-powered spinning mill, weaving shed and ancillary buildings all date from the mid to late 19th century. The site was converted to electric drive in the early 20th century and finally ceased working, as an integrated cotton-waste mill, in 1988

B: carding engines in the ground floor of the spinning mill were powered from line shafting which was driven by an electric motor

C: these mules in the upper floors ranged in date from the early to mid 20th century. They were powered by line shafting which was rope driven by an electric motor

D: other preparation machinery in the adjoining ancillary buildings also dated from the early 20th century.

three line shafts, the central one attached to the columns, which were powered from a 160 horsepower motor located outside the south end wall. A gabled shed attached to the west side contained additional cards and a doubling frame driven by another line shaft powered from the same motor (Fig 176d). The mules were driven from a separate 175 horsepower motor situated outside the west wall. Power was transmitted to transverse line shafts in the upper floors by means of a rope-drive system, with the ropes passing through traps cut into the floors.

## (306)   Beehive Mill, Ancoats, Manchester

Beehive Mill is a room and power mill built in the early 1820s with later additions. It incorporates both heavy timber-floored and fireproof construction and includes unusual examples of the innovative use of cast and wrought iron. The site comprises three attached multi-storeyed blocks built on the south side of the Bengal Arm of the Rochdale Canal. The first two blocks were of six storeys built to an L-shaped plan, with a thirteen-bay range along Radium Street and a three-bay wing added later on Jersey Street (Fig 177). The third, a five-storeyed mill of thirteen bays on Bengal Street, was built *c.*1848 (Fig 178). Most of the occupiers were connected with the cotton trade.[16] Like the contemporary Islington Mill, Salford

Figure 177. Beehive Mill, Manchester, is notable for its unusual types of internal construction. The main block dates from the early 1820s, with the wing on the left added in 1824.

Figure 178. The Bengal Street block of Beehive Mill, Manchester, on the right, was added in c.1848. The site was built at the end of a branch of the Rochdale Canal, which formerly passed from left to right in front of the mills.

Figure 179. The 1824 wing of Beehive Mill, Manchester, is of fireproof construction with flag floors laid on a grid of interlocking cast-iron beams. Its roof is a cast and wrought-iron spaceframe structure. The main block has heavy timber floors and a roof comprising timber principal rafters supported by curved cast-iron ribs.

(829*), however, the site contains no special features to indicate that it was built for room and power.

The large block along Radium Street was the first building on the site and is shown on a map of the early 1820s with a short canal basin by its west side, now the mill yard.[17] It is of heavy timber-floored construction, with two rows of cast-iron columns supporting heavy transverse beams with thick floorboards laid directly on top. Two line shafts in each floor were attached to the columns. The attic was also powered and has distinctive roof trusses comprising curved cast-iron ribs supporting timber principal rafters (Figs 53, 54). The power system was typical of the 1820s, with an internal beam engine housed in the north end and segregated by a cross-wall containing the upright shaft. As in Chorlton New Mill, Manchester (323*), the original fireproof internal circular staircase was

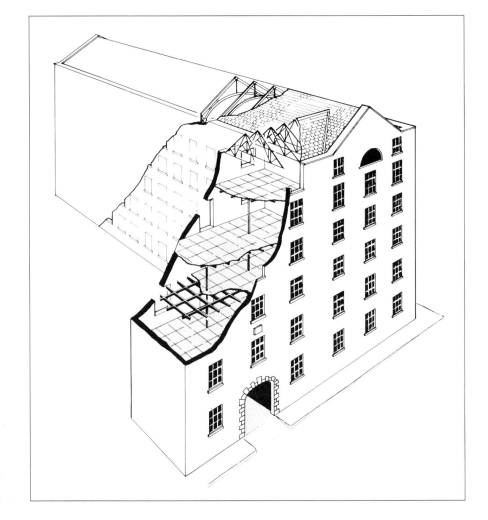

located beyond the end wall of the engine house. At Beehive Mill, however, the stairs enclosed the circular brick chimney, an internal variation of the external combined chimney and stair tower.

The smaller Jersey Street block has an 1824 datestone and is the same height as the earlier range (Fig 179). The north side wall originally contained double taking-in doors to the upper floors, suggesting that the wing was mainly used for warehousing. The ground floor contains a passage leading to the yard. This building features a novel type of fireproof construction, containing no structural timber. The floors are of stone flags laid on a grid of T-section cast-iron beams supported by two columns in each storey (Fig 50). The beams include primary, secondary and tertiary components arranged in a grid pattern similar to that used on a much larger scale in the framing of late 19th-century fireproof mills. Other less sophisticated examples of this type of construction occurred up to the 1830s.[18] The roof is also fireproof, supported by cast-iron trusses held under tension by wrought-iron ties (Fig 55). This is now a rare example of what was an advanced type of roof construction, utilising the different structural properties of cast and wrought iron. A similar type of roof formerly survived at Chepstow Street Mill, Manchester (322*), and possibly at Chorlton New Mill (323*).

The nearby Bengal Street block of 1848 was damaged by fire and partly rebuilt in 1861; a distinctive feature is the small full-height towers located between each bay in the north side wall, possibly part of a heating or ventilation system (Fig 178). See also Fig 43.

## (315)   Brownsfield Mill, Ancoats, Manchester

Brownsfield Mill is a well-preserved room and power mill built *c.*1825, of heavy timber-floored construction similar to that at Beehive Mill, Manchester (306*). It is closely associated with the former canal system, standing at the junction of the Rochdale Canal with two branch canals on the west side of Great Ancoats Street. It is slightly smaller than the other Ancoats mills, comprising two multi-storeyed wings built to an L-shaped plan (Fig 180). The main block (A in Fig 181) of seven storeys and twelve bays dates from 1825. The smaller wing (C), added a few years later, is of six storeys and seven bays. Despite having one storey less than the earlier block it has taller ceilings and is of the same overall height. An unusual feature of the site is the split-level yard, with a lower covered section alongside the mill allowing direct access from street level to the basement.

Up to the late 19th century there seem to have been just one or two occupiers at any time, all in the cotton-spinning trade. By the end of the 19th century, however, the mill was occupied by a large number of small firms in a wide range of trades. By 1912 the occupiers included the aircraft pioneer A. V. Roe, who used part of the mill for the design and construction of early biplanes and triplanes.[19]

The main block was used for powered processes, and contains the engine house. The smaller wing contained line shafting in the upper floors

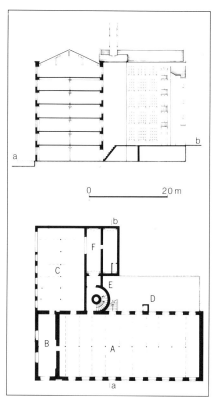

but was partly used for warehousing. Its east side contains a full-height row of taking-in doors with a projecting hoist beam at the top. The west side, overlooking the site of a former branch canal, contains a stone-arched 'shipping hole', presumably to allow access into the basement by canal boats. The floor construction throughout the mill consists of timber beams, supported by a single row of slender cast-iron columns, with thick boards laid directly on top of the beams without joists (Fig 51). Additional columns have been inserted beneath the beams in the basement. The gabled roofs have timber queen-post trusses (Fig 52).

The power system was typical of the period, comprising an internal engine house (B) in the west end of the main block with power transmitted via upright shafts in both wings to line shafting attached to the columns. The boilers were probably located in a detached fireproof room (F) situated beneath the yard, and used water from the canal. The chimney is incorporated in a well-preserved external chimney and stair tower (E) in the corner between the two wings overlooking the yard (Figs 59, 60). This is Manchester's oldest surviving mill chimney. Both wings also have narrow full-height privy towers (D), that to the west wing attached to a second stair tower added in the mid 19th century.

## (316)  Brunswick Mill, Manchester

Brunswick Mill, built *c.*1840, forms part of an impressive group of early to mid 19th-century cotton mills along the banks of the Ashton Canal to

Figure 180 (top left). Brownsfield Mill, Manchester, was built in *c.*1825 at the junction of the Rochdale Canal with two branch canals. It was a room and power mill of heavy timber-floored construction.

Figure 181 (above). Cross-section and basement plan of Brownsfield Mill.
A:  original mill
B:  engine house
C:  wing
D:  privy tower
E:  combined chimney and stair tower
F:  probable site of boilers

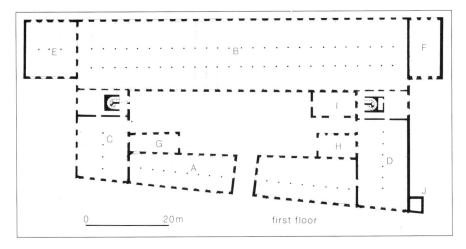

Figure 182 (above). Brunswick Mill, Manchester, first-floor plan.
A.   front block
B.   main spinning mill
C.   east wing
D.   west wing
E.   waste house
F.   engine house
G, H.   loading bays
I.   electricity transformer house
J.   added dust flue

Figure 183 (top right). Brunswick Mill. The front block between the two wings was raised from three to four storeys at the end of the 19th century. The tower in the foreground is the dust flue, added at about the same time.

Figure 184 (right). The yard of Brunswick Mill, with the main spinning mill to the right.

the east of Manchester. It is one of the largest mid 19th-century mills in the county and was built in one principal phase to an unusual quadrangular layout (Fig 70). The seven-storeyed main block alongside the canal (B in Fig 182) is of twenty-eight bays with full-height wings extending northwards from both ends (C and D; Fig 183). The ends of the wings are linked by a lower block fronting Bradford Road (A) which contains the arched main entrance (Fig 74) leading through to an enclosed yard in the centre of the site (Fig 184). The main block and the wings were entered from the yard, semi-circular staircases being situated in both wings (Fig 75).

The main block was used for spinning with preparation in the second storey and self-acting mules in the storeys above.[20] The original mules, which on average had about 400 spindles each, were located transversely, one to each bay of the mill. The wings were used for a combination of

**155**

spinning and ancillary processes, such as yarn winding, while the front block was used primarily for warehousing and offices. The mill was powered by a large double-beam engine in an external engine house (F) attached to the west end of the main block. In the 1850s the machinery included 276 carding engines, twenty drawing frames, fifty slubbing frames, eighty-one roving frames and a total of 77,000 mule spindles.

All the main buildings are of typical fireproof construction for the period, with transverse ceiling vaults supported by Hodgkinson-type cast-iron beams and two rows of columns. The mill was constructed by the firm of David Bellhouse, which was responsible for a number of early to mid 19th-century fireproof mills in the Manchester area, although the deeds indicate that the design of the beams and columns was subject to the approval of William Fairbairn.[21] The distinctive site plan is similar to other mills known to have been designed by Fairbairn (e.g. Orrells Mill, Stockport (907)), which suggests that Fairbairn might also have been involved with the overall design of Brunswick Mill.

In the late 19th century the mill was taken over by the firm of Henry Bannerman, which also operated cotton mills in Stalybridge and Hyde and a large warehouse in Manchester.[22] A horizontal engine with a rope-drive system was added, and the original mules were replaced by larger mules arranged longitudinally in the main block. In 1909 the steam engines were replaced by electric motors housed in two steel and glass towers overlooking the yard.[23] A transformer house was built in the yard (I), electricity being obtained from the Manchester Corporation mains. This was said to be the first conversion of a steam-powered mill to electric drive in Manchester, although purpose-built electrically powered mills were being constructed at about the same time (see Murrays Mills, Manchester (358*)). From the 1920s the mill was converted to ring spinning under the management of the Lancashire Cotton Corporation.[24] This required strengthening of the original cast-iron floor structure (Fig 152). Brunswick Mill ceased to be used for cotton production in the mid 1960s. See also Figs 160, 161.

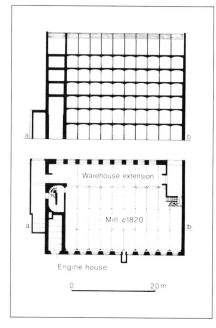

## (322)   Chepstow Street Mill, Manchester

Chepstow Street Mill was a seven-storeyed fireproof mill built some time between 1813 and 1820 and demolished in 1990. It was eleven bays long with a plan measuring 33.4 by 16.3 metres (Figs 185 and 186). The original mill's roof was of exceptional interest as one of the earliest and largest known examples of cast and wrought-iron truss construction. At the end of the 19th century the front elevation was removed and the building extended outwards by about 5 metres, disguising its origins when viewed from the street.[25]

Floor construction was similar to that in other contemporary fireproof mills such as Chorlton New Mill, Manchester (323*), and Sedgwick Mill, Manchester (372*), with brick ceiling vaults, cast-iron beams of inverted-T cross-section and two rows of cast-iron columns.

Figures 185 and 186. Chepstow Street Mill, Manchester, was built before 1820. It was of similar fireproof construction to contemporary mills but with a triple-span cast and wrought-iron roof. One of the original side walls was replaced when the mill was converted into a warehouse.

The power system comprised an internal engine house for a beam engine in the east end bay with the chimney flue built into one corner. The external boiler house did not survive but the stone support for the base of the upright shaft was still *in situ* in the ground floor. Also in the east end bay was the oval fireproof staircase. The north elevation had an external privy tower (Fig 185).

Fragments of the roof were salvaged during demolition enabling a graphical reconstruction of the original structure (Fig 187). The mill had a triple-span roof using cast and wrought-iron trusses. The compressional components were of cast iron and those in tension were of wrought iron. Cast iron was used for the principals, the angled struts, the purlins, the two valley gutters and a separate framework which supported the ridge tiles. Wrought iron was used for the vertical and horizontal tie-rods. All the components were carefully designed, taking into account their function in

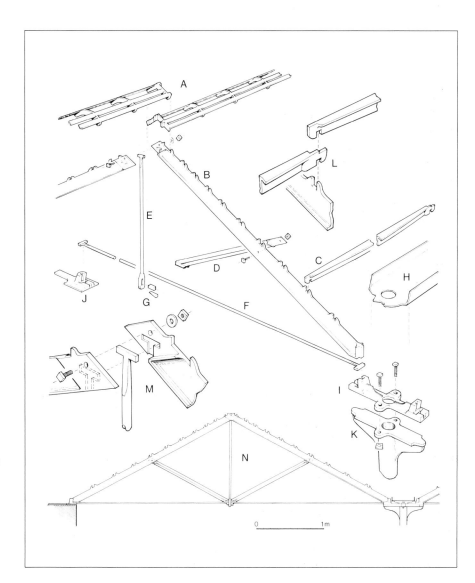

Figure 187. Chepstow Street Mill, Manchester, details of roof truss construction.

A:   frame to support ridge tiles
B:   cast-iron principal
C:   cast-iron purlin
D:   cast-iron strut
E, F:   wrought-iron tie-rods
G:   wedges to secure tie-rods
H:   cast-iron valley gutter with drain-hole
I:   double-ended shoe on column
J:   single-ended shoe on wall
K:   column top plate
L:   details of purlins overlapping on principal
M:   details of apex
N:   reconstructed elevation

supporting the roof and the type of iron used. The principals, for example, were lapped at the apex and joined by a single bolt. Their upper edge had slots to accept the purlins, while their feet were shaped to fit into cast-iron shoes mounted in the walls and on the column tops. The purlins had a fish-bellied long profile and specially shaped ends which overlapped in the notches on the principals. The two valley gutters of this roof drained into the hollow centres of some of the columns.

## (323)   Chorlton New Mill, Chorlton on Medlock

In the early 19th century Chorlton New Mill was one of Manchester's largest spinning mills and was technically advanced in its construction and power system. It is also very well documented, with over sixty drawings held in the Boulton and Watt collection in Birmingham.[26] Some aspects of the mill's design became obsolete by the mid 19th century, so this site represents a transitional stage in the development of the cotton factory. It consists of three large multi-storeyed blocks built in phases to an L-shaped plan alongside Cambridge Street and Hulme Street in Chorlton on Medlock (Fig 188). This area, like Ancoats, was developed as an industrial suburb of Manchester from the 1790s. The River Medlock provided water for steam engines and boilers. The mill was built by members of the Birley family who moved to Manchester in the early 19th century after establishing a successful 'putting-out' business in north Lancashire.[27] It was later ex-

Figure 188. Chorlton New Mill, Manchester. The original 1814 mill is on the left, with the 1818 wing to the right and the 1845 block in the centre.

tended into an integrated mill, a modification which was common in Manchester spinning mills in the 1820s.

The eight-storeyed block on the east side of Cambridge Street, which includes two storeys below street level, is of twenty bays and was built in 1814. It may be the oldest surviving example of fireproof mill construction in Greater Manchester, although some parts of the building are not original. In each storey three rows of cylindrical cast-iron columns support narrow cast-iron beams and brick-vaulted ceilings (Figs 48, 49). This is the only known early fireproof mill in Greater Manchester to have been built with three rows of columns. The roof was probably originally iron-framed (Fig 56), similar perhaps to the nearby Chepstow Street Mill,

Figure 189. The cross wall in the original part of Chorlton New Mill, Manchester, contained ducts for the upright shaft, ventilation flues and a hoist.

Manchester (322*). The mill was powered by a 100 horsepower Boulton and Watt beam engine in a 24 metre high internal engine house near the north end. The engine was segregated from the main part of the mill by a substantial cross-wall which incorporated ducts for the upright shaft, a ventilation system and a hoist (Fig 189). The fireproof staircase was located behind the cross-wall, beyond the west end of the engine house. The type of cross-wall used in this mill thus served several purposes and later became a common feature in mills with internal engines. One feature of the mill which soon fell out of fashion, however, was the internal location of the gas retorts and gas holders. Early gas-lighting systems were used at a number of the more advanced fireproof mills in this period.[28] At Chorlton New Mill gas was manufactured in the basement, close to the boilers, and was stored in three gas holders in a specially built room next to the engine house in the north end of the building (Fig 67). Original drawings indicate that gas was circulated around the mill using the hollow centres of the cast-iron columns which supported the floors.

In 1818 a second fireproof wing of twelve bays was added along Hulme Street. This was originally driven by a horizontal shaft from the 1814 engine but later had its own external engine house. In 1829 a large powerloom weaving shed containing 600 looms was added to the north end of the site. It was powered by an unusual side-lever engine located in the former gas holder room in the end of the 1814 block. The late 19th-century finishing works of Robert Peel and Co now stands on the site of the weaving shed. In 1845 a third full-height fireproof block of six bays was added between the end walls of the two earlier wings at the southwest corner of the site. This included an internal engine house containing a double-beam engine which drove shafting in all three multi-storeyed blocks. In the 1860s the site was taken over by Charles Macintosh and Co, and together with other nearby mills was used for the production of rubberised cloth. The basements of Chorlton New Mill were linked to those of the surrounding mills by a system of tunnels beneath Cambridge Street and Hulme Street (Fig 41). See Figs 40, 85.

## (358)  Murray's Mills, Ancoats, Manchester

The brothers Adam and George Murray migrated from southern Scotland to Manchester in the 1780s. They established a successful business as textile machinery makers and cotton spinners in a number of room and

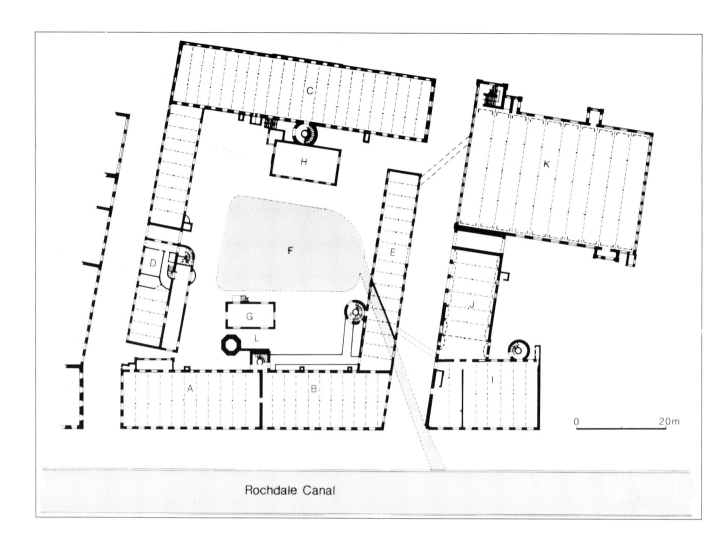

power mills around Manchester before concentrating on fine cotton spinning at the Ancoats site.[29] Other important early industrialists also migrated from southern Scotland to Manchester in this period; yarn produced cheaply using the new factory system was sent back to Scotland to meet the huge demand from handloom weavers.[30] The resulting profits led to the construction of some of Manchester's largest early factories by Scottish entrepreneurs, including McConnel and Kennedy who built large mills on the adjacent site to the Murrays (Fig 38).

## (362, 333, 359)   Old Mill, Decker Mill, New Mill

The original part of the Murray's Mills complex comprises four multi-storeyed blocks erected in phases between 1798 and 1806, including Old Mill (362), the last mill to survive from Manchester's boom in factory building in the late 1790s. The site was enormous by contemporary standards, with an unprecedented 84,000 mule spindles and 1,300 operatives. The four principal buildings are arranged in a quadrangle enclosing a central yard. The seven-storeyed block to the south of the yard

Figure 190. Murray's Mills, Manchester, ground-floor plan.
A:   Old Mill, of 1798
B:   Decker Mill, of 1802
C:   New Mill, of 1804
D:   Murray Street block of *c*.1804–6
E:   Bengal Street block of *c*.1804–6
F:   canal basin
G:   mid 19th-century engine house
H:   partly rebuilt engine house of New Mill
I:   Doubling Mill, of 1842
J:   Fireproof Mill, of *c*.1842
K:   New Little Mill, of 1908
L:   site of former engine house of 1802

Figure 191. The twenty-one bay south elevation of Old Mill, and Decker Mill, built 1798–1802 and now the oldest extant cotton mill in Manchester. To the right is the detached Doubling Mill, added in 1842.

Figure 192. New Mill, Manchester, of 1804, was the largest building at Murray's site.

comprises the original eleven bays of Old Mill, built in 1798 (A in Fig 190), with the ten further bays of Decker Mill (B) added to its east end in 1802 (Fig 191). To the north of the yard the six-storeyed New Mill (C), twenty-two bays long, was added in 1804 (Fig 192). Both blocks were used for spinning. Two narrower blocks (D, E), originally both four-storeyed and used mainly for warehousing, were added by 1806 to form the east and west sides of the yard. The entrance to each of the principal buildings faced the yard. The yard itself was only entered from Murray Street, so the main entrance passage controlled access to all parts of the site (Fig 45). Of particular interest is the high level of integration with the canal network, which was built in the same period. Most of the yard was occupied by a private canal basin (F), used for the transportation of raw cotton, coal and yarn (Fig 193). The basin was entered by boats from the Rochdale Canal via a tunnel passing beneath one of the mills and the adjacent street. The warehouse block on Murray Street included offices alongside the main entrance, distinguished

Figure 193. The yard of Murray's Mills, Manchester, with the site of the former canal basin in the foreground. Two heating or ventilation towers can be seen attached to the side of Decker Mill.

by oriel windows overlooking the yard. All the buildings except the Murray Street block had external fireproof stair towers.

The whole site, except for the stair towers, was of non-fireproof construction with joisted timber floors supported by slender cast-iron columns of cruciform cross-section, although some of the original columns were later replaced (Fig 47).

The two spinning blocks were powered by Boulton and Watt beam engines in external engine houses (G, H) located mid-way along the side walls facing the yard (Fig 39). Both had adjoining boiler houses which used water from the canal basin.[31] Upright shafts were situated in the middle of the mills, geared to line shafting to either side in each storey, in a similar power-transmission system to that used in some double mills. Narrow full-height towers were attached to the sides of the spinning mills and may have formed part of an early ventilation system.[32] See also Figs 42, 44, 46, 62.

### (334, 335, 351)   Doubling Mill, Fireproof Mill, Little Mill

Three smaller mills were later added to the original site. Little Mill was built to the north-east in the 1820s and was replaced by another mill in 1908. Doubling Mill and Fireproof Mill (I, J in Fig 190; Fig 194) were added to the east of the main site in 1842, powered by a single internal beam engine and linked to the earlier buildings by tunnels beneath Bengal Street. They were probably used for doubling yarn and warehousing. Fireproof Mill has typical fireproof construction for 1842, with ceilings of transverse brick vaults supported by cast-iron beams of the Hodgkinson type. In 1908 a concrete-floored mill (K) was built on the site of Little Mill in Accrington brick and was powered by electric motors housed in an external tower (Fig 159). This was probably Manchester's first electrically powered mill designed to use current from the corporation mains.[33]

Figure 196 (opposite). McConnel and Kennedy's Mills, ground-floor plan.
A:   Sedgwick Mill, main block of 1818–20
B:   Sedgwick Mill west wing of 1818–20
C:   Sedgwick Mill east wing of *c.*1820
D:   Sedgwick Mill north block of *c.*1820
E:   Sedgwick New Mill, of 1868
F:   Royal Mill, of 1912
G:   Paragon Mill, of 1912
H:   site of former yard

Figure 194. The southern aspect of the
Ancoats mills, Manchester (see also Fig
38). In the background is Brownsfield
Mill, with, from left to right, Royal Mill,
Sedgwick Mill, Old Mill, Decker Mill
and Doubling Mill.

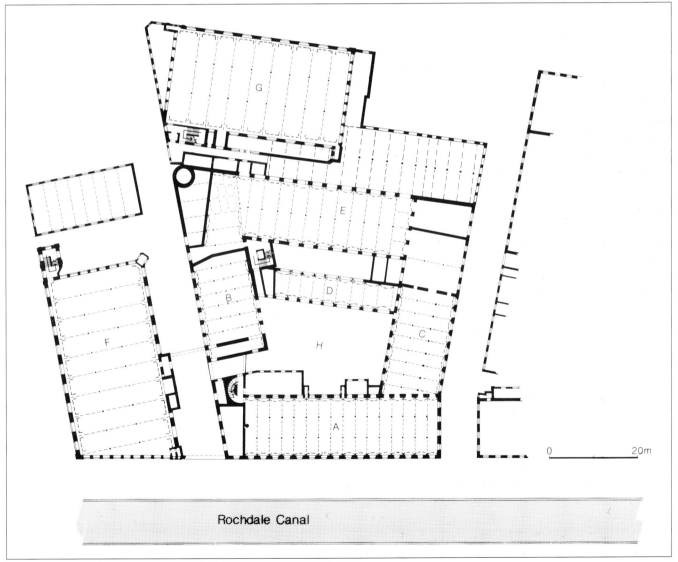

Rochdale Canal

## McConnel and Kennedy's Mills, Ancoats, Manchester

James McConnel and John Kennedy, like the Murray brothers, migrated to Manchester from Scotland in the 1780s. The partners in the two firms were well acquainted and the firms had similar early histories before building large mills on adjacent sites in Ancoats.[34] Both started as manufacturers of textile machinery, acquiring a technical understanding of cotton spinning which gave them a competitive advantage over other firms, and both supplied factory-produced fine cotton yarn to the hand-loom weavers of Scotland. John Kennedy in particular is reputed to have made significant improvements to the mule.[35] The firm of McConnel and Kennedy was founded in 1790, expanding to become one of the most successful and best-known businesses in the Lancashire cotton industry. The expansion of their Ancoats mills continued from the 1790s until the early 20th century, resulting in an unusually complex site (Figs 57, 195, 196). The extensive early records of the firm are preserved in the John Rylands Library, Deansgate, Manchester.

### (372)   Sedgwick Mill

Sedgwick Mill is an impressive eight-storeyed mill built between 1818 and 1820 next to Murray's Mills (358*) on Redhill Street, and is the oldest extant part of McConnel and Kennedy's site (Fig 197). It was built to a U-shaped plan, comprising a seventeen-bay block fronting Redhill Street (A, Fig 196) with wings of eight bays to the north (B and C). The west wing includes the original entrance, a passage which led from the public

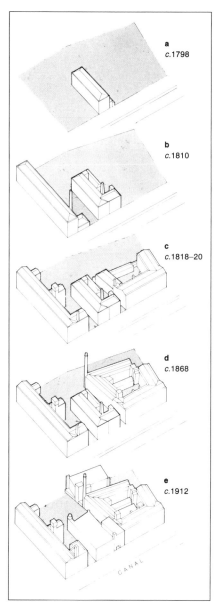

Figure 195. The development of McConnel and Kennedy's Mills, 1798–1912.
A.   Old Mill
B.   Long Mill added
C.   Sedgwick Mill added
D.   Sedgwick New Mill added
E.   Old Mill rebuilt as Royal Mill, Paragon Mill added.
Long Mill is not extant.

Figure 197. The eight-storeyed Sedgwick Mill, Manchester, was one of the tallest early 19th-century fireproof mills.

road to the enclosed yard, and the fireproof stair tower attached to the main block. The site was of similar fireproof construction to the earlier Chorlton New Mill, Manchester (323*), but had a timber roof. The power system was also similar, with a Boulton and Watt beam engine in an internal engine house at the west end of the main block.[36] The engine house was segregated from the rest of the mill by a full-height cross-wall supporting the upright shaft. The boilers were in the ground floor of the west wing (B) and gas retorts were located alongside a separate smaller block forming the north side of the yard (D).[37]

McConnel and Kennedy's original mill at the Ancoats site, Old Mill (363), was built in 1798 and was possibly the first mill designed to accommodate steam-powered mules. The surviving early inventories of Sedgwick Mill indicate that it followed the same principles of internal organisation. Preparation machinery was located in the lower two storeys and mules of around 348 spindles each in the upper six. The mules were positioned transversely, each one fitting neatly between the columns supporting the floor beams, and received power from a single central line shaft running the full length of each storey. This internal layout became commonplace throughout the Lancashire cotton industry, influencing both the shape and the power system of spinning mills.

In the early 1860s the existing mules in Sedgwick Mill were replaced by new self-acting mules of between 800 and 1,000 spindles which because of their increased length had to be installed longitudinally in the upper six floors. The most efficient use of the available floorspace with the new mule layout was obtained by moving one of the two rows of columns outwards by a few feet, the joint in the floor beams being supported with distinctive wide brackets at the column tops (Fig 115). The delicate task of cutting and replacing the original columns was carried out without stopping production in the mill by the firm of William Fairbairn.[38] See also Fig 38.

## (373)   Sedgwick New Mill

As the largest cotton-spinning firm in Manchester, McConnel and Kennedy were largely immune from the worst effects of the Cotton Famine in the 1860s. At about this time new mules were installed in Sedgwick Mill (372*) and in 1868 a new five-storeyed building, Sedgwick New Mill, was built on the site of a nearby street and housing (Fig 198; E in Fig 196). The new mill, of fifteen bays, was attached to the original west wing and was primarily used for doubling the yarn which had been spun in the firm's other mills.[39] The construction of mills to specialise in the doubling of cotton yarn increased in the late 19th century, partly as a consequence of the spread of the sewing machine and the increased use of sewing thread. The internal construction of Sedgwick New Mill (Fig 110) was relatively conservative in comparison with the larger contemporary mills being erected in Bolton and Oldham, but nevertheless contrasts with that of the original Sedgwick Mill built between 1818 and 1820. The building is of similar length to the main block of Sedgwick Mill but has larger bays,

Figure 198. Sedgwick New Mill, centre, was added in 1868 and used for yarn doubling.

and is wider with higher ceilings and larger windows. The beams supporting the transverse ceiling vaults are probably of cast iron but of deeper cross-section and the columns are thicker. The new mill was probably powered by a horizontal steam engine located in the modified basement of an adjoining earlier building (adjacent to D, Fig 196).[40] The engine was geared to the main upright shaft which was located in an external stair tower. The unusual layout of the power system was determined by the constricted nature of the site.

### (364, 370)   Paragon Mill, Royal Mill

The McConnel and Kennedy site was expanded in 1912 with the construction of two spinning mills of advanced design driven by electric motors utilising the Manchester Corporation mains. Both mills are of six storeys and nine bays (Fig 142). Paragon Mill (G in Fig 196) marked a further

Figures 199 and 200. Paragon Mill (above) and Royal Mill (left), Manchester, of 1912 were built for electrically powered mule spinning using the mains supply. In their embellishment and reinforced-concrete floor construction they are typical of contemporary mills but their size was limited by the constricted nature of the site.

extension of the complex into the surrounding streets but Royal Mill (F) was a rebuilding of Old Mill (363), built 1798, and was named following a visit by the King in 1942. Both mills are in Accrington brick with similar distinctive embellishment in sandstone and terracotta (Figs 199 and 200), and both have concrete floors supported by transverse steel beams and cast-iron columns (Fig 150). Their dimensions were largely determined by the constricted nature of this site. They were built to contain mules of over 1,000 spindles each but are smaller than other early 20th-century mills. In this case the mules were located longitudinally and powered from transverse line shafts.[41]

The electric motors were segregated from the main spinning area in external full-height towers attached to the side walls. A single large motor powered the line shaft in each of the mule-spinning rooms, a similar arrangement to that used at Kearsley Mill, (89*). The ground floor of Paragon Mill included a large shed extension for preparation machinery. External dust flues were located alongside the motor towers and linked to dust chambers on the roof. Both mills had external privy towers and stair towers in contrasting architectural style with sprinkler tanks in the top.

## (400)   Anchor Mill, Westwood, Oldham

Anchor Mill was built in 1881 by the newly formed Anchor Spinning Co for spinning medium to coarse counts of cotton on mules. It was designed by Joseph Stott[42] and like many mills of the 1870s and 1880s has both traditional and advanced features. It is of five storeys including a basement and eighteen bays in length with floors supported by five rows of columns. The mill is smaller than other contemporary Oldham mills and has a power system more typical of the mid 19th century. The plan is notably wide in proportion to its length, being designed to accommodate 1,064 spindle mules installed transversely in the upper floors (Fig 91).[43] The ground floor was used for preparation and included a full-width rear shed extension (Fig 95). Internal construction is a development of the traditional brick-vaulted ceilings still used elsewhere, comprising longitudinal and transverse primary beams supporting a pair of transverse vaults in each bay (Fig 112). This enables the longitudinal spacing of the columns to be greater and the windows to be larger.

The power system originally comprised an internal engine house, identifiable by its large embellished arched window, an attached external boiler house and a free-standing chimney. A system of reservoirs was built to the east of the mill. The shaft transmission system was attached to an internal cross-wall which also contained flues for the ventilation system. The upright shaft was located close to the centre-line of the mill and was driven from the engine's flywheel by a horizontal shaft, which in addition drove the multiple line shafts of the ground-floor preparation area. A two-storeyed office block was attached to the mill against the internal stair tower. The basement included a yarn-conditioning cellar (Fig 124). See also Fig 103.

## (478)   Kent Mill, Chadderton, Oldham

Kent Mill, built in 1908, was designed by the Oldham-based architect George Stott and is typical of the scale, materials and internal layout commonly found in Edwardian cotton-spinning mills (Fig 138).[44] Mills of this period in the Oldham area are distinguished by their great size and by the use of hard red Accrington brick. The overall proportions and layout of the mill reflect the original complement of transversely located mules with a total of around 90,000 spindles in the upper floors, although the mules were later replaced by ring frames. The ground floor was used mainly for carding and preparation with the blowing room located in a segregated part of the basement. The only unusual feature at Kent Mill is the absence of a lateral extension to the ground-floor preparation area.

The site consists of a five-storeyed block (A in Fig 201), including a basement, of twelve bays with attached stair towers (H, I, J), engine house (B) and

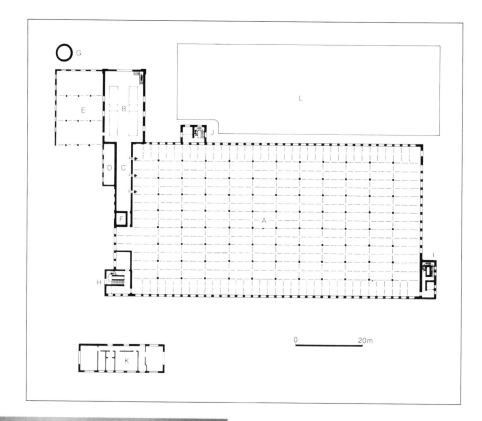

Figure 201. Kent Mill, Chadderton.
A: main block
B: engine house
C: rope race
D: pump house
E: boiler house
F: dust flue
G: chimney
H: main tower
I: north end tower
J: lap hoist tower
K: offices
L: reservoir

Figure 202. The layout and appearance of Kent Mill, Chadderton, designed by George Stott in 1908, is typical of Edwardian steam-powered spinning mills.

boiler house (E) and a detached chimney (G), offices (K) and reservoir (L). The offices, the main stair tower and the power features have more embellishment and are prominently grouped together behind the entrance (Fig 202). Visitors to the site could also see the company name from the entrance, displayed in large white brick lettering on the stair tower and the chimney. The spinning rooms in the upper storeys occupy the full length of the mill and are approximately 84.6 metres long by 43.9 metres wide.

Internal construction reflects the greater size of early 20th-century mills and utilises a combination of advanced and traditional materials. Cast-iron columns support longitudinal and transverse steel beams and ceilings of multiple brick vaults (Fig 149). The steel and cast-iron framework supports most of the weight of the building enabling the windows to occupy a high proportion of the wall area, essential in spinning mills of this width, although in this case the windows are smaller than those of concrete-floored mills. The ceiling vaults adjacent to the side walls are oriented transversely, with one vault to each window, but those in the middle of the floors are longitudinal. Above the vaults is a layer of coke breeze and wooden floorboards; concrete was used to reinforce the flooring beneath the position of the heavy mule headstocks. The flat roof is another characteristic feature of the period and, as in many cases, was probably used as a reservoir to supply the sprinkler tank at the top of the main stair tower.

The large external engine house contained a horizontal cross-compound engine of 1,500 horsepower.[45] Steam was supplied by Lancashire boilers in the attached boiler house (Fig 203). The reservoir along the north side of the mill originally included a long iron trough to assist the cooling of water from the engine. The rope race (C) was built into the end wall of the mill in line with the position of the central longitudinal line shafts required by the mules in the upper storeys (Fig 157). The end of the rope race bay was segregated to form the main dust flue (F), linked to a dust chamber in the basement which was fed by ducting under the floor of the blowing room.

The presence of three external stair towers, each of which also contained a goods hoist, reflects the greater importance of efficient internal organisation in cotton mill design in this period. One tower (J) was built specifically to carry the cotton laps from the blowing room to the ground-floor preparation area. See also Fig 143.

Figure 203. Surviving features of the power system at Kent Mill, Chadderton, comprise the chimney, external engine house, attached boiler house and the rope race in the end bay of the mill itself. The reservoir is located behind the engine house.

## (507)   Nile Mill, Chadderton, Oldham

Nile Mill, built *c.*1898, was designed by the Oldham architect P. S. Stott and was claimed to be the largest ring-spinning mill in the world.[46] It was laid out as a double mill, powered from a central engine house but with a continuous flat roof (Fig 204). It was also probably the last mill to be powered by a beam engine and the last to be designed for an upright shaft transmission system. Ring frames were smaller and heavier than mules and required more power so ring-spinning mills tended to be narrower and

Figure 204. Nile Mill, Chadderton was built *c.*1898 as a double mill powered by an unusual triple-expansion beam engine of 2,400 horsepower. It was claimed to be the largest ring-spinning mill in the world.

Figure 205. Front and rear elevations of Nile Mill, Chadderton. Another storey was added in 1905 (*The Textile Manufacturer*, 1898, 455).

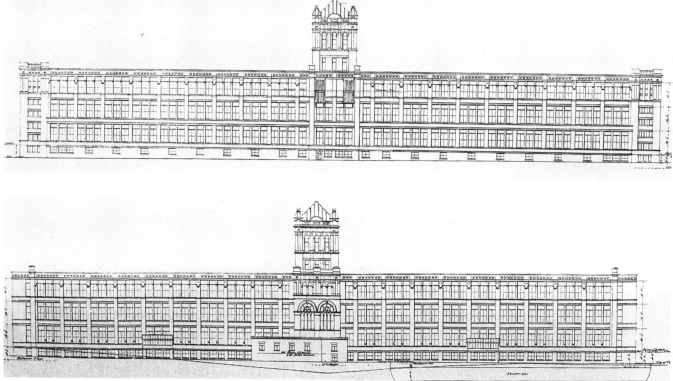

of fewer storeys. The general layout of machinery was similar, however, with preparation usually in the ground floor and spinning in the upper floors.

Nile Mill was originally of three storeys and a basement with a full-length cardroom extension along one side (Fig 205). It comprises two blocks attached end to end resulting in an unusually long and narrow plan. An extra storey was added in 1905 and by 1910 the mill contained 94,000 ring spindles for spinning and 14,000 doubling spindles.[47] The ground floor was used for preparation with multiple line shafts, while in the upper floors separate line shafts drove two rows of transversely located ring frames used for spinning and doubling. The central engine house extended beyond the back wall and contained an unusual triple-expansion beam engine of 2,400 horsepower which was geared to separate upright and horizontal main shafts in each half of the mill (Fig 129).[48] Above the roof of the engine house a tower contained the water tank for the sprinkler system and beyond the engine house end wall, close to the centre of the mill, were the flues for the ventilation system. The opening and scutching of raw cotton were carried out in segregated rooms in front of the dust flues and extended into a tower projecting from the front wall.

## (524)   Prince of Wales Mill, Oldham

Oldham experienced a series of mill-building booms in the second half of the 19th century characterised by the construction of large fireproof mills for spinning coarse to medium counts of cotton yarn. Prince of Wales Mill was built in 1875 during one of these booms. It was designed by Edward Potts for around 70,000 mule spindles[49] and represents a transitional stage in the development of the cotton-spinning mill (Fig 92). Potts used a new form of fireproof construction but the use of an upright shaft transmission system was more typical of the mid 19th century.

When built this was one of Oldham's largest mills, comprising five storeys, including a basement, and twenty-six bays (Fig 206). The internal dimensions of the main block (A and B in Fig 207) are approximately 87.4 metres long by 39.8 metres wide. The method of construction is very similar to that in the spinning block at Gilnow Mill, Bolton (71*), and the 1884 block at Wear Mill, Stockport (934*). Heavy transverse cast-iron beams support lighter longitudinal beams from which are sprung narrow longitudinal brick vaults. In comparison with earlier fireproof mills with transverse brick vaults the ceilings are higher, the windows larger and the building is wider in proportion to its length. The square stair tower is located internally and encloses a dust flue; the hoist is attached to the side of the stair case.

Although Prince of Wales Mill was built with an external engine house (C, the original engine was replaced *c*.1909), it also contains the full-height cross-wall found in mills with internal engines. The cross-wall supported the shaft transmission system and subdivided the internal floorspace to create a segregated area for processes with a high fire risk (B). Internal cross-walls were first used in the early 19th century to segregate internal engine houses, but the layout of Prince of Wales Mill suggests that by the late 19th century they had been developed to serve a number of other important functions, and so were retained after the introduction of the external engine house. See also Fig 133.

Figure 206. The engine house and boiler house of Prince of Wales Mill, Oldham. When completed in 1875 this was one of the largest mills in Oldham.

Figure 207. Prince of Wales Mill, Oldham, ground-floor plan.
A: main spinning room
B: segregated area
C: engine house
D: boiler house
E: shed extension
F: offices
G: warehouse

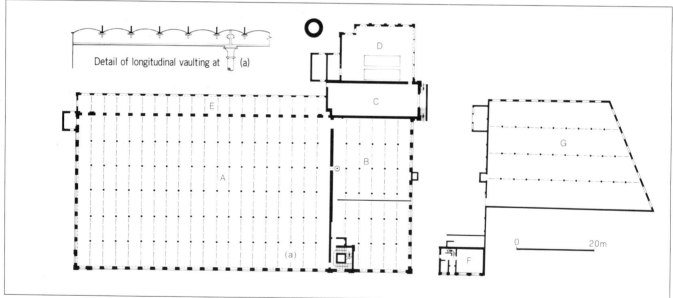

Detail of longitudinal vaulting at (a)

## (627)   Crimble Mill, near Heywood, Rochdale

Crimble Mill, built *c.*1829 for cotton spinning by Charles Stott, is probably the last water-powered cotton mill to survive in Greater Manchester and contrasts with earlier vernacular water-powered mills in its scale, proportions and materials. It is of comparable size to contemporary steam-powered mills in urban areas but is of non-fireproof construction. In the late 19th century it was purchased by the Kenyon family and,

Figure 208. Crimble Mill, near Heywood, was originally water-powered but was later converted to steam power with the addition of a beam-engine house to the right end.

unusually, converted into an integrated woollen mill.[50] The original five-storeyed block of sixteen bays was built at the end of a large reservoir taking water from the River Roch (Fig 208). It was powered by two undershot waterwheels located in the centre of the basement.[51] Water entered the wheel chamber through wide arches in the east side wall and the tailrace was culverted beneath the yard fronting the west side of the mill.

In the mid 19th century a tall external beam-engine house was added to the south end of the mill, driving line shafting by means of an upright shaft. At about the same time a four-storeyed warehouse with fireproof brick-vaulted ceilings was also added to the south end. Smaller ancillary blocks were added to the north end and detached offices built on the river bank in front of the mill.

During the Cotton Famine of the 1860s second-hand machinery for woollen production was installed. Fulling stocks were located in the basement, carding engines and mules in the second and third storeys with weaving above.[52] In the early 20th century the site was further extended and converted into its present use as a dye and finishing works. See p. 45

## (695)   Martin's Mill, Norden, Rochdale

Martin's Mill was built in the mid 19th century as a cotton-weaving shed. It was occupied by the Bagslate Manufacturing Company and by 1910 contained 534 looms.[53] It had a typical weaving-mill layout, with a north-light shed and two-storeyed buildings attached to the sides (Fig 72). The latter contained offices, warehousing and ancillary processes.[54] A tall

Figure 209 (far left). The beam-engine house and boiler house of Martin's Mill, Rochdale, during demolition.

Figures 210 (above) and 211 (left). The interior of the engine house of Martin's Mill was well preserved, with the engine beds, entablature and cast-iron staircase leading to the entablature floor all *in situ*. The cast-iron working beam itself was still mounted above the entablature.

narrow engine house containing a beam engine was attached to the south-east corner, with an adjoining boiler house containing a single Lancashire boiler (Fig 209). The engine, made by J. Petrie and Company of Rochdale, was dismantled around 1960 but the cast-iron working beam, the entablature floor with its fluted supporting columns and the engine beds were all left *in situ* (Figs 210 and 211). In 1884 the original engine was compounded by the addition of a horizontal high-pressure cylinder and the boiler house extended. The line shafting in the shed was gear-driven from a main horizontal shaft attached to the east end wall. A pinion wheel on the end of the main shaft was driven by a toothed rim attached to the engine's flywheel.[55] Demolished.

## (752)   Spotland Bridge New Mill, Rochdale

Spotland Bridge New Mill[56] provides a good illustration of mill development between the early 1830s, the date of the earlier building on the site, and the early 20th century, when a new mill was added (Figs 68, 212). The original mill, of five storeys and an attic and of thirteen bays, has typical proportions for a spinning mill of the early 1830s (Fig 213). It is of non-fireproof construction with joisted timber floors, supported by two rows of columns (Fig 78), and timber queen-strut roof trusses (Fig 81). A square fireproof external stair tower is attached to the north end and a

Figure 212 (above). Spotland Bridge New Mill, Rochdale. Ground-floor plan and cross-section. The original non-fireproof mill, on the left, was built in the 1830s. The concrete-floored mill on the right was added in the early 20th century.

A:   engine house
B:   boiler house
C:   privy tower
D:   store room
E:   stair tower
F:   offices

Figure 213 (top right). The original mill with a privy tower in the centre and the stair tower at the left end.

Figure 214. The mill was powered by a double-beam engine, in an external engine house. The lower boiler house and the chimney lie to the left. The original buildings on the site have corner pilasters and plain parapets, typical embellishment for the mid 19th century.

Figure 215. A two-storeyed office block was added to the base of the stair tower of Spotland Bridge New Mill in the late 19th century. The early 20th-century mill on the left, in red Accrington brick, was probably electrically powered.

privy tower to the west side. A large external engine house for a double-beam engine and a contemporary boiler house are attached to the south end. The detached octagonal brick chimney may also be original (Fig 214). A small office block had been added to the north end by the 1870s.[57]

The second mill, of four storeys and nine bays, was probably built for electric power using the mains supply. Materials and construction are typical of the early 20th century. The walls are of red Accrington brick with large segmental-headed windows (Fig 215). The floors are of concrete supported by steel beams and cast-iron columns and the roof is flat. The square plan is unusual, however, the number of bays being limited by the size of the site. See also Fig 80.

## (829)   Islington Mill, Salford

Islington Mill was built in 1823 as a seven-storeyed room and power mill of twelve bays (Fig 216). Most of the tenants were involved in cotton spinning. It was constructed by the building firm of David Bellhouse, responsible for a number of Manchester's early to mid 19th-century mills. The absence of any special plan features in room and power mills suggests that builders were trying to provide the most flexible type of factory space in the early 19th century. The power system consisted of a single-cylinder beam engine in an internal engine house near the north end driving an upright shaft attached to a full-height cross-wall. An external chimney and stair tower, no longer extant, was attached to the west side wall adjacent to the engine house.

Figure 216. Islington Mill, Salford, a steam-powered fireproof room and power mill of 1823. In 1824 a faulty cast-iron floor beam gave way causing the partial collapse of the mill and the loss of twenty-one lives.

Figure 217. The attic of Islington Mill, showing the queen-post roof trusses.

Figure 218. A contemporary engraving depicting the partial collapse of Islington Mill in 1824. After the accident the mill was rebuilt and strengthened by the addition of two extra rows of columns (*The Portfolio*, 23 October 1824).

Figure 219 (below). In the late 19th century these detached offices with adjoining stables were added to the entrance of Islington Mill, Salford.

# DREADFUL ACCIDENT AT MANCHESTER.

The mill was of fireproof construction with beams and columns of similar form to those in other contemporary mills and a queen-post roof (Fig 217). Unusually, however, the floor beams were only supported by a single row of columns. One year after the completion of Islington Mill a cast-iron floor beam suddenly gave way under the weight of heavy machinery in the north end of the top storey, resulting in the successive collapse of the lower storeys and the loss of twenty-one lives (Fig 218).[58] The inquiry following the disaster blamed inefficient casting techniques. The damage was repaired by the late 1820s simply by the insertion of two extra rows of columns beneath the beams to either side of the original row.

The site was later extended with the construction of a smaller mid 19th-century steam-powered mill to the west and a late 19th-century office and stable block to the south (Fig 219). In 1908 a large detached engine house and a boiler house were added to the rear.[59] By this date the mill was used for specialised cotton yarn doubling.

## (899)   Houldsworth's Mill, Reddish, Stockport

Houldsworth's Mill, built in 1865, was one of the largest double mills to be built in the 1860s, its construction reflecting the success of the Houldsworth's cotton-spinning firm. The firm was first established in Manchester by Thomas Houldsworth in the 1790s and by 1809 was the sixth-largest cotton firm in the town with around 25,000 mule spindles.[60] Early success led to the building of a large mill in Glasgow and the expansion of the Manchester site. In the 1860s and 1870s the scale of the business was such that two new mill complexes were built during the Cotton Famine on 'greenfield' sites at Reddish by Henry Houldsworth, the nephew of the founder.[61] A large complex of housing and other buildings for the firm's employees was built near to the mills, creating a relatively clean and pleasant working environment.

Houldsworth's 1865 mill was designed by A. H. Stott of Oldham,[62] its symmetrical Italianate façade rising dramatically above the rows of workers' housing to the east (Fig 97). The mill consists of two five-storeyed blocks of eighteen bays used for spinning, separated by a narrower central block of nine bays containing warehousing, offices and the main entrance. The central block

Figure 220. The central warehouse and office block of Houldsworth's Mill, Reddish. The mill is distinguished by an unusual level of architectural treatment, reflecting the status of the firm in the 1860s.

is flanked by two Italianate stair towers and features a large clock and cupola on the parapet (Fig 220). Cotton was prepared for spinning in the ground floors of the mills and the upper four floors contained mules with a total of 138,000 spindles. Both blocks are notably wider than earlier spinning mills, reflecting the greater length of mules in use by the 1860s. All the principal buildings are of fireproof construction, with transverse brick-vaulted ceilings supported by cast-iron beams and columns.

Behind the central block is the original detached engine house from which horizontal shafts drove the main upright shafts located in towers attached to the ends of the spinning blocks. The engine house and the unusually tall chimney are located exactly on the centre-line of the site. In the early 20th century the two spinning blocks were re-equipped with separate inverted-compound engines in new engine houses, and rope drives in external rope races replaced the original upright shafts (Fig 80).[63] See also Figs 105, 126b.

## (934)    Wear Mill, Stockport

Wear Mill has the widest chronological range of structures of any mill site in Greater Manchester. It includes relatively early surviving examples of the full range of buildings found at an integrated cotton works. The complex is beside the River Mersey beneath the arches of the Stockport railway viaduct (Fig 221). It stood at one end of an extensive group of textile mills built along the Mersey further to the east. The original water-powered mill was built *c*.1790 by John Collier, a cotton manufacturer, but in 1824 it was taken over by Thomas Fernley, remaining in family hands throughout the 19th century.[64]

Figure 221. The Wear Mill complex, Stockport, on the banks of the River Mersey. Partly beneath the railway viaduct is the *c*.1831 fireproof mill, with the *c*.1840 extension attached to its right end. Further right is the 1884 mill.

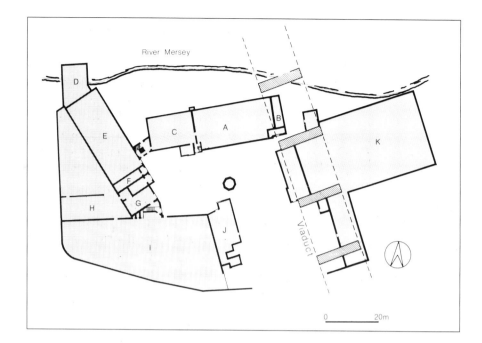

Figure 222. Wear Mill, Stockport, block plan.
A.  *c.*1831 fireproof mill
B:  engine house
C:  full-height extension
D:  three-bay block incorporating part of original wheelhouse
E:  1884 mill
F:  engine house
G:  engine house
H, I:  one and two-storeyed ancillary buildings
J:  early 20th-century offices
K:  mid 19th-century weaving shed

Of the first mill of *c.*1790 only part of the wheelhouse survives (D in Fig 222; Fig 223). By the early 19th century Wear Mill comprised two multi-storeyed spinning mills with attached sheds and was probably used as an integrated cotton works. One of these mills was the original water-powered structure, but this was largely rebuilt in 1884 (E).[65] The other was destroyed by fire in 1831 and replaced with a fireproof mill.[66] This is of six storeys and eleven bays and is of typical fireproof construction, with transverse brick-vaulted ceilings supported by cast-iron beams and columns (A). It is the same length as the earlier mill but slightly wider. A beam engine was located in an internal engine house at the east end (B) and the main upright shaft in the north-east corner. A full-height six-bay fireproof extension (C) with external stair and privy towers was added *c.*1840 to the west end. The extension has Hodgkinson-type cast-iron floor beams with parabolic bottom flanges (Fig 77) and was powered from the existing engine house. The roof has timber principal rafters mounted on cast-iron wall brackets with collars supported by a row of cast-iron columns, creating a spacious attic which was probably used for storage.

The early 19th-century sheds are not extant. A detached north-light weaving shed (K) was added in the mid 19th century, however, and survives partly beneath the arches of the viaduct. The timber roof trusses and tie-beams are supported by cast-iron columns and the north lights by cast-iron mullions (Fig 82). The shed was shaft-driven from an external engine house built against one of the piers of the viaduct. Line shafts were clamped to each row of columns and geared to a horizontal main shaft attached to the north end wall. The 1884 spinning mill (E) is of fireproof floor construction with narrow longitudinal vaults springing from iron joists (Fig 114), similar to that used at Prince of Wales Mill, Oldham (524*). See also Fig 100.

Figure 223. The three-bay block attached to the 1884 mill at Wear Mill, Stockport, incorporates part of the late 18th-century wheelhouse in its basement.

## (963)   Carrs Mill, Ashton under Lyne, Tameside

In the late 19th century cotton weaving was increasingly concentrated in north-east Lancashire although some weaving sheds continued to be built in the Greater Manchester area. Carrs Mill, later re-named Stamford Commercial Mill, was built in 1884 in an area which had many weaving and integrated firms earlier in the 19th century. By the 1880s, however, this was an unusual location for a large weaving mill. One of the benefits of the area cited by the original owners, the Carrs Manufacturing Company, was the better communications with Manchester in comparison with the north Lancashire weaving firms.[67]

The mill was originally entirely of one storey with a north-light roof supported by cast-iron columns and cast-iron trusses (Figs 102, 106). The main weaving area was an unobstructed shed occupying the northern two-thirds of the site. By 1896 1,400 looms were in use.[68] The southern one-third was segregated by a pair of closely spaced cross-walls stretching across the mill, between which was the main horizontal transmission shaft (Fig 136). The southern end of the mill was subdivided by further internal walls and was used for a combination of ancillary processes, warehousing and offices. The attached engine house was the tallest building on the site and contained a horizontal cross-compound engine.[69] A floor has been inserted but the original panelled ceiling still survives (Fig 224). The flywheel drove a horizontal main shaft which was bevel-geared to line shafts attached to each row of columns, a typical arrangement in a weaving mill.

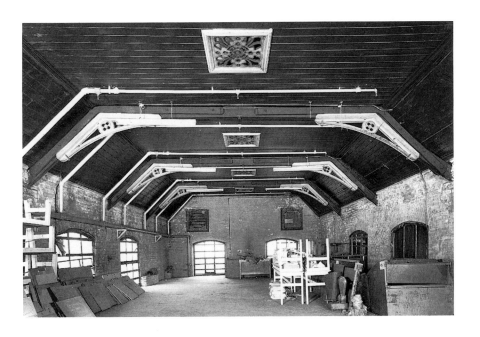

Figure 224. The intact engine house ceiling at Carrs Mill, Ashton under Lyne. The floor was inserted after the removal of the engine.

## (970)   Copley Mill, near Stalybridge, Tameside

Copley Mill is a large stone-built cotton-spinning mill of *c*.1827 with associated workers' housing standing in an elevated position outside Stalybridge (Fig 225). The original mill was built by James Wilkinson, a handloom weaver who began spinning after acquiring a textile machinery business in Stalybridge.[70]

The mill was built in five phases between *c*.1827 and 1871 and is of fireproof construction throughout, with transverse brick-vaulted ceilings supported by cast-iron columns and beams. The mill of *c*.1827 (A, Fig

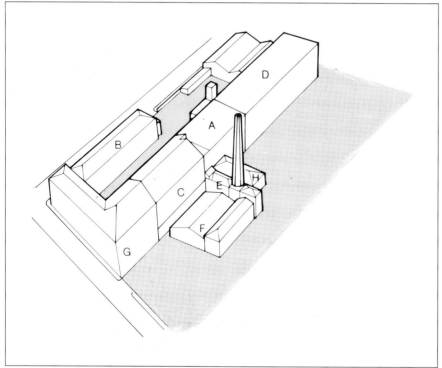

Figure 225. Copley Mill, near Stalybridge, south elevation. The original c.1827 mill is behind the chimney. Later extensions to both ends of the mill were matched by modifications to the power system.

Figure 226. The development of Copley Mill.
A:   original mill
B:   original warehouse
C:   first extension to mill
D:   second extension to mill
E:   extension to original internal engine house
F:   boiler house
G:   final extension to mill and warehouse
H:   1871 engine house

226) originally comprised a five-storeyed building of nine bays. It had an internal beam-engine house and stair tower, an external boiler house and a separate warehouse block (B). A full-height extension above the boiler house (C), added before 1845, converted the original mill into a double-mill layout, with a central engine and shaft transmission system. Another

larger addition (D), of similar date, was matched by modifications to the power system with an extension to the engine house (E) and a new boiler house (F). The rows of columns in the earlier phases were moved to match the wider column spacing in the latest addition, possibly to assist the internal location of new machinery. Another L-shaped extension was added by 1845 and used mainly for warehousing (G). In 1871 a new horizontal cross-compound engine was added in an external engine house (H), and used in conjunction with the earlier beam engine. By the 1880s the mill contained 51,000 spindles.[71]

## (979)   Good Hope Mill, Ashton under Lyne

Good Hope Mill, first built in the 1820s for cotton spinning, is representative of the smaller scale of early cotton-mill building in the Ashton area (Fig 227).[72] It was later more than doubled in size and had a series of owner-occupiers by the middle of the 19th century when it was an integrated mill used for both spinning and weaving.[73] In the late 19th century it was again used as a specialised spinning mill containing 27,000 spindles.[74] It was converted to its present use as a tannery in the 1890s.[75]

The original part of the mill (A in Fig 228) has non-fireproof joisted timber floors and a simpler layout than that used in larger contemporary Manchester mills (Fig 229). The west end bay of the five-storeyed main block contained the beam-engine house (D) and the fireproof staircase. The mill did not have a full-height cross-wall, so the upper-storey rooms

Figure 227. The front block of Good Hope Mill, Ashton under Lyne, was added in the late 19th century to provide a boiler room, blowing room, warehousing and offices. The site as a whole reflects the smaller scale of mill building in Ashton under Lyne up to the mid 19th century.

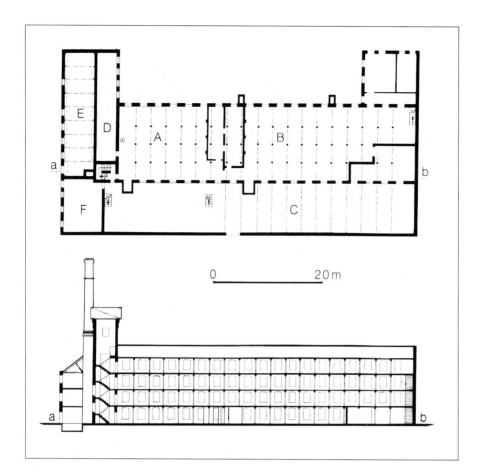

Figure 228. Good Hope Mill, Ashton under Lyne, ground-floor plan and long section.
A: original 1820s mill
B: mid 19th-century extension
C: later shed extension
D: engine house
E: fireproof end block
F: offices

extended above the engine house. Processes involving a high fire risk were probably located in small attached buildings. The chimney was attached to the outside of the west end wall (Fig 89). Power was transmitted to the upper floors by an upright shaft located to the east of the engine house. In the mid 19th century the east end wall was completely removed and a full-height extension added (B). The extension was of heavy timber-floored construction.

In the late 19th century the engine house was lengthened to contain a horizontal compound engine, a block of three-storeyed buildings was added in phases to the west end (E) and the chimney rebuilt. Part of the west end block was of fireproof construction, with ceilings of transverse brick vaults and roof trusses of cast and wrought iron (Fig 230). It contained a boiler room and a blowing room. The offices (F) and main entrance are also located in the west end block, the entrance giving access to the original fireproof staircase.

## (1060)   Barnfield Mills, Tyldesley, Wigan

This large concrete-floored mule-spinning mill was built in 1894 on the site of an earlier mill destroyed by fire in 1891.[76] It was the last and is the

Figure 229. Non-fireproof construction in the original part of Good Hope Mill, Ashton under Lyne.

Figure 230. The cast and wrought-iron roof of the north end of the fireproof block of Good Hope Mill, Ashton under Lyne (E in Figure 228).

only surviving member of a large complex of cotton mills built by Caleb Wright and Co,[77] and was distinguished by architectural details typical of the Bolton architects Bradshaw and Gass (Figs 93, 231). It is of six storeys and ten bays, with overall internal dimensions of approximately 65.2 metres by 40.2 metres. It was built to contain transversely located mules for fine spinning in the upper floors with preparation mainly in the ground floor. Internal construction in the main block consists of concrete floors supported by steel beams and cast-iron columns. In contrast with earlier concrete-floored mills, such as Atlas No. 6 Mill, Bolton (17*), the floor

Figure 231. Barnfield Mills, Tyldesley, was a state-of-the-art cotton-spinning mill when built in 1894, employing an internal layout, floor construction and architectural embellishment more characteristic of early 20th-century mills. The embellishment suggests that the architects were Bradshaw, Gass and Hope.

beams are encased and the columns are more widely spaced (Fig 119). A north-light shed extension added to the north side provided further ground-floor space for carding. Other multi-storeyed extensions were used for warehousing and ancillary processes. The slate roof comprises multiple transverse ridges. The external engine house was retained from the earlier mill, but later a second much larger external engine house was added to the opposite end. The mill thus appears to have two power systems and two rope races, although it is unlikely that they were both used at the same time.

Other details of Barnfield Mills suggest that its design foreshadows that adopted in many early 20th-century mills. The main block is wider in proportion to its length than in earlier mills and the spinning rooms occupied the full length and width of the mill, there being no internal cross-wall. The horizontal-rectangular flat-headed windows occupy most of the wall surface area, the main staircase is contained in a projecting tower topped with an ornamental dome (Fig 104) and the mill was built with an external dust flue (Fig 125), all typical features found in large early 20th-century mills. See also Fig 99.

# Gazetteer

The Gazetteer is a name index of the surviving mills which were recorded in 1985–6. Sites of mills were identified using large-scale OS maps ranging in date from c.1845 to c.1930 and surviving mills located on the latest 1:25,000 maps. A small number of mills were missed owing to gaps in the coverage of the available large-scale maps. Sites which have had more than one name have separate entries under each name. Also included are mills which were demolished prior to 1985 but which are mentioned in the text. Thus the total number of entries in the gazetteer exceeds the total number of recorded mills. The Districts of Greater Manchester are arranged in alphabetical order with the mills listed alphabetically within each District. Each entry is identified by a separate number and contains the following information: the mill name, the National Buildings Record file number, a date category, the grid reference, the economic branch of the site and an indication of the type of record that was made of the mill. Numbers which include an asterisk indicate that the mill is described in more detail in the Inventory.

## Name

The names of mills have been obtained chiefly from large-scale maps; all the known names of each mill have been included. Mills which are not named on maps have been named for the gazetteer after the street which gives access to the mill. Up to seven different names may refer to the same site. The name may refer to a mill on the same site which pre-dated the extant buildings.

## National Buildings Record file number

The archive created during the mill survey is structured as part of the NBR, which is itself part of the National Monuments Record based at Fortress House, 23 Savile Row, London W1X 2JQ. Requests for information, historical documents or photographs of any mill should quote the appropriate NBR number and the District in which the mill is located. NBR numbers were not allocated to mills which were not extant at the time of the survey.

## Date

Dates are categorised into E (early), M (mid) and L (late) with the appropriate century given as 18, 19 or 20 (e.g. E19). Each category is thus one-third of a century (e.g. E19 = 1800 to 1833; M19 = 1834 to 1866). The date refers to the observed buildings at a site; many mill sites were occupied by earlier buildings before the extant mill was built. Where the buildings cover more than one date category a range of dates is indicated (e.g. L18–M19).

## Grid reference

This gives the approximate location of a site. In congested parts of the county large-scale maps are needed to find the exact position of a mill.

## Economic branch

OS maps of 25 inches to 1 mile or greater give the economic branch of mills in parentheses after the name. The branch refers to the nature of the business in the mill at the time the map was surveyed. It is not unusual for a mill to be identified as belonging to different branches of the textile trade on maps of different dates. The gazetteer gives the branch which is closest to the date of the extant buildings.

## Archive

At the end of each entry is a coded indication of the level of information about the mill held in the project archive. The archive contains four levels of information:

A. Site selected for detailed recording. File contains a full written report, a surveyed plan and elevation, a chronology of documentary information, photocopies of plans and documents, 35mm photographs, large-format photographs, aerial photographs.

B. Site selected for detailed recording but without full written report. File contains a chronology of documentary information with various combinations of plans and photographs.

C. Site recorded in the initial survey and added to the county Sites and Monuments Record database at GMAU. Archive contains a printout of the database giving a description of the site, cross-referenced to cartographic sources, 35mm photographs and aerial photographs.

D. Mill demolished prior to the initial survey but mentioned in the text.

Table 2

Analysis of Gazetteer entries by economic branch

| | Gazetteer entries | Extant sites* | Cotton | | Cotton waste | | Woollen | | Silk | | Bleach, dye, print or finished works | |
|---|---|---|---|---|---|---|---|---|---|---|---|---|
| Bolton | 154 | 143 | 122 | (79%) | 3 | (2%) | 1 | (0.7%) | 0 | | 27 | (17%) |
| Bury | 140 | 130 | 81 | (58%) | 3 | (2.1%) | 7 | (5%) | 0 | | 39 | (28%) |
| Manchester | 95 | 73 | 59 | (62%) | 5 | (5.3%) | 0 | | 4 | (4.2%) | 17 | (18%) |
| Oldham | 187 | 170 | 143 | (76%) | 5 | (2.7%) | 27 | (14%) | 0 | | 8 | (4.3%) |
| Rochdale | 229 | 203 | 139 | (61%) | 2 | (0.9%) | 37 | (16%) | 1 | (0.4%) | 40 | (17%) |
| Salford | 54 | 44 | 39 | (72%) | 0 | | 0 | | 2 | (3.7%) | 11 | (20%) |
| Stockport | 79 | 77 | 53 | (67%) | 3 | (3.8%) | 1 | (1.3%) | 0 | | 12 | (15%) |
| Tameside | 117 | 116 | 96 | (82%) | 3 | (2.6%) | 4 | (3.4%) | 0 | | 10 | (8.5%) |
| Wigan | 56 | 49 | 47 | (84%) | 0 | | 0 | | 1 | (1.8%) | 3 | (5.4%) |
| TOTAL | 1,111 | 1,005 | 779 | (70%) | 24 | (2.2%) | 77 | (6.9%) | 8 | (0.7%) | 167 | (15%) |

* Extant sites which had more than one name have separate Gazetteer entries under each name. The Gazetteer also includes entries for non-extant mills which are mentioned in the text.

Economic branch is calculated from the total number of Gazetteer entries. 57 entries (5 per cent) were of 'other' or unknown eonomic branch.

# Bolton

1. Albert Mill?, 53729, L19, SD 639 119, Cotton, C.
2. Albert Mills, 53765, L19, SD 715 099, Cotton, C.
3. Albert Mills, 53839, L19, SD 735 062, Cotton, C.
4. Albert Road Mill, 53835, M19–L19, SD 735 056, Finishing works, C.
5. Albion Mill, 53794, L19, SD 718 083, Cotton, C.
6. Albion Mill, 53833, L19?, SD 733 064, Cotton, C.
7. Allenby Mill, 53802, E20, SD 649 054, Cotton, C.
8. Alma Mills, 53857, M19?, SD 702 076, Cotton, C.
9. Asia Mill, 53819, L19, SD 723 075, Cotton, C.
10. Astley Bridge Mill, 53742, E20, SD 716 123, Cotton, C.
11. Astley Dye & Chemical Co, 53744, E20, SD 717 114, Dyeworks?, C.
12. Atlas No.1 Mill, 53761, M19–L19, SD 702 101, Cotton, C.
13*. Atlas No.2 Mill, 53771, L19, SD 702 099, Cotton, A.
14. Atlas No.3 Mill, 53762, L19, SD 701 101, Cotton, C.
15*. Atlas No.4 Mill, 53739, L19, SD 701 100, Cotton, A.
16. Atlas No.5 Mill, 53770, L19, SD 703 097, Cotton, C.
17*. Atlas No.6 Mill, 53737, L19, SD 700 101, Cotton, A.
18. Atlas No.7 Mill, 53738, L19, SD 699 100, Cotton, C.
19. Atlas No.8 Mill, 53736, M19–L19, SD 699 102, Cotton, C.
20. Bankfield Mill, 53789, E20, SD 704 083, Cotton, C.
21. Beehive Mills, 53740, L19, SD 654 096, Cotton, C.
22. Beehive Mills, 53827, L19–E20, SD 726 073, Cotton, C.
23. Bent Mill, 53821, M19, SD 744 054, Cotton, C.
24. Bolton Road Mill, 53803, L19, SD 659 064, Cotton, C.
25. Bolton Textile Mill No.2, 53831, L19, SD 732 064, Cotton, C.
26. Bolton Textile Mill No.3, 53837, E20?, SD 731 063, Cotton waste, C.
27. Bolton Union Mills, 53748, L19, SD 722 107, Cotton, C.
28. Bower Mill, 53838, L19, SD 734 064, Cotton, C.
29. Bradford Mill, 53817, L19, SD 721 077, Cotton, C.
30. Bradley Mill, 53834, L19?, SD 755 076, Cotton, C.
31 Bradshaw Works, 53741, M19–L19, SD 734 128, Bleach, dye and print works, B.
32. Breightmet Fold Works, 53776, L19, SD 752 099, Bleachworks, C.
33. Breightmet Mill, 53799, M19–L19, SD 753 093, Cotton, C.
34. Breightmet Works, 53776, L19, SD 752 098, Bleachworks, C.
35. Bridge Street Works, 53728, E19–L19, SD 642 115, Bleachworks, C.
36. Bridgewater Mill, 53861, L19, SD 741 056, Cotton, C.
37. Brownlow Fold Mills, 53759, L19–E20, SD 709 104, Cotton, C.
38. Burnden Works, 53798, L19, SD 728 081, Bleachworks, C.
39. Caledonia Mill, 53730, L19?, SD 635 117, Cotton, C.
40. Causeway Mill, 53845, L19, SD 740 055, Cotton, C.
41. Cawdor Mill, 53829, L19, SD 733 065, Cotton, C.
42. Century Ring Spinning Mill, 53842, E20, SD 729 055, Cotton, C.
43. Chew Moor Mill, 53863, E19?, SD 669 077, Cotton, C.
44. Clyde Mill, 53757, L19, SD 712 106, Cotton, C.
45. Cobden Mill, 53752, M19–L19, SD 715 107, Cotton, C.
46. Cobden Mill, 53836, L19, SD 732 063, Cotton, C.
47. Columbia Mills, 53768, L19, SD 705 097, Cotton, C.
48. Croal Mill, 53784, E20, SD 701 085, Cotton, C.
49. Daubhill Mill, 53857, M19?, SD 702 076, Cotton, C.
50. Deane Mill, 53784, E20, SD 701 085, Cotton, C.
51. Deane Mill, 53800, M20, SD 694 079, Weaving, C.
52. Deane Road Mill, 53787, L19, SD 710 086, Cotton, C.
53. Denmark Mill, 53832, L19, SD 733 065, Cotton, C.
54. Derby Mill, 53820, L19, SD 709 079, Cotton, C.
55. Derby Mill, 53850, M19–L19, SD 708 082, Cotton, C.
56. Derby Street Mill, 53790, M19, SD 710 083, Cotton, C.
57. Dixon Green Mill, 53825, M19–E20, SD 731 060, Cotton, C.
58. Dove Mill, 53801, E20, SD 696 077, Cotton, C.
59. Drake Mill, 53824, E20?, SD 737 049, Cotton, C.
60. Dunscar Works, 53854, M19–L19, SD 713 134, Bleachworks, C.
61. Eagle Mill, 53788, L19, SD 711 085, Cotton, C.
62. Eagley Mills, 53856, L19–E20, SD 718 131, Cotton, C.
63. Egerton Mill, 53830, L19, SD 733 065, Cotton waste, B.
64. Egerton Works, 53855, L19, SD 707 145, Cotton and dye, C.
65. Egyptian Mills, 53772, L19, SD 716 100, Cotton, C.
66. Falcon Mill, 53756, E20, SD 707 111, Cotton, C.
67. Flash Street Mills, 53785, M19–L19, SD 714 088, Cotton, C.
68. Folds Mill, 53747, M19–L19, SD 724 100, Cotton, C.
69. German Mill, 53851, L19, SD 710 081, Cotton, C.
70. Gibraltar Mill, 53783, L19, SD 705 087, Cotton, C.
71*. Gilnow Mill, 53781, M19–L19, SD 704 089, Cotton, A.
72. Globe Mills, 53806, L19, SD 656 060, Cotton weaving, C.
73. Gower Street Mill, 53841, L19–E20, SD 733 063, Cotton, C.
74. Grecian Mills, 53814, L19, SD 717 078, Cotton, C.
75. Green Vale Works, 53866, L19, SD 660 046, Print works, C.
76. Halliwell Cotton Works, 53769, L19, SD 704 097, Cotton, C.
77. Halliwell Mills (part of), 53753, L19, SD 711 110, Cotton, C.
78. Halliwell Mills (part of), 53754, L19–E20, SD 709 109, Cotton, C.
79. Halliwell Works (part of), 53732, M19, SD 695 114, Bleachworks, C.
80. Halliwell Works (part of), 53848, M19–L19, SD 698 113, Bleachworks, C.
81. Harrowby Mill, 53840, L19, SD 734 058, Cotton, C.
82. Haslam Mill, 53792, L19, SD 711 080, Cotton, C.
83. Hill Mill, 53849, M19–E20, SD 707 113, Bleachworks, C.
84. Hillfold Mill, 53743, E20?, SD 713 119, Cotton, C.
85. Hope Mill, 53823, M19–L19, SD 740 052, Cotton, B.
86. Horrockses Mill, 53828, E20, SD 733 067, Cotton, C.
87. Horwich Works, 53728, E19–L19, SD 642 116, Bleachworks, C.
88. Industrial Mill, 53805, E20, SD 659 065, Cotton, C.
89*. Kearsley Mill, 53846, E20, SD 752 057, Cotton, C.
90. Lark Hill Mill, 53822, L19, SD 741 052, Cotton, C.
91. Lark Mill, 53845, L19, SD 740 055, Cotton, C.
92. Lee Mill, 53730, L19?, SD 635 117, Cotton, C.
93. Lever Bridge Mills, 53797, L19–E20, SD 734 083, Cotton, C.
94. Lever Street Mill, 53815, L19, SD 718 080, Cotton, C.
95. Lincoln Mill, 53782, M19–L19, SD 704 087, Quilt, C.
96. Little Bolton Works, 53745, M19–M20, SD 721 103, Bleachworks, C.
97. Marsh Fold Mill, 53770, L19, SD 703 097, Cotton, C.
98. Martin Mill, 53793, L19, SD 714 085, Cotton, C.
99. Mather Street Mill, 53793, L19, SD 714 085, Cotton, C.
100. Meeting Of The Waters Works, 53749, M19–L19, SD 721 112, Bleachworks, B.
101. Mill Hill Mills, 53780, L19, SD 725 095, Cotton, C.
102. Milton Mills, 53779, M19–L19, SD 724 094, Cotton, C.
103. Moor Mills, 53791, M19–L19, SD 712 082, Cotton, C.
104. Moorfield Mill, 53844, M19–L19, SD 738 054, Cotton, C.
105. Moorland Mills, 53750, L19, SD 715 104, Cotton, C.
106. Moss Rose Mill, 53847, M19?, SD 753 047, Cotton, C.
107. Mossfield Mill, 53764, L19, SD 713 098, Cotton, C.
108. Nelson Mills, 53758, L19, SD 709 100, Cotton, C.
109. New Stone Mill, 53766, M19–E20, SD 717 099, Cotton, C.
110. Oaken Bottom Mill, 53795, E19–L19, SD 735 090, Cotton, C.
111. Orient Mill, 53811, L19–E20, SD 703 077, Cotton, C.
112. Park Mill, 53775, L19, SD 708 098, Cotton, C.

113. Peakes Place Works, 53755, L19, SD 709 112, Cotton, C.
114. Peel No.1 Mill, 53767, M19–L19, SD 720 100, Cotton, C.
115. Peel No.2 Mill, 53746, E20?, SD 721 101, Cotton, C.
116. Perseverance Mill, 53804, L19, SD 659 064, Cotton, C.
117. Perseverence Mill, 53838, L19, SD 733 064, Cotton, C.
118. Persian Mills, 53774, L19, SD 708 097, Cotton, C.
119. Prospect Mill, 53751, L19, SD 715 106, Cotton, C.
120. Prospect Works?, 53868, M19–L19, SD 696 114, Bleachworks, C.
121. Raikes Works, 53826, M19–L19, SD 733 079, Bleachworks, C.
122. Red Bridge Mill, 53777, L19, SD 751 100, Cotton weaving, C.
123. Refuses Works, 53773, M19–L19, SD 736 097, Bleachworks, B.
124. Riverside Mill, 53852, L19, SD 735 080, Cotton, C.
125. Robin Hood Mills, 53815, L19, SD 718 080, Cotton, C.
126. Rose Mill, 53847, M19?, SD 753 048, Cotton, C.
127. Round Hill Mills, 53767, M19–L19, SD 720 100, Cotton, C.
128. Rumworth Mill, 53810, L19–E20, SD 703 076, Cotton, C.
129*. Saint Helena Mill, 53778, E19, SD 713 094, Cotton waste?, A.
130. Saint Paul's Mill, 53812, E20, SD 707 077, Worsted, C.
131. Saville Mill, 53786, L19, SD 722 090, Cotton, C.
132. Shipton Mill, 53736, M19–L19, SD 699 102, Cotton, C.
133. Spa Mill, 53865, E19, SD 712 093, Cotton, C.
134. Spring Field Works, 53853, L19, SD 708 132, Bleachworks, C.
135. Springside Mill, 53859, M19, SD 757 073, Cotton, C.
136. Star Works, 53733, L19, SD 627 112, Bleachworks, C.
137. Sunnyside Mill, 53809, L19, SD 704 074, Cotton, C.
138*. Swan Lane No.1 and No.2 Mills, 53813, E20, SD 708 076, Cotton, B.
139. Swan Lane No.3 Mill, 53813, E20, SD 708 077, Cotton, B.
140. Telford Mills, 53735, E20?, SD 645 107, Cotton, C.
141. Tonge Fold Works, 53796, L19, SD 734 092, Cotton, C.
142. Undershore Works, 53773, M19–L19, SD 736 097, Bleachworks, B.
143. Vale Works, 53733, L19, SD 627 112, Bleachworks, C.
144. Vernon Mills, 53763, L19–E20, SD 712 097, Cotton, C.
145. Victoria Mill, 53862, L19–E20, SD 653 069, Cotton, C.
146. Victoria Mill, 53734, E20, SD 646 104, Cotton, C.
147. Victoria Mill, 53843, L19, SD 735 053, Cotton, B.
148. Victoria Mills, 53818, E20, SD 722 079, Cotton, C.
149. Victoria Street Works, 53807, L19, SD 656 058, Cotton reeling, C.
150. Victoria Works?, 53732, M19, SD 695 114, Bleachworks, C.
151. Wallsuches Works, 53727, E19–L19, SD 654 117, Bleachworks, B.
152. Wallsuches Works, 53731, E19–L19, SD 653 118, Bleachworks, B.
153. Waterloo Mill, 53750, L19, SD 715 104, Cotton, C.
154. Waters Meeting Works, 53749, M19–L19, SD 721 112, Bleachworks, B.

# Bury

155. Ainsworth Mercerising Works, 53621, L19, SD 753 094, Finishing, C.
156. Ainsworth Mills, 53619, M19–L19, SD 756 092, Bleach and dyeworks, C.
157. Ainsworth Vale Works, 53620, L19, SD 753 093, Bleach and dyeworks, C.
158. Albert Mill, 53684, M19?, SD 817 060, Cotton, C.
159. Albert Mill, 53717, M20, SD 783 072, Cotton, C.
160. Albert New Mill, 53685, L19?, SD 811 059, Cotton, C.
161. Albert Works, 53673, L19, SD 783 076, Finishing works, B.
162. Albion Mill, 53688, L19, SD 824 039, Cotton, C.
163. Albion Mills, 53614, M19?, SD 796 108, Cotton, C.
164. Alexandra Mill, 53631, L19, SD 808 114, Cotton, C.
165. Bankside Works, 53683, L19, SD 792 061, Finishing works, C.
166. Barn Brook Mills, 53705, L19, SD 812 110, Cotton, C.

167. Beech Mill, 53713, L19–E20, SD 813 102, Cotton, C.
168. Beehive Works, 53662, M19–L19, SD 819 076, Cotton, C.
169. Bentley & Lumn Mills, 53625, L19?, SD 810 138, Print works, C.
170. Bevis Green Works, 53625, L19?, SD 810 138, Print works, C.
171. Black Lane Mills, 53622, L19, SD 777 088, Cotton, C.
172. Bleaklow Mill, 53692, L19–E20, SD 765 149, Cotton, C.
173. Bolholt Mills, 53602, M19–L19, SD 785 117, Print works, C.
174. Brickhouse Mills, 53709, M19, SD 813 110, Cotton, C.
175. Bridge Hall Works, 53642, L19, SD 824 106, Dyeworks, C.
176. Bridge Mills, 53615, E19–M19, SD 797 111, Cotton, C.
177. Bridge Street Mill, 53632, L19, SD 812 113, Braid, C.
178. Britannia Mill, 53605, L19, SD 789 120, Cotton, C.
179. Britannia Mill?, 53686, L19, SD 812 039, Smallware, C.
180. Britannia Mills, 53633, E20, SD 813 114, Cotton, C.
181. Britannia Mills, 53716, E20, SD 782 074, Finishing works, C.
182. Brookhouse Mill, 53597, L19?, SD 776 137, Cotton, C.
183. Brooksbottoms Mill, 53694, L19, SD 794 152, Cotton, C.
184. Burrs Mill, 53701, M19?, SD 799 126, Bleachworks, C.
185. California Mill, 53710, M19, SD 809 107, Cotton, C.
186. Canal Mill, 53670, E20, SD 779 074, Cotton, C.
187. Chesham Mills?, 53637, L19, SD 813 118, Woollen, C.
188. Cobden Mill, 53658, M19–L19, SD 792 166, Cotton, C.
189. Commercial Mill, 53630, M19?, SD 806 115, Cotton, C.
190. Cross Mill, 53666, L19, SD 794 078, Cotton, C.
191. Crow Oaks Works, 53664, L19–M20, SD 795 064, Bleach, dye and finishing works, C.
192*. Crown Mill, 53691, M19, SD 762 150, Cotton, A.
193. Crystal Mills, 53678, L19, SD 784 068, Cotton, C.
194. Derby Street Mill, 53704, M19, SD 809 109, ?, C.
195. Dingle Vale Works, 53680, L19, SD 778 069, Dyeworks, C.
196. Dumers Lane Mill, 53647, E20?, SD 803 083, Cotton weaving, C.
197. Egyptian Mills, 53611, L19, SD 794 102, Cotton weaving, C.
198. Elton Cop Works, 53609, L19, SD 791 114, Dyeworks, C.
199. Elton Fold Mills, 53610, L19, SD 792 113, Cotton, C.
200. Elton Vale Works, 53616, M19–L19, SD 787 110, Bleachworks, C.
201. Fern Grove Mills, 53641, M19, SD 822 115, Cotton, C.
202. Fernhill Mill, 53630, M19?, SD 806 115, Cotton, C.
203. Fernhill Mills, 53628, L19, SD 807 117, Woollen, B.
204. Fernhill Mills, 53629, L19, SD 807 116, Woollen, B.
205*. Field Mill, 53651, M19–L19, SD 794 171, Cotton waste, B
206. Fold Mill, 53618, L19, SD 757 084, Cotton, C.
207. Foundry Mills?, 53675, L19, SD 781 068, Cotton, C.
208. Fountain Street North Mill, 53706, L19, SD 813 110, Cotton waste, B.
209. Glen Mill, 53604, L19, SD 783 122, Cotton weaving, C.
210. Gollinrod Mill?, 53689, M19, SD 800 155, Woollen, C.
211. Heap Bridge Mills, 53643, L19, SD 824 106, Woollen, C.
212. Higher Mills, 53635, M19–L19, SD 812 113, Cotton, C.
213. Hollins Vale Works (part of), 53644, L19, SD 813 085, Bleachworks, C.
214. Hollins Vale Works (part of), 53645, L19?, SD 814 085, Dyeworks, C.
215. Hollins Vale Works (part of), 53646, L19, SD 815 085, Bleachworks, C.
216. Holly Bank Mills, 53668, L19, SD 778 073, Dyeworks, C.
217. Holme Mill, 53650, E20?, SD 792 163, Cotton, C.
218. Hope Mill, 53595, M19?, SD 801 187, Cotton, C.
219. Hope Mill, 53679, M19, SD 778 074, Cotton, B.
220. Hope Works, 53660, L19, SD 788 162, Bleach, dye and finishing works, C.
221. Hudcar Mills, 53638, L19, SD 812 117, Cotton, C.
222. Irwell Bridge Mills, 53615, E19–M19, SD 797 111, Cotton, C.

223. Irwell Bridge Mills, 53652, M19–L19, SD 794 168, Cotton, C.
224. Irwell Vale Works, 53718, L19, SD 789 070, Dyeing and finishing, B.
225. Irwell Works, 53649, L19–E20, SD 799 085, Bleach and dyeworks, C.
226. Kenyon Street Mill, 53690, M19–L19, SD 793 172, Cotton, C.
227. Kenyons Mill, 53691, M19, SD 762 150, Cotton, A.
228. Kersal Vale Mill?, 53720, L19–M20, SD 809 018, Bleach, dye and finishing works, C.
229. Kilnecroft Mill, 53662, M19–L19, SD 819 076, Cotton, C.
230. Kirklees Works, 53601, L19–L20, SD 784 128, Artificial silk, C.
231. Kirklees Works (part of), 53721, L19, SD 784 129, ?, C.
232. Leemans Mill, 53604, L19, SD 783 122, Cotton weaving, C.
233. London Vale Works, 53720, L19–M20, SD 809 018, Bleach, dye and finishing works, C.
234. Lower Croft Works, 53617, M19–L19, SD 776 110, Bleach and finishing works, C.
235. Lumn Mills, 53625, L19?, SD 810 138, Print works, C.
236. Meadow Mill, 53659, M19?, SD 793 167, Cotton, C.
237. Moorside Mill, 53698, L19, SD 767 104, Cotton, C.
238. Moorside Works, 53703, L19, SD 811 111, Cotton, C.
239. Moss Lane Works?, 53723, E20, SD 811 058, ?, C.
240. Mossfield Mills, 53640, E19–L19, SD 819 114, Woollen, B.
241. Mount Pleasant Mill, 53596, E19–L19, SD 810 151, Cotton, A.
242. Mount Sion Works, 53715, M19–L19, SD 767 067, Bleachworks, C.
243. New Road Mills?, 53664, L19–M20, SD 795 064, Bleach, dye and finishing works, C.
244. New Victoria Mills, 53613, L19, SD 796 105, Cotton, C.
245. Nursery Mills, 53719, M19–L19, SD 790 061, Smallware, C.
246. Old Ground Mill, 53655, M19?, SD 791 167, Cotton, C.
247. Olive Bank Mill, 53605, L19, SD 789 120, Cotton, C.
248. Parkside Mill, 53687, L19, SD 823 041, Cotton, C.
249. Parr's Fold Mill, 53661, M19, SD 816 068, Cotton and dye, C.
250. Peel Mills, 53627, L19–E20, SD 803 114, Cotton, C.
251. Phoenix Mills, 53678, L19, SD 784 068, Cotton, C.
252. Pilot Mill, 53714, E20, SD 813 101, Cotton, C.
253. Pimhole Mill, 53713, L19–E20, SD 813 102, Cotton, C.
254. Pioneer Mill, 53663, E20, SD 792 072, Cotton, C.
255. Polka Shed, 53704, M19, SD 809 109, Cotton, C.
256. Premier Mills, 53608, L19, SD 789 113, Woollen, C.
257. Railway Mill, 53657, M19, SD 792 168, Cotton, C.
258. Ramsbottom Mills?, 53653, M19?, SD 792 172, Cotton, C.
259. Reddisher Works, 53696, L19, SD 778 155, Bleach and dyeworks, C.
260. Roach Bank Mills, 53712, L19?, SD 814 105, Cotton, C.
261. Rose Mill?, 53656, M19?, SD 792 168, Cotton, C.
262. Smyrna Works, 53671, L19, SD 780 076, Dye and finishing works, C.
263. Spider Mill, 53669, L19, SD 778 072, Cotton, C.
264. Spring Mill, 53600, L19?, SD 775 129, Cotton, C.
265. Springfield Mill, 53636, M19, SD 813 117, Cotton, C.
266. Springfield Mills, 53667, L19–E20, SD 785 066, Finishing works, C.
267. Stormer Hill, 53598, M19–L19, SD 777 136, Bleach and finishing works, B.
268. Summerseat Works, 53695, L19, SD 790 147, Dye and print works, C.
269. Sun Mills, 53674, L19, SD 784 075, Cotton, C.
270. Sunny Bank Mill, 53681, L19, SD 774 067, Cotton, C.
271. Tagg Wood Works?, 53693, L19, SD 785 160, ?, C.
272. Tower Works, 53677, L19, SD 795 076, Bleach and dyeworks, C.

273. Union Mill, 53670, E20, SD 779 074, Cotton, C.
274. Victoria Mill, 53603, L19–E20, SD 776 117, Cotton, C.
275. Victoria Mill, 53654, M19?, SD 792 175, Cotton, C.
276. Victoria Mill, 53661, M19, SD 816 068, Cotton and dye, C.
277. Victoria Mill, 53682, L19, SD 783 074, ?, C.
278. Victoria Works?, 53676, L19, SD 784 067, Finishing works, C.
279. Virginia Mill, 53707, L19, SD 811 108, ?, C.
280. Warth Mills, 53623, L19, SD 797 092, Cotton, C.
281. Water Lane Mill, 53672, L19, SD 783 075, Cotton, C.
282. Waterside Mill, 53699, M19–L19, SD 794 099, Cotton?, logwood, C.
283. Waterside Mill, 53700, M19–L19, SD 794 098, Cotton?, logwood, C.
284. Wellington Mills, 53612, M19, SD 794 104, Cotton, C.
285. Wilton Mill, 53665, E20, SD 791 073, Cotton, C.
286. Windley Works, 53682, L19, SD 783 074, ?, C.
287. Windsor Mill, 53722, L19, SD 771 074, Cotton, C.
288. Withins Mill, 53624, L19?, SD 791 081, Cotton, C.
289. Wood Road Mill, 53599, E19?, SD 795 141, Cotton, C.
290. Wood Street Mill, 53713, L19–E20, SD 813 102, Cotton, C.
291. Woodhill Mills, 53607, M19, SD 797 116, Cotton, C.
292. Woodhill Works, 53702, E19?, SD 798 112, Bleachworks, C.
293. Woolford Works, 53606, L19, SD 791 116, Dyeworks, C.
294. York Street Mill, 53648, L19, SD 800 084, Cotton weaving, C.
295. York Street Mill, 53708, L19, SD 812 108, Cotton waste, C.

## Manchester

296. Albany Works, 53326, E19?, SD 882 007, Silk, C.
297. Albert Mill, 53321, E20?, SJ 875 941, Carpet, C.
298. Albion Mill, E19, SJ 837 976, Cotton, D.
299. Alexandre Works, 53282, L19, SD 855 022, ?, C.
300. Anchor Works, 53285, M19–L19, SD 854 013, Bleachworks, C.
301. Aquatite Mills, 53294, M20, SJ 839 999, ?, C.
302. Ashenhurst Works, 53280, L19?, SD 847 030, Dyeworks, C.
303. Atlantic Works, 53284, M20?, SD 838 000, Garment waterproofing, C.
304. Atlas Mills, 53320, L19, SJ 876 942, Cotton?, C.
305. Bank of England Mills, 53301, L19, SJ 857 984, Cotton, C.
306*. Beehive Mill, 53329, E19, SJ 851 987, Cotton, A.
307. Beswick Street Mills, 53302, E19–L19, SJ 858 985, Silk, C.
308. Beswick Works, 53308, L19, SJ 863 986, Cotton weaving?, C.
309. Big Cotton Mill?, 53320, L19, SJ 876 942, Cotton?, C.
310. Bowker Bank Works, 53279, M19–L19, SD 847 030, Bleach, dye and finishing works, B.
311. Bradford Mill, 53312, M19–L19, SJ 872 986, Cotton, C.
312. Bradford Road Mill, 53336, E19–M19, SJ 857 986, Cotton, C.
313. Bridge Mill, 53303, L19, SJ 856 985, Cotton and hemming, C.
314. Broom House, 53322, L19–E20, SJ 882 940, Carpet works, C.
315*. Brownsfield Mill, 53327, E19, SJ 849 984, Cotton, A.
316*. Brunswick Mill, 53304, M19, SJ 859 987, Cotton, A.
317. Cambridge Street India Rubber Works, 53345, E19–L19, SJ 837 974, Cotton, later rubber works, C.
318. Chain Bar Mill, 53275, L19, SD 882 031, Cotton waste?, C.
319. Chapeltown Street Mills, 53342, M19, SJ 851 980, Cotton?, C.
320. Chatham Mill, 53341, E19, SJ 840 973, Cotton, C.
321. Chatsworth Mill, 53319, L19, SJ 882 961, ?, C.
322*. Chepstow Street Mill, 55019, E19–L19, SJ 838 978, Cotton, A.
323*. Chorlton New Mill, 53338, E19–M19, SJ 838 974, Cotton, A.
324. Chorlton New Mill (north end), 53339, L19, SJ 838 974, Finishing works, A.
325. Chorlton Old Mill (site of), 53315, L19, SJ 839 973, Cotton,

later india rubber works, C.

326. Chorlton Twist Mill, E19, SJ 842 973, Cotton, D.
327. City Corn Mill, 53329, E19, SJ 851 987, Cotton, A.
328. Clayton Works, 53313, L19, SJ 879 984, Finishing works, C.
329. Collyhurst Works, 53295, L19, SJ 849 998, Finishing works, B.
330. Crumpsall Mill, 53281, M19, SD 855 021, Cotton, C.
331. Culcheth Lane Mill, 53291, L19, SD 884 001, Cotton, C.
332. Daisy Bank Mill, 53292, L19?, SD 887 002, Linen and cotton, C.
333*. Decker Mill, 53297, E19, SJ 851 986, Cotton, A.
334*. Doubling Mill, 53297, M19, SJ 851 986, Cotton, A.
335*. Fireproof Mill, 53297, M19, SJ 851 986, Cotton, A.
336. Garratt Mill, M18–E19, SJ 843 975, Cotton, D.
337. Gorebrook Works, 53318, L19, SJ 875 956, Dyeworks?, C.
338. Gorton Wadding Works, 53317, L19, SJ 891 966, Cotton waste?, C.
339. Great Bridgewater Street Mills, 53293, E19–M19, SJ 837 975, Cotton, dye and silk, C.
340. Great Marlborough Street Works, 53340, L19, SJ 840 974, Finishing works?, C.
341. Hanover Mill, 53316, M19?, SJ 849 976, Cotton, C.
342. Harpurhey Dyeworks, 53286, M19–L19, SD 854 014, Dye and print works, C.
343. Havelock Mills, 53293, E19–M19, SJ 837 975, Cotton, dye and silk, C.
344. Heaton Mills, 53277, M19–L19, SD 844 046, Bleachworks, B.
345. Holt Town Works?, 53307, L19, SJ 862 986, Finishing and calendering works, C.
346. Hope Mills, 53334, M19, SJ 857 985, Cotton, C.
347. Jackson Street Mills, 53335, L19–E20, SJ 847 976, Cotton, C.
348. Knutsford Vale Works, 53318, L19, SJ 875 956, Print and bleach works, C.
349. Levenshulme Works, 53323, L19, SJ 883 946, Print and finishing works, C.
350. Little Green Works, 53289, M19–L19, SD 849 001, Dyeworks, C.
351*. Little Mill, 53297, E20, SJ 851 986, Cotton, A.
352. Lloydsfield Mill, 53311, L19, SJ 856 991, Cotton, C.
353. Marsland's Mill, 53346, E19?, SJ 840 973, Cotton, C.
354. Medlock Mill, 55018, E19–M19, SJ 838 973, Cotton, C.
355. Monsall Mills, 53324, M19?, SD 863 009, Dyeworks, C.
356. Moston Mill, 53276, E20, SD 885 027, Cotton, C.
357. Murray Street Mills, 53297, L18–E20, SJ 851 986, Cotton, A.
358*. Murray's Mills, 53297, L18–E20, SJ 851 986, Cotton, A.
359*. New Mill, 53297, E19, SJ 851 986, Cotton, A.
360. New Old Mill, 53296, E20, SJ 850 985, Cotton, A.
361. Newton Silk Mill, 53326, E19?, SD 882 007, Silk, C.
362*. Old Mill, 53297, L18, SJ 851 986, Cotton, A.
363. Old Mill, 53296, L18, SJ 849 985, Cotton, D.
364*. Paragon Mill, 53328, E20, SJ 849 985, Cotton, A.
365. Phoenix Mill, 53333, M19?, SJ 855 984, Cotton, C.
366. Piccadilly Mill, L18, SJ 845 979, Cotton, D.
367. Pin Mill, 53343, M19, SJ 856 976, Cotton, later finishing and engraving, C.
368. Reservoir Mill, 53309, L19?, SJ 865 987, Cotton, C.
369. Rhodes Mill?, 53300, M19?, SJ 857 984, Cotton, C.
370*. Royal Mill, 53296, E20, SJ 849 985, Cotton, A.
371. Salvin's Factory, L18–E19, SJ 852 984, Cotton, D.
372*. Sedgwick Mill, 53328, E19–L19, SJ 850 985, Cotton, A.
373*. Sedgwick New Mill, 53328, L19, SJ 850 985, Cotton, A.
374. Shudehill Mill, L18, SJ 844 989, Cotton, D.
375. Smedley Vale Works, 53288, E19?, SD 850 011, Dye, bleach, weaving works, B.
376. Smedley Works, 53287, E20, SD 850 012, ?, C.
377. Soho Iron Works site, 53299, L19, SJ 855 983, Cotton waste

(part of), C.

378. Supreme Mills, 53344, E20, SJ 852 987, Cotton? warehouse?, C.
379. Talbot Mill, 53314, M19, SJ 827 974, Cotton, C.
380. Ten Acres Mill, 53290, L19, SD 873 003, Cotton, C.
381. Thistle Mill, 53281, M19, SD 855 021, Cotton, C.
382. Union & Bengal Mills, 53306, L19–E20, SJ 861 988, Cotton, C.
383. Victoria Mill, 53310, L19, SJ 859 993, Cotton, B.
384. Victoria Mills, 53331, M19?, SJ 856 985, ?, C.
385. Waterside Works, 53278, L19, SD 839 034, Bleachworks, C.
386. Waulk Mill, 53306, L19–E20, SJ 861 988, Cotton, C.
387. Wellington Mill, 53305, M19, SJ 859 987, Cotton, C.
388. Wellington Mill, 53325, E19?, SD 866 003, Cotton, C.
389. Wellington Mills, 53337, E20, SJ 832 976, Cotton waste, C.
390. York Mill, 53298, L19, SJ 854 983, Cotton waste, C.

# Oldham

391. Abbey Mill, L19, SD 913 053, Cotton, D.
392. Ace Mill, 54190, E20, SD 897 037, Cotton, C.
393. Acorn Mill, 54158, E19–L19, SD 953 047, Cotton, C.
394. Acorn Mill, 54180, L19, SD 909 038, Cotton waste, C.
395. Albert Mill, 54145, L19, SD 934 059, Cotton, C.
396. Albert Mills, 54268, L19, SD 906 022, Cotton, C.
397. Albion Mill, 54243, M19, SD 998 057, Cotton, woollen, B.
398. Alexandra Mill, 54241, M19?, SD 997 055, Woollen, B.
399. Alliance Mill, 54155, L19, SD 934 055, Cotton waste, C.
400*. Anchor Mill, 54206, L19, SD 917 053, Cotton, A.
401. Andrew Mill, 54245, E19–L19, SD 999 041, Woollen, C.
402. Ashley Mill, 54204, L19, SD 915 055, Cotton, C.
403. Athens Mill, 54161, E20, SD 951 047, Cotton, C.
404. Austerlands Mill, 54163, M19, SD 959 055, Cotton, C.
405. Bailey Mills, 55007, L19?, SD 986 074, Woollen, C.
406. Baytree Mill, 54135, E20, SD 888 053, Cotton, C.
407. Bee Mill, 54138, L19, SD 926 075, Cotton, C.
408. Belgrave Mills, 54194, E20, SD 931 034, Cotton, C.
409. Bell Mill, 54157, L19, SD 935 053, Cotton, C.
410. Bell Mill, 54218, E20, SD 927 028, Cotton, C.
411. Birchen Lee Mill, 55003, L19, SD 909 071, Bleachworks, C.
412. Booth Hill Mill, 54143, M19, SD 922 064, Cotton, C.
413. Borough Mill, 54198, L19, SD 925 037, Cotton, C.
414. Borough Mill, 54197, L19, SD 918 046, Cotton, A.
415. Briar Mill, 54253, E20, SD 942 088, Cotton, C.
416. Britannia Mill, 54156, M19, SD 934 054, Cotton waste, C.
417. Brook Mills No.2, 54178, L19, SD 915 030, Cotton, C.
418. Brunswick House, 54151, L19, SD 925 047, Cotton, C.
419. Buckley New Mill, 54234, M19–L19, SD 997 059, Woollen, C.
420. Cairo Mill, 54166, E20, SD 952 057, Cotton, C.
421. Cambridge Mill, 54207, M19–L19, SD 916 057, Cotton, C.
422. Cape Mill, 54129, L19, SD 939 085, Cotton, C.
423. Castle Mill, 54199, L19, SD 924 035, Cotton, C.
424. Chadderton Mill, 54182, L19, SD 907 045, Cotton, C.
425. Chamber Mill, 54176, L19, SD 913 035, Cotton, C.
426. Clough Mill, 54254, E19–L19, SD 946 089, Cotton, C.
427. Cocker Mill (site of), 55001, L19–E20, SD 929 082, Cotton, C.
428. Court Mill, 54232, E19, SE 008 084, Woollen, C.
429. Cromford Mill, 54258, M19, SD 934 058, Cotton, C.
430. Dam Head Mill, 54243, M19, SD 998 057, Woollen, B.
431. Dawn Mill, 54131, E20, SD 940 089, Cotton, C.
432. Delph Scribbling Mill, 55018, L18, SD 986 079, Woollen, B.
433. Delta Mill, 54140, L19, SD 918 073, Cotton, C.
434. Denshaw Vale Works, 55000, M19–L19, SD 974 102, Print works, C.

435. Devon Mill, 54266, E20, SD 912 029, Cotton, C.
436. Diggle Mill, 54249, E19?, SE 017 081, Woollen, C.
437. Diggle New Mill, 54249, E19?, SE 017 081, Woollen, C.
438. Dob Lane End Mill, 54224, L19, SD 885 009, Cotton, C.
439. Duke Mill, 54130, L19, SD 940 087, Cotton, C.
440. Durban Mill, 54177, E20, SD 915 031, Cotton, C.
441. Eagle Mills, 55005, M19, SD 985 081, Woollen, C.
442. Earl Mill, 55006, L19, SD 929 032, Cotton, C.
443. Elk Mill, 55012, E20, SD 911 068, Cotton, C.
444. Elm Mill, 54251, L19, SD 944 094, Cotton, C.
445. Failsworth Mill, 54222, L19, SD 895 013, Cotton, C.
446. Falcon Mill, 54211, L19, SD 911 057, Velvet, C.
447. Fernhurst Mill, 55011, E20, SD 911 064, Cotton, C.
448. Fir Mill, 54127, E20, SD 923 079, Cotton, C.
449. Firs Mill, 54217, M19, SD 896 015, Cotton, C.
450. Forge Mill, 54147, M19–L19, SD 938 053, Cotton, C.
451. Fountain Mill, 54146, L19, SD 936 056, Cotton, C.
452. Fox Mill, 54270, E20, SD 912 025, Cotton, C.
453. Garland Mill, 54154, M19, SD 934 054, Cotton waste, C.
454. Gatehead Mill, 55008, L19–E20, SD 986 072, Woollen, C.
455. Gem Mill, 54186, E20, SD 904 040, Cotton, C.
456. Gorse Mill, 54189, E20, SD 897 037, Cotton, C.
457. Gorse Mill No.2, 54189, E20, SD 898 039, Cotton, C.
458. Granville Mill, 54149, L19, SD 941 060, Cotton, C.
459. Grape Mill, 54259, E20, SD 917 073, Cotton, C.
460. Greenfield Mills, 54274, L19?, SE 009 037, Cotton, C.
461. Greengate Mill, 54265, L19?, SD 906 028, Cotton waste, C.
462. Gresham Mill, 54205, L19, SD 915 053, Cotton, C.
463. Harbour Lane Mill, 54173, L19, SD 907 032, Reeling, C.
464. Harrop Court Mill, 54232, E19, SE 008 084, Woollen, C.
465. Hartford Mill, 54191, E20, SD 911 045, Cotton, C.
466. Hathershaw Mill, 54196, E20, SD 925 031, Cotton, C.
467. Hawk Mill, 55017, E20, SD 940 096, Cotton, C.
468. Haybottoms Mill, 54238, M19–L19, SD 995 043, Bleachworks, C.
469. Heron Mill, 54179, E20, SD 917 031, Cotton, C.
470. Hey Lane Mill, 54159, E19–L19, SD 953 047, Cotton, C.
471. Holden Fold Mills, 54272, E19–L19, SD 914 068, Cotton, C.
472. Hope Mills, 54148, L19, SD 939 053, Cotton, C.
473. Hull Mill, 54230, L18, SD 988 085, Cotton, C.
474. Iris Mill, 54196, E20, SD 925 031, Cotton, C.
475. Ivy Mill, 54216, L19, SD 897 017, Cotton, B.
476. Jubilee Mill, 54167, M19, SD 951 058, Cotton, C.
477. Junction Mill, 54136, L19, SD 890 049, Cotton, C.
478*. Kent Mill, 54213, E20, SD 912 060, Cotton, A.
479. Kinders Mill, 54236, E19–L19, SD 998 045, Woollen, C.
480. Knarr Mills, 55009, E19–E20, SD 981 069, Woollen, C.
481. Lane End Mill, 55004, E19–L19, SD 916 074, Cotton, C.
482. Laurel Mill, 54134, E20, SD 889 055, Cotton, C.
483. Lees Brook Mill, 54262, L19, SD 949 044, Cotton, C.
484. Lilac Mill, 55010, E20, SD 943 086, Cotton, C.
485. Lily Mills, 54252, E20, SD 943 092, Cotton, C.
486. Lime Mill, 54267, L19, SD 907 024, Cotton, C.
487. Lion Mill, 54139, L19, SD 927 076, Cotton, C.
488. Longrange Mill, 54165, E20, SD 952 057, Cotton, C.
489. Lower Mill, 54164, E20, SD 953 057, Cotton, C.
490. Lumb Mill, 54228, L19–E20, SD 988 076, Print works, C.
491. Lydgate Mill, 54264, L18–L19, SD 973 042, Cotton, C.
492. Lyon Mill, 54132, L19, SD 936 088, Cotton, C.
493. Majestic Mill, 54164, E20, SD 953 057, Cotton, C.
494. Malta Mill, 54133, E20, SD 889 058, Cotton, C.
495. Manor Mill, 54212, E20, SD 911 058, Cotton, C.
496. Maple Mill, 54195, E20, SD 930 033, Cotton, C.

497. Marlborough Mills, 54225, E20, SD 889 009, Cotton, C.
498. Marsland Mill, 54197, L19, SD 918 046, Cotton, B.
499. Meadow Mills, 54227, M19–L19, SD 885 008, Cotton, C.
500. Mona Mill, 54183, E20, SD 906 043, Cotton, C.
501. Monarch Mill, 54141, E20, SD 919 068, Cotton, C.
502. Moorside Mills, 54255, M19–L19, SD 951 074, Cotton, C.
503. Morton Mill, 54223, L19, SD 884 010, Cotton, C.
504. Napier Mill, 54207, M19–L19, SD 916 057, Cotton, C.
505. Newbreck Mills, 54168, L19–E20, SD 945 057, Cotton, C.
506. Newby Mill, 54251, L19, SD 944 094, Cotton, C.
507*. Nile Mill, 54185, L19–E20, SD 905 043, Cotton, B.
508. Oak View Mills, 54244, M19–L19, SD 994 040, Woollen, C.
509. Oldham Mill, 54260, L19?, SD 980 061, Woollen, C.
510. Orb Mill, 54170, E20, SD 953 060, Cotton, C.
511. Orine Mill, 54165, E20, SD 952 057, Cotton, C.
512. Osbourne Mill, 54203, L19–E20, SD 914 057, Cotton, C.
513. Owl Mill, 54160, L19, SD 952 047, Cotton, C.
514. Palm Mill, L19, SD 905 050, Cotton, D.
515. Paradise Mills, 54153, L19?, SD 933 053, Cotton, C.
516. Park and Sandy Lane No.2 Mill, 54125, E20, SD 919 083, Cotton, C.
517. Park Bridge Mill?, 54219, L19?, SD 939 025, Cotton, C.
518. Park Bridge Works, 54220, L19, SD 938 023, Bleachworks?, C.
519. Park No.1 Mill, 53330, L19–E20, SD 919 081, Cotton, C.
520. Park No.2 Mill, 54126, E20, SD 921 082, Cotton, C.
521. Park-Woodend Mill, 54200, L19, SD 944 101, Cotton, C.
522. Phoenix Mill, 54151, L19, SD 925 047, Cotton, C.
523. Pingle Mill, 55015, M19–L19, SD 979 081, Woollen, C.
524*. Prince Of Wales Mill, 54169, L19, SD 942 059, Cotton, A.
525. Ram Mill, 54188, E20, SD 896 041, Cotton, B.
526. Ramsey Mill, 54184, E20, SD 906 042, Cotton, C.
527. Rasping Mills, 54229, L19, SD 987 078, Woollen, C.
528. Raven Mill, 54193, E20, SD 903 042, Cotton, C.
529. Regent Mill, 54221, E20, SD 895 013, Cotton, C.
530. Ridgefield Mill, 54226, L19, SD 891 010, Cotton, C.
531. Rome Mill, 54162, E20, SD 960 047, Cotton, C.
532. Roscoe Mill, 54150, L19, SD 932 050, Cotton, C.
533. Rose Mill, 54172, L19, SD 904 033, Cotton, C.
534. Royal George Mill, 54202, E19–L19, SD 984 040, Woollen, C.
535. Royd Mill, 54175, E20, SD 913 034, Cotton, C.
536. Royton Lane Mill, 55004, E19–L19, SD 916 074, Cotton, C.
537. Royton Ring Mill, 54142, E20, SD 923 065, Cotton, C.
538. Rugby Mill, 54187, E20, SD 896 039, Cotton, C.
539. Rutland Mill, 54250, E20, SD 943 094, Cotton, A.
540. Shaw Mills, 54131, E20, SD 940 089, Cotton, C.
541. Shaw Side Mills, 54128, L19, SD 937 083, Cotton, C.
542. Shore Mill, 55018, L18, SD 986 079, Woollen, B.
543. Slackcote Mills, 55016, M19–L19, SD 970 092, Woollen, C.
544. Spring Hey Mill, 54171, E19–M19, SD 949 059, Cotton, C.
545. Spring Meadows Works, 54246, M19?, SE 002 056, Bleachworks, C.
546. Spring Mill, 54242, E19?, SD 996 057, Woollen, C.
547. Spring Mill, 54171, E19–M19, SD 949 059, Cotton, C.
548. Springfield Works, 54214, L19, SD 895 017, Sponge cloth, C.
549. Springside Mill, 54262, L19, SD 949 044, Cotton, C.
550. Stockfield Mill, 54208, L19, SD 907 052, Cotton, C.
551. Stone Bottom Mills, 54233, L19, SD 996 066, Woollen, C.
552. Street Bridge Works, 55002, L19, SD 907 073, Bleachworks, C.
553. Sun Mill, L19, SD 908 052, Cotton, D.
554. Swan Mill, 54137, L19, SD 890 047, Cotton, C.
555. Tame Water Mill, 54271, M19–E20, SD 987 066, Woollen, C.
556. Textile Mill, 54209, L19, SD 908 052, Cotton, C.
557. Thornham Mill, 54124, L19, SD 914 086, Cotton, C.

558. Tunstead Clough Mill, 54247, L18?, SE 004 042, ?, C.
559. United Mill, 54181, L19, SD 909 039, Cotton, C.
560. Vale Mill, 54174, L19–E20, SD 911 032, Cotton, C.
561. Vale Mill, 54210, L19, SD 909 050, Cotton, C.
562. Vale Mills, 54261, M19–L19, SD 927 047, Cotton, C.
563. Victoria Mills, 54240, M19?, SD 996 055, Woollen, C.
564. Vine Mill, 55014, L19, SD 917 074, Cotton, C.
565. Walk Mill, 54235, M19?, SD 988 063, Dyeworks, C.
566. Wall Hall Mill, 54260, L19?, SD 980 061, Woollen, C.
567. Warth Mill, 54231, L19–E20, SE 004 078, Cotton, C.
568. Waterside Mill, 54248, M19–L19, SE 003 038, Cotton, C.
569. Wellington Mills, 54239, M19–L19, SD 994 046, Cotton, C.
570. Werneth Mill, 54192, L19–E20, SD 915 043, Cotton, C.
571. Werneth Mills, 54256, L19, SD 918 059, Cotton, C.
572. Westhulme Mills, 54257, M19–L19, SD 919 060, Cotton, C.
573. Willowbank Mill, 54144, L19, SD 920 062, Cotton, C.
574. Windsor Mill, 54269, L19, SD 905 024, Cotton, C.
575. Woodend Mills, 54263, L19, SD 957 044, Cotton, C.
576. Wright Mill, 54201, E19?, SD 980 037, Woollen, C.
577. Wrigley Head Mills, 54215, L19, SD 897 019, Cotton, C.

# Rochdale

578. Albert Mill, 54005, E19–L19, SD 865 101, Cotton, C.
579. Albert Mill, 54030, L19?, SD 906 125, Cotton, C.
580. Albert New Mill, 54006, L19, SD 863 101, Cotton, C.
581. Albion Mill, 53936, L19, SD 931 161, Cotton, C.
582. Albion Mill, 54089, L19?, SD 883 103, Cotton, C.
583. Alma Mill, 54016, L19, SD 900 142, Cotton?, C.
584. Arrow Vale Mill, 54093, E20, SD 887 109, Cotton, C.
585. Ashbrook Hey Mill, 53941, L19?, SD 913 157, Cotton?, C.
586. Ashrook Hey Works, 53942, M19–L19, SD 914 158, Dyeworks, C.
587. Baitings Mill, 54064, L19, SD 852 148, Fustian, Cotton, B.
588. Balderstone Mill, 54043, E20?, SD 905 110, Cotton, C.
589. Bamford Mills, 53968, L19, SD 862 127, Woollen, C.
590. Bankfield Mills, 54029, M19?, SD 909 125, Woollen, C.
591. Barchant Mill, 54021, M19–L19, SD 901 132, Cotton, C.
592. Beal Works, 54098, L19?, SD 922 136, Bleachworks, C.
593. Belfield Mill, 54115, M19?, SD 917 139, Woollen, C.
594. Belfield Mill (part of), 54096, L19, SD 918 139, Cotton waste?, C.
595. Belfield Mill (part of), 54119, E19?, SD 918 140, Woollen, C.
596. Belgrave Works, 54082, M19–L19, SD 844 109, Cotton, C.
597. Birch Mill, 54008, L19, SD 853 082, Cotton, C.
598. Birtle Works, 53963, M19?, SD 836 124, Bleachworks, B.
599. Bluepits Mill, 54091, M19, SD 885 107, Cotton, B.
600. Boarshaw Clough Works, 54046, L19, SD 877 068, Bleach and dyeworks, C.
601. Boarshaw Mill, 54048, L19, SD 876 066, Raising and finishing, C.
602. Boarshaw Works, 54046, L19, SD 877 068, Bleach and dyeworks, C.
603. Booth Hollings Mill, 54099, L18–M19, SD 952 139, Woollen, B.
604. Bowlee Mill, 54111, L19?, SD 846 067, ?, C.
605. Bridgefield Street Mill, 54121, L19, SD 889 131, ?, C.
606. Brimrod Mill, 53956, L19, SD 888 128, Cotton, C.
607. Broadfield Mill, 53981, L19, SD 850 104, Cotton, C.
608. Brook Mills, 53985, M19–E20, SD 851 107, Cotton, C.
609. Brookside Mill, 54059, L19, SD 873 061, Cotton, C.
610. Buckley Brook Mills, 53991, L19, SD 907 149, Cotton, C.
611. Buckley Lower Mill, 54075, M19, SD 905 147, Woollen, C.
612. Buckley Mill, 53950, M19–L19, SD 907 151, Woollen, C.
613. Burnedge Mill, 54110, M19?, SD 919 104, Cotton, C.
614. Butterworth Hall Mill, 54104, E20, SD 934 123, Cotton, C.

615. Caldershaw Mills, 53924, L19–M20, SD 878 145, Dye and finishing works, C.
616. Calliards Mill, 54077, M19?, SD 925 156, Woollen, C.
617. Canal Street Mill, 54036, M19–L19, SD 903 122, Cotton, C.
618. Castleton Old Mill, 53978, L19, SD 892 118, Cotton, C.
619. Castleton Works, 54094, M19?, SD 888 101, Print works?, C.
620. Cheesden Lumb Mill, 53988, E19, SD 824 161, Woollen, B.
621. Church Street Mill, 54102, M19–L19, SD 928 127, Cotton, B.
622. Clegg Hall Mill, 54113, E19–L19, SD 923 145, Cotton, B.
623. Clover Mill?, 54009, E20, SD 908 139, Dyeworks, C.
624. Coral Mill, 54109, L19–E20, SD 938 115, Cotton, C.
625. Crawford Mills, 54025, L19, SD 910 125, Cotton, C.
626. Crest Mill, 53974, E20, SD 889 112, Cotton, C.
627*. Crimble Mill, 53966, E19–E20, SD 866 116, Cotton, A.
628. Croft Mill, 54010, E20, SD 908 140, Cotton, C.
629. Cromer Mill, 54057, L19?, SD 878 063, Cotton, C.
630. Cross Street Works, 54112, M19–L19, SD 866 059, Finishing works, B.
631. Crossfield Mill, 54032, M19, SD 904 124, Cotton, C.
632. Dale Mill, 53949, E20, SD 909 144, Cotton, C.
633. Dawson Hill Mill, 53987, M19, SD 854 107, Cotton, C.
634. Dicken Green Mill, 54037, M19–E20, SD 901 119, Cotton, C.
635. Dob Wheel Mill, 53945, L18–L19, SD 916 151, Woollen, cotton, A.
636. Don Mill, 54054, E20, SD 884 062, Cotton, C.
637. Doris Mill, 54081, L19, SD 842 108, Cotton, C.
638. Drydock Mill, 53938, M19, SD 927 161, Woollen, C.
639. Duke Street Mill, 54116, L19, SD 898 139, Cotton?, C.
640. Dunlop Mills, 53973, E20, SD 887 114, Cotton, C.
641. Durn Mills, 53929, L19, SD 943 164, Woollen, C.
642. Ealees Mill, 53928, L19, SD 942 162, Bleach, dye and finishing works, C
643. Eclipse Mill, 53993, M19, SD 905 148, Cotton, C.
644. Ellenroad Mill, 54105, E20, SD 931 116, Cotton, C.
645. Ensor Mill, 53975, E20?, SD 888 111, Cotton, C.
646. Fairfield Mill, 54012, E20, SD 909 140, Cotton, C.
647. Featherstall Mill, 53937, L19, SD 929 162, Woollen, C.
648. Fieldhouse Mills, 53964, L19, SD 898 147, Cotton, C.
649. Fielding Street Mill, 54047, L19–E20, SD 873 068, Dyeworks, C.
650. Gale Works, 54073, L19–E20, SD 942 173, Print works, C.
651. Garrison Mill, 53982, L19, SD 850 104, Cotton, C.
652. Glendale Mills, 53996, L19–E20, SD 863 107, Cotton, C.
653. Grange Mill, 54095, L19, SD 891 100, Print works, C.
654. Grange Mill (part of), 54095, M19?, SD 891 100, Print works, C.
655. Green Grove Mill, 53944, E19–M19, SD 913 152, Cotton, C.
656. Green Mill, 54038, L19, SD 903 117, Woollen, C.
657. Green Mill, 53945, L18–L19, SD 916 150, Woollen, cotton, A.
658. Green Vale Mill, 54071, L19?, SD 947 177, Cotton, C.
659. Gregge Street Mill, 54004, L19, SD 864 101, Cotton, C.
660. Grove Mills, 54035, L19?, SD 902 125, Cotton, C.
661. Grove Works, 54069, L19?, SD 945 177, Dye and finishing works, C.
662. Hamer Lane Mill, 54013, M19?, SD 908 141, Woollen, B.
663. Hamer Mill, 54014, M19?, SD 908 141, Cotton, C.
664. Hamer Vale Mills, 53994, L19, SD 905 147, Cotton, C.
665. Hare Hill Mills, 53930, L19, SD 936 166, Woollen, C.
666. Harp Mill, 54092, L19–E20, SD 887 108, Cotton, C.
667. Healey Hall Mills, 53920, M19–L19, SD 880 156, Dye and finishing works, C
668. Healey Mill, 53919, L19, SD 888 158, Cotton, C.
669. Heybrook Mill, 54120, E19–M19, SD 906 142, Woollen, C.
670. Higher Two Bridge Mill, 54107, M19–L19, SD 939 114,

Cotton, C.
671. Highfield Mill, 54082, M19–L19, SD 844 109, Cotton, C.
672. Hooley Bridge Mill, 53971, E19–L19, SD 854 116, Cotton, C.
673. Hope Street Mills, 54118, M19–E20, SD 896 138, ?, C.
674. Howarth Cross Mill, 53947, E19?, SD 913 147, Cotton, C.
675. Jennings Mills, 54019, L19, SD 901 136, Cotton, C.
676. John Street Works, 54083, L19, SD 858 109, Dyeworks, C.
677. Jubilee Mill, 54044, M19–L19, SD 943 110, Woollen, C.
678. Kitcliffe Mill, 54041, E19, SD 957 125, Woollen, C.
679. Lady House Mill?, 54103, E19–L19, SD 929 123, Cotton, C.
680. Lane End Mill, 54086, M19?, SD 859 106, Cotton, A.
681. Lawflat Mill, 53927, M19?, SD 911 165, Woollen, C.
682. Lincouth Bridge Mills, 54098, L19?, SD 922 136, Woollen, C.
683. Linden Mill, 54090, M19–L19, SD 884 105, Cotton, C.
684. Lodge Mill, 53925, M19, SD 913 168, Woollen, C.
685. Lodge Mill, 54059, L19, SD 873 061, Cotton, C.
686. Low Flat Mill, 53927, M19?, SD 911 165, Woollen, C.
687. Low Hill Mills, 53943, L19, SD 911 154, Woollen, C.
688. Lower Mill, 54077, M19?, SD 925 156, Woollen, C.
689. Lower Two Bridge Mill?, 54106, E19?, SD 936 113, Cotton, C.
690. Lowfield Mill, 54018, L19, SD 917 136, Cotton, C.
691. Lydgate Mill, 53940, E19–L19, SD 953 166, Woollen, B.
692. Manchester Old Road Works, 54051, L19, SD 854 052, Print works, C.
693. Marland Mill, 54087, E20, SD 878 111, Cotton, C.
694. Mars Mill, 53976, E20, SD 878 112, Cotton, C.
695*. Martin's Mill, 54066, M19, SD 866 145, Cotton, A.
696. Mayfield Mill, 54015, L19, SD 909 142, Cotton, C.
697. Mellor Street Mill, 53959, E20, SD 886 136, Cotton waste, C.
698. Millers Brook Mill, 53999, L19–E20, SD 859 109, Cotton, C.
699. Milnrow Mills, 54102, M19–L19, SD 928 127, Cotton, B.
700. Mitchell Hey Mills, 53951, L19, SD 890 133, Cotton, C.
701. Morning Side Mill, 54031, M19–L19, SD 904 124, Woollen, C.
702. Moss Mill, 54022, E20, SD 908 124, Cotton, C.
703. Mossfield Mill, 53986, M19–L19, SD 850 109, Cotton, C..
704. Mutual Mills, 53969, L19, SD 863 111, Cotton, B.
705. Mutual Mills, 53997, L19, SD 861 111, Cotton, B.
706. Ned Mill?, 53963, M19?, SD 836 124, Bleachworks, B.
707. New Hey Mill, 54108, M19–L19, SD 939 114, Cotton, C.
708. New Mill, 53948, L19?, SD 915 146, Dyeworks, C.
709. Norwich Street Mills, 54033, L19, SD 902 123, Cotton, C.
710. Oak Mill, 53953, L19, SD 890 132, Cotton, C.
711. Oakenrod Mills, 53955, M19?, SD 887 131, Cotton, C.
712. Ogden Mill, 54039, M19–L19, SD 950 121, Bleach and finishing works, C
713. Oxford Mill, 53922, L19–M20, SD 893 149, Cotton, C.
714. Park Mill, 53970, M19–E20, SD 856 115, Cotton, C.
715. Park Mill, 53992, L19, SD 906 149, Cotton, C.
716. Parkfield Works, 54052, L19–E20, SD 865 058, Bleach and dyeworks, C
717. Passmonds Mill, 53961, M19?, SD 879 139, Cotton, C.
718. Perseverance Mill, 54007, M19–E20, SD 864 103, Cotton, C.
719. Phoenix Mill, 53999, L19–E20, SD 859 109, Cotton, C.
720. Princess Mill, 54003, L19?, SD 863 101, Cotton, C.
721. Providence Mill, 54101, M19, SD 926 126, Woollen, C.
722. Python Mill, 53935, L19–E20, SD 933 163, Artificial silk, C.
723. Quarry Mill, 53921, L19, SD 893 154, Cotton, C.
724. Rainshore Mill, 54063, L19–E20, SD 852 154, Bleachworks, C.
725. Rainshore Upper Mill, 54063, L19–E20, SD 852 154, Bleachworks, C.
726. Rakewood Lower Mill, 54079, L19, SD 945 143, Cotton and woollen, C.

727. Rakewood Mill, 54100, M19–E20, SD 945 142, Cotton, C.
728. Rakewood Mill, 54079, L19, SD 945 143, Cotton and woollen, C.
729. Red Brook Mill, 53954, M19, SD 889 132, Woollen, B.
730. Red Lumb Mill, 54062, E19–L19, SD 842 156, Cotton, B.
731. Regent Mill, 54017, L19, SD 900 141, ?, C.
732. Rex Mill, 54045, E20, SD 883 064, Cotton, C.
733. Rhodes Works, 54050, L19, SD 847 052, Cotton, bleach and dye, C.
734. Riley's Mill?, 54028, L19, SD 909 126, Cotton?, C.
735. Riverside Mill, 53946, M19–L19, SD 916 149, Cotton, C.
736. Roach Vale Mill, 54076, L19, SD 913 148, Cotton, C.
737. Rock Nook Mill, 54070, L19, SD 947 179, Cotton, C.
738. Roe Acre Works, 53995, E20, SD 862 108, Dyeworks, C.
739. Roeacre Mills, 53996, L19, SD 863 107, Cotton, C.
740. Rose Hill Mill, 53983, L19, SD 846 107, Cotton, C.
741. Rose Mill, 54049, L19, SD 872 064, Silk, B.
742. Royle Works?, 53973, E20, SD 887 114, Cotton, C.
743. Salt Pye Mill, 54109, L19–E20, SD 938 115, Cotton, C.
744. Shore Mills, 53933, L19, SD 927 170, Cotton, C.
745. Simpson Clough Fulling Mill, 53972, L19, SD 852 121, Bleach and dyeworks, C.
746. Simpson Clough, 53972, L19, SD 852 121, Bleach and dyeworks, C
747. Sladen Mill, 53939, L19, SD 950 174, Cotton and finishing, C.
748. Sladen Wood Mill, 54068, L19, SD 947 182, Cotton, C.
749. Soudan Mills (part of), 54055, E20, SD 882 063, Cotton, C.
750. Soudan Mills (part of), 54056, E20, SD 883 062, Cotton, C.
751. Spodden Mill, 53951, L19, SD 890 133, Cotton, C.
752*. Spotland Bridge New Mill, 53960, M19–E20, SD 885 138, Cotton, A.
753. Spotland New Mill, 53957, L19, SD 888 137, Cotton, C.
754. Spotland Works, 53958, L19, SD 887 135, Finishing works, C.
755. Spring Mill, 53984, E20, SD 845 107, Cotton, C.
756. Spring Mill, 54040, M19?, SD 953 123, ?, C.
757. Springfield Mill, 54122, L19, SD 911 112, ?, C.
758. Stanley Mill?, 53990, M19?, SD 856 105, Cotton, C.
759. Stansfield Works, 54067, M19, SD 942 180, Dyeworks, print works, C.
760. Stansfield Works?, 54069, L19?, SD 945 177, Bleachworks, C.
761. State Mill, 54026, E20, SD 909 124, Cotton, C.
762. Sudden Mills, 53977, L19?, SD 884 118, Cotton and dye, C.
763. Sun Mill, 53937, L19, SD 929 163, Woollen, C.
764. Sunny Brook Mill, 53952, L19, SD 890 132, Cotton, C.
765. Syke Mill?, 54123, L18–E19, SD 898 159, Cotton, C.
766. Tack Lee Works, 53962, M19–L19, SD 839 121, Bleachworks, C.
767. Times Coloured Spinning Company, 53989, L19, SD 854 109, Cotton, C.
768. Times Mill, 54061, L19–E20, SD 878 055, Cotton, C.
769. Times Mill, 53989, L19, SD 854 109, Cotton, C.
770. Tonge Mill, 54058, L19–E20, SD 874 059, Cotton, C.
771. Tonge Works, 54053, L19, SD 868 056, Dyeworks, C.
772. Town House Mill, 53931, M19?, SD 935 172, Cotton, C.
773. Town House Shed Mill, 53931, M19?, SD 935 172, Cotton, C.
774. Trafalgar Mill, 54020, L19, SD 904 135, Cotton, C.
775. Trafalgar Mill, 54078, L19, SD 924 153, Woollen, C.
776. Trows Fulling Mill?, 54094, M19?, SD 888 101, Woollen, C.
777. Trows Upper Works, 54095, L19, SD 891 100, Print works, C.
778. Twin Mill, 54001, L19, SD 862 102, Cotton, C.
779. Two Bridges Mill, 54107, M19–L19, SD 939 114, Cotton, C.
780. Two Bridges Mill, 54109, L19–E20, SD 938 115, Cotton, C.
781. Tyne Mill, 53935, L19–E20, SD 933 163, Cotton, C.
782. Union Mill, 53978, L19, SD 892 118, Cotton, C.

783. Union Ring Mill, 53978, L19, SD 892 118, Cotton, C.
784. Unity Mill, 53980, E20, SD 846 101, Cotton, C.
785. Vale Mill, 54019, M19–L19, SD 901 135, Cotton, C.
786. Vale Mill, 54085, M19–L19, SD 863 106, Cotton, C.
787. Vale Mills, 54120, E19–M19, SD 906 142, Woollen, C.
788. Valley Ring Mill, 53979, E20?, SD 892 117, Cotton, C.
789. Victoria Mill, 54002, L19, SD 863 102, Cotton, C.
790. Victoria Mill, 54023, L19?, SD 905 123, Cotton, C.
791. Victoria Mill, 54034, M19, SD 903 125, Woollen, C.
792. Wardle Mill, 54072, E19, SD 911 171, Woollen, C.
793. Warwick Mill, 54060, E20, SD 872 057, Cotton, C.
794. Wash Mill, 54080, E20?, SD 836 123, ?, C.
795. Wasp Mill, 53926, M19–L19, SD 913 167, Woollen, C.
796. Waterside Mill, 54011, E20, SD 909 140, Cotton, C.
797. Wellfield Mill, 54027, M19–E20, SD 904 124, Cotton, C.
798. Wellfield Mill, 54036, M19–L19, SD 903 122, Cotton, C.
799. Westbrooke Mill, 54088, M19–L19, SD 884 102, Cotton, C.
800. White Lees Mill, 53934, E19–E20, SD 933 165,
     Finishing works, C.
801. Wicken Hall Works, 54042, L19, SD 955 118, Print works, C.
802. Willow Street Mill, 53998, L19, SD 858 109, Cotton, C.
803. Woodfield Mill, 54084, L19, SD 859 110, ?, C.
804. Woodhouse Mills, 54065, M19–L19, SD 857 147, Dye and
     finishing works, C.
805. Yew Vale Mill, 54019, L19, SD 901 136, Cotton, C.
806. Yew Vale Mill, 54120, E19–M19, SD 906 142, Woollen, C.

## Salford

807. Acme Mills, 53441, L19–E20, SD 785 016, Cotton, C.
808. Agecroft Works, 53450, L19, SD 807 012, Print works, B.
809. Albert Mill, 53449, L19, SJ 778 983, Cotton, C.
810. Albert Mill, 53455, L19, SD 808 003, Cotton, C.
811. Albert Mill, 53365, M19–E20, SJ 825 984, Cotton?, C.
812. Albion Mill, 53441, L19, SD 785 016, Cotton, C.
813. Bank Mill, 53460, L19, SJ 815 997, Cotton, C.
814. Beddingate Mill, 53448, M19–L19, SJ 762 984, Silk, cotton, B.
815. Bridge Mill, 53454, L19, SD 810 001, Cotton, C.
816. Bridgewater Mill, 53433, L19, SD 739 029, Cotton, B.
817. Bridgewater Mill, 53438, L19, SD 776 028, Cotton, C.
818. Clegg's Lane Mill, 53431, M19?, SD 720 043, Cotton, C.
819. Clough Works, 53463, L19?, SJ 830 994, Finishing works, C.
820. Deans Mill, 53444, L19, SD 771 015, Cotton, C.
821. Eccles Spinning & Manufacturing Co, 53445, E20, SJ 762 990,
     Cotton, C.
822. Egerton Works, 53447, L19, SJ 762 985, Dyeworks, C.
823. Glazebury Mill, 53443, L19, SJ 764 982, Cotton, C.
824. Granville Mill, 53429, L19, SD 735 036, Cotton, C.
825. Grecian Mill, 53467, L19, SD 736 046, Cotton, C.
826. Hope Mill, 53432, E20, SD 739 028, Cotton, C.
827. Hope Mill, 53442, M19, SD 779 018, Cotton, C.
828. Irwell Works, 53453, L19, SD 815 004, Bleachworks, B.
829*. Islington Mill, 53462, E19–E20, SJ 826 984, Cotton, A.
830. King Street Mill, 53466, M19?, SJ 835 989, Cotton?, C.
831. Kingston Mills, 53456, L19, SJ 811 998, Cotton, C.
832. Lakefield Mills, 53431, M19?, SD 720 043, Cotton, C.
833. Lakefield Mills, 53468, L19, SD 736 045, Cotton, C.
834. Linnyshaw Mill, 53434, L19, SD 747 031, Cotton, C.
835. London Place Works, 53450, L19, SD 807 012, Print works, B.
836. Monton Mill, 53446, E20, SJ 763 994, Cotton, C.
837. Moorside Road Mill, 53437, L19–M20, SD 769 022, Cotton, C.
838. Moss House Works, 53461, L19, SJ 823 992, Dye and

finishing works, C.
839. Moss Side Mills, 53439, M19–L19, SD 778 028, Cotton, C.
840. Mossley Mill, 53459, L19, SJ 814 996, Cotton, C.
841. Nassau Mills, 53469, M19–L19, SJ 765 983, Cotton, C.
842. Newtown Mill, 53440, L19, SD 778 024, Cotton, C.
843. Overbridge Mills, 53465, M19, SJ 834 995, Cotton, C.
844. Park Mill, 53428, L19–E20, SD 734 036, Cotton, C.
845. Parkhouse Works, 53451, L19, SD 807 008, Dyeworks, B.
846. Pendleton New Mills, 53458, M19–L19, SJ 813 998, Cotton, B.
847. Primrose Mill, 53430, L19, SD 735 034, Cotton, C.
848. Riverside Works, 53452, M19–L19, SD 810 007, Dye and finishing
     works, C.
849. Salford Twist Mill, L18–E19, SJ 834 985, Cotton, D.
850. Salford Works, 53461, L19, SJ 823 992, Dye and finishing works, C.
851. Springfield Mills, 53465, M19, SJ 834 995, Cotton, C.
852. Trafford Mill, 53457, E20?, SJ 811 999, Cotton, C.
853. Victoria Lane Mill, 53436, L19, SD 767 016, Cotton, C.
854. Victoria Mills, 53464, L19, SJ 834 995, ?, C.
855. Victoria Mills, 53470, L19, SJ 798 986, Bleach and dyeworks, C.
856. Victoria Mills, 53443, L19, SJ 764 982, Cotton, C.
857. Walker's Silk Mill, 53471, E19?, SJ 825 983, Silk, B.
858. Wardley Mills, 53435, L19–E20, SD 749 031, Cotton, C.
859. Waverley Mills, 53472, L19, SJ 833 994, ?, C.
860. Willow Bank Works, 53452, M19–L19, SD 810 007, Dye and
     finishing works, C.

## Stockport

861. Alligator Mills, 53384, L19, SJ 898 910, Cotton, C.
862. Aqueduct Works, 53403, L19?, SJ 956 990, Dyeworks, C.
863. Avondale Works, 53358, M20, SJ 878 894, Ribbon weaving, C.
864. Bankside Mill, 53380, E20, SJ 893 916, Cotton, C.
865. Beehive Mill, 53384, L19, SJ 898 910, Cotton, C.
866. Botany Mill, 53364, L19, SJ 933 927, ?, C.
867. Brewery Street Mill?, 53384, L19, SJ 898 910, Cotton, C.
868. Brewery Street Mills, 53385, L19, SJ 898 909, Cotton, C.
869. Brinksway Mill, 53420, E19–L19, SJ 884 899, Cotton, dyeworks, C.
870. Britannia Mill?, 53391, L19, SJ 891 917, Cotton, C.
871. Broadstone Mill, 53349, E20, SJ 892 930, Cotton, C.
872. California Mill, 53397, M19–L19, SJ 900 899, Cotton waste?, C.
873. Cataract Bridge Mills, 53413, L19, SJ 970 888, Cotton, C.
874. Chadkirk Works, 53417, L19, SJ 938 895, Print works, B.
875. Cheadle Works, 53359, L19, SJ 855 890, Bleachworks, C.
876. Churchgate Mill, 53368, L19?, SJ 899 902, ?, C.
877. Compstall Mills, 53408, M19–L19, SJ 965 908, Cotton, B.
878. Compstall Works, 53389, M19, SJ 965 908, Print works, B.
879. Coronation Mill, 53381, M19–E20, SJ 894 916, Cotton, C.
880. Coronation Mill, 53380, E20, SJ 893 916, Cotton, C.
881. Croft Mills, 53372, L19, SJ 905 904, Cotton, C.
882. Demmings Works, 53360, E20, SJ 866 881, Bleach and
     dyeworks, C.
883. Demmings Works (part of?), 53423, E20, SJ 867 881, ?, C.
884. Dysart Street Shed, 53421, E20, SJ 909 883, Cotton, C.
885. East Bank Mill, 53376, L19, SJ 907 910, Cotton, C.
886. Edgeley Works, 53354, L19, SJ 885 890, Bleachworks, C.
887. Elder Mill, 53388, L19, SJ 936 907, Cotton, C.
888. Faulder's Mill, 53386, L19, SJ 898 908, Cotton, C.
889. Foggbrook Mill, 53401, E19, SJ 927 888, Print works? (part of), C.
890. Gorsey Bank Mill, 53357, L19–E20, SJ 878 898, Cotton, C.
891. Goyt Mill, 53419, E20, SJ 957 876, Cotton, C.
892. Hallam Mill, 53411, L19?, SJ 900 887, Cotton?, C.
893. Hampstead Mill, 53404, M19–L19, SJ 910 883, Cotton weaving, C.

894. Heap Riding Mill, 53418, M19–L19, SJ 886 902, Cotton, C.
895. Heaton Mersey Works, 53353, M19–L19, SJ 867 901, Bleachworks, B.
896. Hempshaw Lane Works, 53393, L19?, SJ 908 895, Dyeworks, C.
897. Hollins Mill, 53402, L19?, SJ 959 887, Cotton, C.
898. Hope Mill, 53383, M19, SJ 897 910, Woollen, cotton, C.
899*. Houldsworth's Mill, 53348, L19, SJ 891 933, Cotton, A.
900. Kingston Mill, 53350, M19, SJ 889 902, Cotton, C.
901. Lower Carrs Mill, 53369, E19–M19, SJ 898 902, Cotton, B.
902. Marriott Street Mills, 53396, L19, SJ 897 897, ?, C.
903. Meadow Mill, 53382, L19, SJ 899 912, Cotton, C.
904. New Bridge Lane Mills, 53375, E19, SJ 904 907, Cotton, C.
905. New Bridge Mills, 53367, M19–E20, SJ 900 905, Cotton, C.
906. Oakwood Mill, 53424, E19–E20, SJ 945 905, Cotton?, C.
907. Orrell's Mill, M19, SJ 886 903, Cotton, D.
908. Palmer Mills, 53373, L19, SJ 903 907, Cotton, C.
909. Pear New Mill, 53378, E20, SJ 912 908, Cotton, C.
910. Primrose Mill, 53414, E19?, SJ 978 893, ?, C.
911. Reddish Mills, 53348, L19, SJ 891 933, Cotton, A.
912. Reddish Spinning Co, 53347, L19, SJ 891 937, Cotton, C.
913. Reddish Vale Works, 53361, L19, SJ 905 933, Print works, C.
914. Rivett's Mill, 53379, L19, SJ 893 916, Cotton, C.
915. Shaw Heath Mill, 53395, M19, SJ 895 894, Cotton, C.
916. Spring Bank Mill, 53409, E19, SJ 894 900, Cotton, C.
917. Spring Mount Mill, 53356, M19–L19, SJ 882 898, Cotton, C.
918. Springfield Mill, 53425, L19, SJ 896 984, Cotton, C.
919. Spur Mill, 53415, E20, SJ 894 925, Cotton, B.
920. Squirrel Works, 53411, L19?, SJ 900 887, Cotton?, C.
921. Stockport Ring Mills, 53405, E20, SJ 882 901, Cotton, C.
922. Thorn Works, 53363, L19, SJ 934 925, ?, C.
923. Throstle Bank Mill, 53372, L19, SJ 905 904, Cotton, C.
924. Top Mill, 53362, L19, SJ 935 925, ?, C.
925. Travis Brook Mill, M19, SJ 886 903, Cotton, D.
926. Unity Mills, 53366, M19, SJ 939 930, Cotton, B.
927. Vernon Mills, 53374, L19, SJ 904 907, Cotton, C.
928. Victoria Mill, 53371, M19, SJ 894 926, Cotton, B.
929. Victoria Works, 53400, L19, SJ 900 894, Dyeworks, B.
930. Virginia Mills, 53412, L19, SJ 889 892, ?, C.
931. Wards Hat Factory, 53370, E19, SJ 893 902, Cotton, B.
932. Waterloo Mill, 53397, M19–L19, SJ 900 899, Cotton waste?, C.
933. Waterloo Road Mill, 53390, L19, SJ 901 902, Cotton waste, C.
934*. Wear Mill, 53352, E19–E20, SJ 890 902, Cotton, B.
935. Welkin Ring Mill, 53377, E20, SJ 912 914, Cotton, C.
936. Wellington Hat Factory, 53370, E19, SJ 893 902, Cotton, B.
937. Wellington Mill, 53370, E19, SJ 893 902, Cotton, B.
938. Wellington Mill, 53416, L19?, SJ 927 874, Cotton, C.
939. Woodley Mills, 53426, E19–M19, SJ 937 924, ?, C.

## Tameside

940. Albert Mill, 53554, L19, SJ 943 966, Cotton, C.
941. Albert Mill, 53484, L19, SD 978 018, Cotton, B.
942. Algier Mill, 53492, E20, SJ 947 999, Cotton, C.
943. Angola Mill, 53529, L19, SJ 901 980, Cotton, C.
944. Aniline Works, 53572, L19, SJ 897 976, Dyeworks, C.
945. Atlas Mill Spinning Co, 53490, E20, SD 935 001, Cotton, C.
946. Bank Mill, 53473, L19?, SD 981 033, Cotton, C.
947. Bankfield Mill, 53499, L19, SJ 936 986, Cotton, C.
948. Bankwood Mills, 53527, M19, SJ 968 982, Cotton, C.
949. Bardsley Vale Mills, 53491, M19–L19, SD 931 013, Cotton (part of), C.
950. Barn Meadow Mills, 53573, M19?, SJ 933 970, Cotton, B.
951. Barnfield Mill, 53561, L19, SJ 943 950, Finishing?, C.
952. Bayley Field Mill, 53548, M19–E20, SJ 947 956, Cotton, C.
953. Beetle Works, 53590, L19, SJ 904 986, Dye and finishing works, C.
954. Birch Street Mill, 53533, L19, SJ 928 977, Cotton, C.
955. Bridge Street Mills, 53515, L19, SJ 959 985, Cotton, C.
956. Britannia Mills, 53478, M19, SD 974 022, Cotton, C.
957. Brook Street Mill, 53587, M19?, SJ 933 988, ?, C.
958. Broomstair Mill, 53575, L19, SJ 936 953, Finishing works?, C.
959. Brunswick Mill, 53484, L19, SD 978 018, Cotton, B.
960. Buckton Vale Works, 53583, L19, SD 991 009, Bleach, dye and print works, B.
961. Carrfield Mill, 53549, M19–M20, SJ 946 955, Cotton, C.
962. Carrhill Mills, 53482, E20, SD 976 026, Cotton, C.
963*. Carrs Mill, 53493, L19, SD 952 000, Cotton, A.
964. Castle Street Mills, 53516, E19, SJ 962 985, Cotton, C.
965. Cavendish Mill, 53499, L19, SJ 936 986, Cotton, C.
966. Cedar Mill, 53494, E20, SD 947 001, Cotton, C.
967. Cheethams Mill, 53527, M19, SJ 968 982, Cotton, C.
968. Clarence Mill, 53519, L19, SJ 953 985, Cotton, C.
969. Clock Tower Mill, 53518, E20, SJ 961 983, Cotton, C.
970*. Copley Mill, 53525, M19–L19, SJ 973 988, Cotton, A.
971. Curzon Mill, 53492, E20, SJ 947 999, Cotton, C.
972. Droylsden Mill, 53530, L19, SJ 903 978, Cotton, C.
973. Dukinfield Old Mill, 53506, L19, SJ 945 984, Cotton, C.
974. Duncan Mill, 53533, L19, SJ 928 977, Cotton, C.
975. Fairfield Mills, 53531, L19, SJ 903 982, Cotton, C.
976. Fern Mill, 53497, M19, SJ 926 983, Cotton, C.
977. Free Trade Buildings, 53502, L19, SJ 933 992, Cotton waste, C.
978. Gee Cross Mill, 53559, E20, SJ 942 937, Cotton?, C.
979*. Good Hope Mill, 53501, E19–L19, SJ 934 988, Cotton, A.
980. Greencroft Mills, 53547, L19, SJ 946 951, Cotton, C.
981. Grosvenor Mill, 53536, M19, SJ 932 981, Cotton, C.
982. Grosvenor Street Mills, 53518, E20, SJ 961 983, Cotton, C.
983. Guide Bridge Mill, 53537, L19, SJ 923 978, Cotton, C.
984. Guide Mills, 53532, M19, SJ 926 976, Cotton, C.
985. Harper Mills, 53569, M19, SJ 944 991, Cotton, C.
986. Harrap Street Mill, 53567, M19, SJ 960 985, Cotton, C.
987. Higher Mill, 53570, M19–L19, SJ 967 988, Cotton (part of), C.
988. Hollingworth Cotton Spinning & Manufacturing Co, 53582, L19, SK 006 962, Cotton, C.
989. Hollins Mill, 53485, M19, SD 980 019, Woollen, B.
990. Hurst Mill, 53564, L19, SD 949 002, Cotton, C.
991. Hurst Mount Mill, 53521, M19–L19, SJ 942 996, Cotton, C.
992. Hyde Junction Works, 53555, L19, SJ 971 966, Dyeworks, C.
993. Hyde Mill, 53552, E20, SJ 951 965, Cotton, C.
994. Junction Mills, 53565, L19, SJ 933 984, Cotton, C.
995. Junction Mills, 53566, M19, SJ 934 984, Cotton, C.
996. Kingston Mills, 53544, L19, SJ 941 953, Cotton, C.
997. Leach Street Mill, 53588, E19?, SJ 962 985, ?, C.
998. Lees Street Mill, 53503, E20, SJ 938 996, Cotton waste, C.
999. Limefield Mill, 53585, M19?, SJ 997 935, Cotton, C.
1000. Longdendale Works, 53579, L19, SK 010 959, Bleachworks, C.
1001. Longlands Mill, 53477, M19?, SD 974 021, Cotton, C.
1002. Lumb Mill, 53578, L19, SJ 911 994, Cotton, C.
1003. Mersey Mills, 53580, L19, SK 011 960, Cotton, B.
1004. Milton Mill, 53481, L19, SD 976 025, Cotton, C.
1005. Newton Bank Works, 53550, L19, SJ 952 952, Print works, C.
1006. Newton Moor Mills, 53551, M19?, SJ 953 961, Cotton, C.
1007. Northend Mill, 53570, M19–L19, SJ 967 988, Cotton (part of), C.
1008. Oakwood Mills, 53523, M19–L19, SJ 978 997, Cotton, C.
1009. Old Mill, 53506, L19, SJ 945 984, Cotton, C.
1010. Oxford Mills, 53535, M19, SJ 931 980, Cotton, C.

1011. Park Road Mill, 53507, L19, SJ 946 984, Cotton, dyeworks, C.
1012. Phoenix Mill, 53540, L19, SJ 920 957, Yarn winding, C.
1013. Phoenix Mill?, 53586, M19, SJ 955 981, ?, C.
1014. Premier Mills, 53513, E20?, SJ 952 983, Cotton, C.
1015. Providence Mill, 53558, L19, SJ 944 945, Cotton, C.
1016. Quarry Street Mills, 53539, L19, SJ 958 981, Cotton, C.
1017. Queen Street Mill, 53476, M19?, SD 975 021, Cotton, C.
1018. Ray Mill, 53512, E20, SJ 952 983, Cotton, C.
1019. Ray Mills, 53512, ?, SJ 952 983, Cotton, C.
1020. Rhodes Mill, 53580, L19, SK 011 960, Cotton, B.
1021. River Etherow Works, 53581, L19, SK 010 962, Bleachworks, B.
1022. River Meadow Mills, 53524, L19, SJ 971 993, Cotton, C.
1023. River Mill, 53475, M19?, SD 974 019, Cotton, C.
1024. River Mill, 53508, L19?, SJ 947 984, Cotton, C.
1025. Royal Mill, 53592, L19, SJ 910 991, Cotton, C.
1026. Ryecroft Mills, 53498, M19, SJ 927 983, Cotton, C.
1027. Saxon Mill, 53591, E20, SJ 906 988, Cotton, C.
1028. Slack Mills, 53556, E20, SJ 954 945, Cotton, C.
1029. Smith Street Mill, 53488, M19, SD 969 026, Cotton?, C.
1030. Spring Grove Mill, 53495, M19–L19, SJ 976 999, Woollen, C.
1031. Springfield Works, 53571, L19, SJ 895 976, Print works, C.
1032. Squire Mills, 53486, L19, SD 983 020, Woollen, C.
1033. Staley Mill, 53522, L19, SJ 977 996, Cotton, C.
1034. Stamford Commercial Mill, 53493, L19, SD 952 000, Cotton, A.
1035. Standard Mill, 53566, M19, SJ 934 984, Cotton, C.
1036. Stokes Mill, 53526, M19–L19, SJ 967 987, Cotton waste, C.
1037. Tame Valley Mill, 53510, M19, SJ 950 983, Cotton, C.
1038. Tameside Mills, 53509, L19, SJ 948 983, Cotton, C.
1039. Throstle Bank Mill, 53576, L19, SJ 942 956, Cotton, C.
1040. Tower Mill, 53511, E20?, SJ 951 983, Cotton, C.
1041. Union Mill, 53474, L19, SD 981 033, Cotton, C.
1042. Vale Mill, 53487, M19–L19, SD 984 020, Woollen, C.
1043. Valley Mills, 53489, M19?, SD 969 027, Cotton, C.
1044. Victor Mill, 53514, E20, SJ 953 982, Cotton, C.
1045. Victoria Mill, 53538, L19–E20, SJ 942 967, Cotton (part of), C.
1046. Victoria Mills, 53479, L19?, SD 975 022, Cotton, C.
1047. Victoria Mills, 53528, M19, SJ 901 981, Cotton, C.
1048. Waterside Mill, 53504, L19, SJ 944 985, Cotton, C.
1049. Weir Mill, 53496, L19, SD 973 010, Cotton, C.
1050. Wellington Mills, 53505, L19, SJ 945 986, Cotton, C.
1051. Wellington Mills, 53504, L19, SJ 944 985, Cotton, C.
1052. West End Mill, 53563, M19?, SJ 988 938, Cotton, C.
1053. Wharfe Mill, 53500, E19?, SJ 938 988, Cotton, C.
1054. Whitelands Mill, 53520, L19, SJ 950 986, Cotton, C.
1055. Whitelands Weaving Shed, 53568, L19, SJ 944 985, Cotton, C.
1056. Woodend Mill, 53483, E19–L19, SD 977 026, Cotton, C.

# Wigan

1057. Actons Mill, 53904, E19?, SD 584 051, Cotton, C.
1058. Atherton Mill, 53909, L19, SD 686 022, Cotton, C.
1059. Atherton Mills, 53882, L19, SD 680 033, Cotton, C.
1060*. Barnfield Mills, 53885, L19, SD 689 022, Cotton, A.

1061. Bedford New Mills, 53887, L19, SD 667 001, Cotton and silk, C.
1062. Bradley Mills, 53869, L19, SD 572 112, Cotton?, C.
1063. Britannia Mill, 53903, M19?, SD 576 053, Cotton, C.
1064. Brook Mill, 53889, L19, SD 663 002, Cotton and silk, B.
1065. Brooklands Mill, 53893, L19, SD 664 996, Cotton, C.
1066. Brookside Mill, 53888, L19, SD 661 003, Cotton, C.
1067. Butts Mill, 53896, E20, SJ 667 994, Cotton, B.
1068. Charles Street Mill, 53911, L19, SD 660 003, Silk, C.
1069. Crescent Mill, 53907, L19, SD 597 055, Cotton?, C.
1070. Dan Lane Mills, 53884, L19?, SD 676 030, Cotton, C.
1071. Dicconson Mills, 53878, M19–L19, SD 630 073, Cotton, C.
1072. Douglas Mill, 53869, L19, SD 572 112, Cotton?, C.
1073. Elizabeth Mills, 53915, M19?, SD 582 051, ?, C.
1074. Empress Industrial Estate, 53906, E20, SD 597 053, Cotton weaving?, C.
1075. Ena Mill, 53880, E20, SD 673 035, Cotton, C.
1076. Enfield Mill, 53877, L19, SD 553 043, Cotton, C.
1077. Etherstone Mill, 53901, L19, SJ 651 998, Cotton, C.
1078. Gidlow Works, 53918, L19, SD 579 065, Cotton, C.
1079. Haigh Works, 53871, L19, SD 582 082, Dyeworks, C.
1080. Hall Lane Mill, 53892, L19, SJ 663 996, Cotton, C.
1081. Hindley Green Mills, 53883, L19, SD 635 034, Cotton, C.
1082. Howe Bridge Mills, 53881, L19, SD 673 033, Cotton, C.
1083. Kirkhall Lane Mills, 53891, L19?, SD 657 012, Cotton, C.
1084. Leigh Manufacturing Co, 53898, E20, SD 668 996, Cotton, C.
1085. Leigh Spinners Mills, 53899, E20, SJ 674 997, Cotton, A.
1086. Makerfield Mill, 53886, E20, SD 580 987, Cotton, C.
1087. Mather Lane Mills (part of), 53894, L19, SJ 663 997, Cotton, C.
1088. Mather Lane Mills (part of), 53893, L19, SJ 664 996, Cotton, C.
1089. Parkside Mills, 53913, M19–L19, SJ 605 976, Cotton, C.
1090. Pendle Mill, 53897, E20, SJ 669 995, Cotton, B.
1091. Pennyhurst Mill?, 53903, M19?, SD 576 053, Cotton, C.
1092. Platt Lane Mill, 53879, L19, SD 618 042, Cotton, C.
1093. Princess Street Mill, 53915, M19?, SD 582 051, ?, C.
1094. Prospect Mill, 53879, L19, SD 618 042, Cotton, C.
1095. Resolution Mill, 53885, L19, SD 689 022, Cotton, A.
1096. Sandbrook Mill, 53876, E20, SD 526 041, Cotton, C.
1097. Signal Mill, 53876, E20, SD 526 041, Cotton, C.
1098. Standish Works, 53870, L19, SD 579 101, Bleach and dyeworks, B.
1099. Stanley Mill, 53895, L19, SJ 665 997, Cotton, C.
1100. Swan Meadow Mills, 53874, L19, SD 577 050, Cotton, B.
1101. Swan Meadow Mills, 53875, L19, SD 576 050, Cotton, B.
1102. Trencherfield Mill, 53873, E20, SD 578 051, Cotton, C.
1103. Upper Mills, 53910, L19, SJ 600 979, Cotton, C.
1104. Victoria Mills, 53872, M19–L19, SD 576 053, Cotton, C.
1105. Victoria Mills, 53890, L19, SD 653 009, Cotton, C.
1106. Welch Mill, 53902, L19–E20, SJ 653 999, Cotton, C.
1107. Welsh Hill Mill, 53902, L19–E20, SJ 653 999, Cotton, C.
1108. Western Mills, 53875, L19, SD 576 050, Cotton, C.
1109. Wharfe Mill, 53915, M19?, SD 582 051, ?, C.
1110. Whittaker's Mill, 53918, L19, SD 579 065, Cotton, C.
1111. Williams Street Works, 53912, L19, SD 664 001, Dyeworks, C.
1112. Wood Street Mill, 53904, E19?, SD 584 051, Cotton, C.

# Notes

## 1. Introduction

1. The methodology of the mills survey is discussed in Williams 1987–8*a* and Williams 1987–8*b*.
2. Farnie 1979, Chapter 2. See also Daniels 1927.
3. Farnie 1979, 47–50.
4. For a general description and illustrations of cotton growing in the United States and its export to Liverpool see Mortimer 1894, 95.
5. Farnie 1979, 14–15.
6. Tippett 1969, Chapter 2.
7. The count is the amount of yarn spun from a pound of raw cotton. The length of yarn was measured in units of 840 yards, known as 'hanks'.
8. For a general introduction to textile machinery see Benson 1983. On the historical development of cotton machinery see Mann 1958 and Aspin 1981. A more detailed account of the processes in a 20th-century mill is given in Tippett 1969, Chapter 3. For a contrasting description of processes in the 1840s see A Day at a Cotton Factory, *Supplement to The Penny Magazine*, 1843, 12.
9. The manual willowing of Sea Island cotton, which was used to spin the finest yarns, was still carried out in the 1830s when it was described by an American visitor to Murray's Mills, Manchester (358*). See Allen 1831.
10. The invention and development of the mule are described in Catling 1970.

## 2. The cotton towns of Greater Manchester

1. An estimate for which I am indebted to Dr S. D. Chapman of the University of Nottingham.
2. Chapman 1981–2, 8.
3. [Mallalieu] 1836, 408.
4. Anon 1858, 251.
5. Esher 1981, 274.
6. Ryan 1937, 45, by the daughter of E. C. Montague.
7. *The Textile Mercury*, 29 July 1904, 65 (Beehive No. 2); *Textile Recorder*, August 1905, 115–17 (Cromer); *Magazine of Commerce*, February 1906, 99–102 (Maple, Asia, Durban, Cromer, Don, Soudan); *The Engineer*, December 1906, 652 (Soudan, Heron, Regent, Texas); *Engineering*, 11 January 1907, 50 (Cromer, Nile, Asia, Don).
8. Mills 1921, 12.
9. [Lamb] 1856, 631.
10. Worrall 1893. Greater Manchester comprises the seventeen towns listed in the note on sources appended to Table 1, pp. 46–7.
11. The Fine Cotton Spinners' and Doublers' Association was formed in 1898, the Amalgamated Cotton Mills Trust in 1918, Crosses and Winkworth Consolidated Mills in 1920, and the Lancashire Cotton Corporation as well as Combined Egyptian Mills in 1929.
12. Worrall 1927.
13. Hart 1965, 70, 83, 121–2.
14. Jacobs 1969, 88.
15. Moorhouse 1964, 121, 127. For the author's later recantation see What Manchester does today ...? *The Listener*, 6 March 1980, 300.
16. Stewart 1956.
17. Dodd 1852, 6; Anon 1858, 251. With heavy irony, Dickens dubbed the mills of Coketown 'fairy palaces' in *Hard Times* (1854). The mills of Manchester impressed Taine in 1862 as 'economical and colossal prisons'. Hyams 1957, 219.
18. Bailey 1985 (a thesis of outstanding importance); Lloyd-Jones and Lewis 1988; Walter 1976, 22–3. The last is by the American scholar who in 1975 discovered the volume of 'Plans of all the Spinning Factories within the Township of Manchester' (1821) and secured its transfer to the John Rylands Library.
19. *Factory Inspectors' Reports*, 31 October 1862, 18, where Alexander Redgrave reprints the figure of 2,109 cotton factories in the Lancashire district.
20. Bailey 1984, 3.
21. Chorlton Mills are misleadingly referred to as 'Charlton Mills' in two articles published in *Accounting and Business Research*, **4** (1973), 71 and in the *Economic History Review*, 2nd ser, **42** (November 1989), 487. Manchester's warehouses in 1790–1810 were low-built in contrast to those in Liverpool and were not rebuilt in palatial style until the 1830s.
22. Southey 1951, 213.
23. Bailey 1984, 3.
24. Henderson 1968, 35.
25. Schinkel 1967, 118–19, on the visit paid by the Berlin architect to Manchester on 17 July 1826. 'It makes a horribly dismal impression.'
26. Dodd 1851, 11.
27. Schulze 1853, 266.
28. Ainsworth 1858, 4, 60; [Lowe] 1854, 268–72; Lamb 1872, 170, referring to Ancoats, the 'lowest suburb of Yarndale' as 'Mudlington'.
29. Bailey 1984, 3; Redford 1934, 238; Lewis 1965, 313–14, reveals a marked peak in building in 1853.
30. *The Textile Manufacturer*, 1886, **12**, 562–3; 1892, **18**, 253, Eminent Machinists. Messrs Brooks and Doxey; Farnie 1990*a*, 154.
31. *Factory Inspectors' Reports*, 30 April 1860, 25; Lamb 1866, 95. Lamb's work was a reprint of his 1853 essay on 'Manchester by a Manchester Man'.

32. These dates remain subject to modification in the light of research by local historians.
33. *Wheeler's Manchester Chronicle*, 9 May 1829, 3.
34. Bailey 1985, 76.
35. *Manchester City News*, 4 June 1892, 6ii, Opening of the Ancoats Model Dwellings (a report upon the conversion of Jersey Street Mill into 140 tenements).
36. Nicholas 1945, 51.
37. Brighouse and Forrest 1917, 4. Brighouse presents the most balanced portrait of Salford as it was in 1879 in what originated as a play in 1916, became a novel in 1917 and was then twice filmed, in 1931 and 1953. The most thorough economic history of the borough is provided by V. I. Tomlinson in Bergin *et al* 1975, 19–61.
38. Lowry began to paint industrial scenes from 1912 and mill folk from 1917. *Love on the Dole* was published in 1933, dramatised in 1934 and, after much opposition, filmed in 1941. Shelagh Delaney wrote *A Taste of Honey* as a play, which was first performed in 1958 and filmed in 1961. She then wrote *The White Bus*, which was published in *Sweetly Sings the Donkey* (1964), 123–40, and filmed in 1967. Ewan MacColl (Jimmy Miller) composed *Dirty Old Town* in 1950 and copyrighted it in 1956. *The Classic Slum* was published in 1971.
39. Greenwood 1951, 143–6; Fitton 1989, 146, 149.
40. Salford was the first mill town to erect a public statue to a textile magnate, in the person of the philanthropic spinner Joseph Brotherton (1783–1857).
41. Wright Turner in 1833 at Kingston Mills, Pendleton; Elkanah Armitage in 1836 at Pendleton New Mills, established in 1840; Ermen and Engels at Victoria Mill, Weaste, in 1837; E. R. Langworthy in 1839 at Greengate Mills.
42. Rubinstein 1974, 208, 216, 219.
43. *Factory Inspectors' Reports*, 31 October 1863, 40.
44. Rohde 1979, xix, 134; Nasmith and Nasmith 1909, 164–5, 285–7, a work which was critically reviewed in *Engineering*, 4 November 1910, 619–20.
45. *The Textile Manufacturer*, 1892, **8**, 278; 1894, **10**, 419–21; 1896, **12**, 409–11, showing a five-storeyed mill.
46. Tawney 1968, xii.
47. Hills 1987–8, 32.
48. The mills of Oldknow at the top of Hillgate in 1790, of Orrell in Heaton Norris in 1834 and of Houldsworth (899*), in Reddish in 1865.
49. Chaloner 1949, 132–5, on the sixteen Boulton and Watt engines ordered between 1791 and 1809.
50. Henderson 1968, 136, quoting J. G. May in 1814.
51. Mason 1981, 59–83. The section on Stockport in this chapter has benefited greatly from Dr Mason's helpful comments.
52. Unwin 1924, 29; Simpson 1990, 24, a reference for which I am indebted to Mr Peter Wadsworth; Jeremy 1991, 24–59.
53. Ure 1836, 348.
54. *The Times*, 7 September 1878, 11i.
55. *Stockport Advertiser*, 3 December 1841, 2, quoting the graffito 'Stockport to Let. Enquire of the Town Clerk'; Taylor 1968, 186; *Factory Inspectors' Reports*, 31 October 1862, 142–3; 30 April 1864, 21–5, John Evans 'Historical Summary of the Relief Movement in Stockport'; Coutie 1989, 18–27.
56. *Stockport Advertiser*, 18 March 1881, 7iv; 22 April, 8v; 4 September 1885, 4i; Cotton Mill Building. *The Textile Manufacturer*, 1885, **11**, 411.
57. The three ring-spinning companies established in 1891, 1909 and 1912 under the guidance of Giles Atherton (1852–1931) amalgamated in 1919, with an aggregate of 201,512 ring spindles. The first two companies built what were for their time the largest ring mills in the world, with 53,000 and 72,000 spindles respectively.
58. *Factory Inspectors' Reports*, 31 October 1893, 259.
59. *Stockport Advertiser*, 27 December 1901, 6ii; Crabtree 1907, 18.
60. Gray 1937, 17.
61. Barker 1927, 35.
62. Mills 1924, 56–7.
63. Haynes 1990, 3, 16.
64. Taylor 1968, 227, referring to Stalybridge.
65. *Factory Inspectors' Reports*, 31 October 1851, 10, refers to a new mill intended to hold 126,000 spindles.
66. Taylor 1840, 604.
67. Both Stalybridge and Dukinfield declined in population, as well as Stockport and Glossop.
68. *Ashton under Lyne Reporter*, 7 February 1891, 8iv; Hill 1907, 258; Haynes 1990, 35–6, 41; *Factory Inspectors' Reports*, 31 October 1863, 109, refers to a six-storeyed Manchester mill built in 1863 with a similar plan and dimensions of 40.5 metres by 38.7 metres. *The Textile Manufacturer*, January 1891, 4–5 and February 1891, 55–6, published the 'Plan of a Cotton Mill for Abroad' which was designed by Lancaster & Co of Manchester for 20,000 ring spindles and was almost square in shape, being 100 metres by 99 metres.
69. Haynes 1987, 5–7, 48–53. The seven mills were Minerva (1891), Rock (1891), Atlas (1898), Curzon (1899), Tudor (1901), Cedar (1903) and Texas (1905). Only Tudor Mill had six storeys and Cedar Mill five.
70. *Cotton Factory Times*, 20 February 1885, 5, a paper for operatives published by J. Andrew & Co of Ashton from 1885 to 1937.
71. Hyde established its Technical School in 1899 and its first joint-stock limited in the Hyde Spinning Co Ltd in 1906. In 1903 a peak in building activity was registered for Tameside as a whole (Lewis 1965, 315) and the ring frame was first introduced to the district by the Victor Mill of Stalybridge.
72. Middleton 1952, 447–9, 452–3.
73. Fowler 1979–80.
74. Ure 1836, 346; Jewkes and Gray 1935; Catling 1970, 115–39.
75. Clarke 1893; Madge and Harrisson 1938, 7; Mass Observation 1970; Armstrong 1943, an attribution which I owe to Mr Paul Salveson.
76. *The Textile Manufacturer*, 1876, **2**, 151–2; 1883, **9**, 508.
77. *The Textile Manufacturer*, 1904, **30**, 141; *Textile Mercury*, 10 December 1904, 418.
78. Nasmith and Nasmith 1909, 167; Vose 1919, 136–7.
79. Vose 1919, 62.
80. *Sing as We Go* (1934) had its mill scenes shot at the Denvale Mill, built in 1885 as the Union Mills on Union Road, Tonge Moor. The film of *Love on the Dole* (1941) reportedly had its mill scenes shot in Bolton. Monton Mill (1905) may well have supplied the first interior shot of a cotton mill for the film of *Hindle Wakes* (1931).
81. Tattersall 1914 (1915); 1920 (1921).
82. The thirteen mills built in Leigh between 1902 and 1924 comprised Firs (1902), Alder (1905), Atherton No. 2 (1905), Laburnum (1905, 1914, 1920), Butts (1907), Ena (1907), Leigh Spinners Ltd (1907–13, 1924), Hall Lane (1908–10), Bedford New Mill (1909) and Mill Lane (1912).

83. *The Oxford English Dictionary* dates the first use of 'wigan' in 1875. 'Manchester cloth' referred in the 18th century to fustian, a usage which died out in England but survived in Germany.

84. Dodd 1842, 123–33; Orwell 1937, based upon visits lasting respectively for one day and for two weeks.

85. *Manchester City News*, 15 April 1865, 2; Leigh 1873, 196–7; Farnie 1985, 999–1004. Gidlow Works still remained in use in 1992 with reinforcing cross-ties in its walls dating from a threatened collapse during construction above a colliery in full operation (Figs 25 and 26).

86. Fowler and Wyke 1987, 82, 123.

87. *Oldham Chronicle*, 18 August 1877, 8iii, The Oldham Cotton Trade: the Past and the Present. In 1862 a model of the Sun Mill was displayed at the International Exhibition in London. Today, models of mills may be seen at Styal, at the Oldham Local Studies Centre and at the Bolton Museum.

88. *Oldham Chronicle*, 15 September 1877, 2vi. *The City Lantern*, 11 June 1880, 304, a reference I owe to Mr J. M. Higgins of Royton.

89. *The Textile Manufacturer*, 1890, **16**, 417, 462.

90. Jones 1985, 153–64, 183–94.

91. Tattersall 1898, 8; 1900, 6; Howarth 1975, 17 gives 108,000 spindles; Gurr and Hunt 1989, 42 (see Inventory for description of Nile Mill).

92. Farnie 1984, 506–10.

93. *Oldham Standard*, 14 December 1907, 16iii; 28 November 1908, 12iv; *The Textile Mercury*, 13 June 1908, 455.

94. *Oldham Chronicle*, 3 November 1906, 8viii.

95. *Oldham Chronicle*, 9 October 1920, 14.

96. Gurr and Hunt 1989, 34.

97. *Oldham Chronicle*, 28 May 1898, 7iv.

98. *The Textile Mercury*, 12 May 1906, 349; 21 December 1907, 481; *Oldham Standard*, 6 December 1907, 6vi; *Oldham Chronicle*, 30 May 1908, 12vi.

99. Nasmith and Nasmith 1909, 162; *Textile Recorder*, 15 August 1906, 115.

100. *Oldham Chronicle*, 1 November 1919, 11v; 7 February 1920, 14v; 25 September 1920, 14v; *Textile Recorder*, September 1920, 66; October 1920, 71; December 1920, 79; Hansard, *Parliamentary Debates, House of Commons*, 10 May 1920, 13–14; 21 February 1921, 590–1.

101. Muir 1964.

102. The fly-shuttle in 1733, the drop box in 1760 and the Diggle chain for the drop box in 1845, together with Henry Whitehead's technique of piecing yarn whilst the mule remained in motion, introduced in 1791.

103. *The Textile Manufacturer*, 1885, **11**, 410; *Bury Times*, 21 May 1887, 6vi. The new company added two more mills in 1892 and 1913–15 and so raised its capacity from 68,000 spindles in 1887 to 244,092 in 1915. It ceased cotton spinning in 1975, became a property company as Peel Holdings Ltd in 1981 and acquired a majority shareholding in the Manchester Ship Canal Company in 1987.

104. Howarth 1974.

105. The five other cotton towns which increased their inhabitants between 1911 and 1971 were Leigh, Swinton, Middleton, Glossop and Hyde, under the influence in the latter three cases of the resettlement of 'overspill' population from Manchester.

106. *Rochdale Observer*, 17 May 1890, 5i.

107. *Rochdale Observer*, 10 May 1890, 5i.

108. *Rochdale Observer*, 24 May 1890, 4vi.

109. *Rochdale Observer*, 28 June 1890, 4vi, Milnrow Ring Spinning Companies, on the three companies, the New Ladyhouse (1877), the Haugh (1881) and the Newhey Spinning Companies (1884), which were formally amalgamated only in 1953 as Newhey Rings Ltd.

110. *Rochdale Observer*, 21 December 1889, 6ii; 4 January 1890, 6iv.

111. Atkinson 1973, 309–38; *Textile Recorder*, December 1894, 269, The Ventilation of Cotton Spinning Mills.

112. Nasmith and Nasmith 1909, 169; Platt Bros, 1907, *Catalogue of Cotton Spinning and Weaving Machinery*, 318, included a plan for a two-storeyed ring mill for 74,100 spindles, with basement.

113. *Oldham Chronicle*, 21 February 1920, 14iv; *The Statist*, 11 September 1920, 454. Night-shift working in mule mills was not introduced until 1959, at the Mersey Mill in Failsworth (*Oldham Evening Chronicle*, 30 October 1959, 10).

114. Ashworth 1915, 50–3; Ashworth 1918, 69–80; Ashworth 1919, 109–19.

115. Johnson and Skempton 1955–7, 179–205; Fitton and Wadsworth 1958, 97, 196.

116. Quarry Bank Mill at Styal was transferred to the National Trust in 1939. Cromford Mill was listed in 1950, Masson Mill at Matlock Bath in 1955, the North Mill at Belper in 1966 (the first to be scheduled as a class I monument), the New Lanark Mills in 1971 (relisted in 1973 as Class A monuments) and the Houldsworth's Mill at Reddish (899*), together with the Wellington Mill in Stockport (937), in 1975.

117. Until recently Crimble Mill had a plaque on one building with the following inscription:

> THE FAMILY OF KENYON were landowners and yeoman farmers in this district from the time of Queen Elizabeth I or earlier. A John Kenyon was a fuller and cloth-worker at Castleton in the middle of the 17th century and the family were living at Kenyon Fold in the early years of the 18th century. They soon started on this exact site to follow their trade of fulling, textile processing and subsequently textile manufacture which by the Grace of God they pursued here at Crimble for over 200 years.

> This memorial tablet was erected by James Christopher Kenyon, Chairman of James Kenyon & Son Ltd in December 1970 AD when Kenyons left Crimble.

## 3. Early mills, 1780–1825

1. Although Manchester contains the best-preserved early mills in the county, significant early mill building also took place in other nearby towns. In Stockport, where Wear Mill (934*) was begun *c*.1790, sixty-seven steam engines were in use by 1825, mostly in cotton mills (Ashmore 1975, 13). In Bolton numerous smaller mills were built (Longworth 1986, Chapter 2).

2. Lee 1972, 114.

3. Lloyd-Jones and le Roux 1980, 77.

4. For a discussion of the business structure of Manchester in the early 19th century see Lloyd-Jones and Lewis 1988.

5. Lloyd-Jones and Lewis 1988, 50.

6. A list of Newcomen or Savery engines in use in late 18th-century factories states that Manchester contained twenty-eight, Bolton eight, Stockport four, Oldham four and Salford three (Tann 1970, 91). Manchester's cotton mills probably accounted for at least thirty-two steam engines by 1800, with an estimated total of 430 horsepower (Baines 1835, 226).

7. Lloyd-Jones and Lewis 1988, 88.

8. Peter Drinkwater, for example, had considerable involvement with the design of his Piccadilly Mill, Manchester (366), in the late 1780s; see Chaloner 1954. Another example was the Salford Twist Mill, Salford (849), of 1802, which was in part designed by George Lee of the cotton-spinning firm of Phillips and Lee; see Fitzgerald 1987–8a, 129.

9. For a discussion of the role of the millwright see Tann 1974, 80–9.

10. Fitzgerald 1987–8a, 137.

11. Lloyd-Jones and Lewis 1988, 33.

12. Musson and Robinson 1969, 400.

13. On early steam engines see Dickinson 1963, Chapters 3 and 4 and Hills 1989, Chapters 2 and 3.

14. Musson and Robinson 1969, 400–1.

15. Plans of all the Spinning Factories within the Township of Manchester, c.1822, 107. John Rylands University Library, Manchester.

16. Thompson 1967, 227–9.

17. Chapman 1981–2. Arkwright-type cotton mills were preceded by large water-powered silk mills built earlier in the 18th century, notable examples being Thomas Lombe's Mill in Derby (1718–21), Carrs Mill in Stockport (1732), and Old Mill, Congleton (1752). The last had similar dimensions to Arkwright's Manchester mill and is partially extant, albeit lowered to two storeys (see Calladine and Fricker forthcoming).

18. Chapman 1981–2, Appendix B, 26–7.

19. Tann 1970, 75.

20. Thompson 1967, 227–9.

21. Musson and Robinson 1969, 400–1.

22. Tann 1970, 73.

23. Lee 1972, 9.

24. Tann 1970, 73.

25. Plans of all the Spinning Factories within the Township of Manchester, c.1822, 25. John Rylands University Library, Manchester.

26. See Lee 1972, 104–5, on the economic advantages of mule making for McConnel and Kennedy.

27. Chaloner 1954, 78–102.

28. On the development of rotary condensing engines see Dickinson 1963, Chapters 5 and 6 and Hills 1989, Chapters 4 and 5.

29. Plans of all the Spinning Factories within the Township of Manchester, 53. John Rylands University Library, Manchester.

30. Owen resigned in 1794 and by 1796 had formed the successful Chorlton Twist Company at nearby Chorlton on Medlock. In 1799 he left Manchester to develop the well-known mill community at New Lanark, Scotland. Chaloner 1954, 92–102.

31. Green's *Map of Manchester*, published in 1794, shows the new streets of Ancoats superimposed on the old field boundaries and the undeveloped site of Murray's Mills, Manchester (358*).

32. Boulton and Watt Collection, Portfolio 167, Birmingham Library Services.

33. Extra materials for A and G Murray, March 1802. Boulton and Watt Collection, BVX7 IV, Birmingham Library Services.

34. The following eleven cotton mills dating from 1825 or earlier were extant in Manchester and Salford in June 1991: Murray's Mills, 1798–1806 (358*); the Hulme Street Wing of Chorlton Old Mill, c.1803 but later partly rebuilt (325); Medlock Mill, c.1813 (354); Marsland's Mill, c.1813 but later partly rebuilt (353); Chorlton New Mill, 1814–17 (323*); Sedgwick Mill, part of McConnel and Kennedy's site, 1818–20 (372*); Chatham Mill, c.1823 (320); Islington Mill, Salford, 1823–4 (829*); Beehive Mill, c.1824 (306*); Brownsfield Mill, c.1825 (315*) and possibly parts of the Cambridge Street India Rubber Works, originally a cotton mill, c.1825 (317).

35. Daniels 1927.

36. The close association of early mills with the canal system is shown on Bancks and Co's *Plan of Manchester and Salford*, published 1831.

37. The bricks for McConnel and Kennedy's early mills were fired from clay dug from the mill site in Ancoats (Lee 1972, 102).

38. The means of opening mill windows for ventilation were usually reported in the 1834 Parliamentary survey of working conditions for children in factories. Parliamentary Papers (House of Commons), 1834 (167), *Employment of Children in Factories* XX, D1.

39. This and other installations are illustrated in Tann 1970, 144.

40. For contemporary illustrations of other early ventilation systems see Tann 1970, 117.

41. Freeman 1891, 177.

42. Macleod *et al*, 1988; Johnson and Skempton, 1955–7, 30.

43. Fitzgerald 1987–8a, 128–9; Skempton and Johnson 1962, 131.

44. Fitzgerald 1987–8a, 129.

45. Macleod *et al*, 1988, 63.

46. Fitzgerald 1987–8b, 219–20.

47. The last known example to be built in Manchester is the three lower storeys in the Cotton Mill wing of Great Bridgewater Street Mills (339), probably dating from c.1840.

48. In Manchester this type of construction was also used for the lower three storeys of the Silk Mill in Great Bridgewater Street Mills (339), built c.1828, and for the Wire Mill, an engineering works of c.1820, on Laystall Street.

49. Freeman 1891, 276–7. It was also thought that cast-iron columns could shatter if sprayed with water during a fire; see *The Textile Manufacturer*, 1877, **3**, 6, Fireproof Mill Construction.

50. Candee 1989, 21–34.

51. Crest Ring Mill (626), near Rochdale, demolished 1988. Described in Nasmith and Nasmith 1909, 168–9.

52. For example, at Ebley Mill and Dunkirk Mill, Gloucestershire.

53. Drawings of mill roof for Messrs Birley and Hornby, 1815. Boulton and Watt Collection, Portfolio 449, Birmingham Library Services.

54. Ashmore 1975, 10–11.

55. Fairbairn 1869, 197.

56. Inventories of McConnel and Kennedy 1797–1811. Inventory of Stock and Debts owing to and by McConnel and Kennedy, 4 January 1800, 55–76. John Rylands University Library, Manchester

57. M'Connel 1906, 38–9.

58. *The Textile Manufacturer*, 1876, **2**, 249, The Planning and

Construction of Cotton Mills and Weaving Sheds.

59. Jones 1985, 183.
60. Beehive Mill, Manchester (306*), was built as a slow-burning room and power mill. Islington Mill, Salford (829*), was a fireproof room and power mill.
61. Plans of all the Spinning Factories within the Township of Manchester, c.1822, includes plans of sixty-four sites, external boiler houses being named at twenty-three. John Rylands University Library, Manchester.
62. For example at McConnel and Kennedy's Old Mill, Manchester (363), of 1798; M'Connel 1906, 39.
63. For a general history of the development of the factory chimney see Douet nd.
64. Integral chimneys at McConnel and Kennedy's Old Mill (363) and Sedgwick Mill (372*), Manchester, are illustrated in a watercolour of the site in c.1820; M'Connel 1906, frontispiece.
65. Fitzgerald 1987–8*b*, 222–6.
66. *The Textile Manufacturer*, 1876, **2**, 283, The Planning and Construction of Cotton Mills and Weaving Sheds.
67. Pole 1877, 115.
68. Ewart to Southern, 12 August 1791. Boulton and Watt Collection, Letters Box 19, Birmingham Library Services.
69. Section and Plan with Mr Lee's letter of 26 December 1800, Boulton and Watt Collection, Folio 242, Birmingham Library Services.
70. Hughes 1853, 11; Tann 1970, 124.
71. Chorlton New Mill, Manchester (323*); proposed basement plan for Messrs Birley and Hornby, 2 December 1813, Boulton and Watt Collection, Portfolio 449, Birmingham Library Services. Columns were also used for piping gas at Albion Mill, Manchester (298); Fitzgerald 1987–8*b*, 221.

## 4. Mid nineteenth-century mills, 1825–1860

1. Fitzgerald 1987–8*a*, 139–41. For a Yorkshire example, see Robinwood Mill, Todmorden with Walsden; Giles and Goodall 1992.
2. The machinery in Brunswick Mill, Manchester (316*), is listed in a Schedule included with a Conveyance dated 22 December 1856. Deeds of Brunswick Mill, inspected courtesy of the owners, Leslie Fink Ltd. For Orrell's Mill (907) see Fig 71.
3. Thelwall 1972, introduction.
4. Ure 1836, 296–304.
5. Bellhouse is named as the builder of Islington Mill, Salford (829*), in the *Manchester Guardian*, 16 October 1824, 3. The firm received the contract to build Brunswick Mill in 1839: Specifications of Sundry Works, February 1839, in Deeds of Brunswick Mill. See also Fitzgerald, 1987–8*b*, 206.
6. Clark 1977–8, 213. Bellhouse are recorded as architects in a list of Manchester firms using canal water to supply steam plant in 1820: Rochdale Canal Company Papers, Greater Manchester Record Office.
7. Fairbairn 1865, 114.
8. Ure 1836, 304.
9. For example at Shaddon Mill, Carlisle: see Jones 1985, 58–9.
10. An account of the collapse of Islington Mill, Salford (829*), is included in the Parliamentary Papers (House of Commons), 1845 (c628), *Report on the Fall of the Cotton Mill at Oldham, and part of the prison at Northleach*, XVI, 43–5.
11. Hodgkinson 1831.
12. Freeman 1891, 177.
13. Schedule with Conveyance of 22 December 1856, Deeds of Brunswick Mill, Leslie Fink Ltd, 121 Princess Street, Manchester.
14. Anon 1888, 87.
15. Watkins 1971, 98.
16. Plan of Engine House and Boiler House with Cross-Section of Engine House, for Messrs Birley and Kirk, 10 January 1828. Boulton and Watt Collection, Portfolio 104, Birmingham Library Services.
17. For more information on McNaughted engines see Dickinson 1963, 106–7 and Hills 1989, 157–9.
18. Sales by Auction . . ., *Bury Times*, 14 May 1859, 5.
19. Thelwall 1972, 14.

## 5. Late nineteenth-century mills, 1860–1900

1. *The Textile Manufacturer*, 1876, **2**, 249.
2. Ibid.
3. Farnie 1979, 284–6
4. Fairbairn 1865, 115–16. See also Sington 1892. Cromer Mill, Chadderton (629), was a shed mill built for spinning; see Nasmith and Nasmith 1909, 161. Spur Mill, Reddish (919), was a shed mill built for doubling cotton yarn; see Frank Wightman Collection, No 645, Q19/57/1–2, Greater Manchester Record Office.
5. Nasmith and Nasmith 1909, Chapter 1.
6. This account of the best-known mill architects relies on recently published works: see Jones 1985, Gurr and Hunt 1989 and Holden 1987–8. The largest collection of mill architects' drawings in Greater Manchester is held by the Oldham Local Studies Library.
7. Gurr and Hunt 1989, 35. On the mill architecture of the Stotts see Holden 1987–8, 163–7.
8. Woodhouse was also partly responsible for Bolton Town Hall; see Jones 1985, 147–8.
9. For example the Howe Bridge Mills, Atherton (1082), and probably Barnfield Mills, Tyldesley (1060*); Jones 1985, 165–8, 191.
10. Jones 1985, 159.
11. Gurr and Hunt 1989, 32.
12. Farnie 1989, 9.
13. Manchester's textile warehouses were already noted for their architectural quality in the 1840s; see Archer 1985, 5. For a full discussion of Italianate industrial architecture see Jones 1985, Chapter 7.
14. Nasmith and Nasmith 1909, 70.
15. Freeman 1891.
16. Nasmith and Nasmith 1909, 174.
17. Freeman 1891, 229.
18. Sington 1892, parts 4 and 5.
19. Freeman 1891, 228.
20. Nasmith and Nasmith 1909, 29.
21. Gurr and Hunt 1989, 35.
22. *The Textile Mercury*, 1894, **10**, 373–9.
23. Extant examples of A. H. Stott's construction are the Reddish Spinning Company's Mill, Reddish (912), and part of Swan Meadow Mills, Wigan (1100). A well-known early example was Abbey Mill, Oldham (391), of 1875; see *The Textile Manufacturer*, 1876, **2**, 153–7 and Illustrated Supplement.

24. Freeman 1891, 229–30.
25. Fairbairn 1865, illustration on p. 96.
26. Jones 1985, 146.
27. Freeman 1891, 229.
28. Jones 1985, 159.
29. Freeman 1891, 230.
30. *The Textile Manufacturer*, 1876, **2**, 153–7.
31. *The Textile Manufacturer*, 1876, **2**, 249.
32. Jones 1985, 189.
33. *The Textile Manufacturer*, 1876, **2**, 283.
34. Ibid.
35. Nasmith and Nasmith 1909, 30–1.
36. *The Textile Mercury*, 1894, **10**, 374.
37. Nasmith and Nasmith 1909, 173.
38. Dickinson 1984, Chapter 4; Watkins 1971, 98.
39. Douet nd, 13.
40. Dickinson 1984, 39.
41. Barker 1898 and Dickinson 1984, 32.
42. *The Textile Manufacturer*, 1876, **2**, 157.
43. *The Textile Manufacturer*, 1898, **24**, 421–4.
44. For a summary of the development of the late 19th-century mill engine see Dickinson 1984, Chapter 2; for further examples of late 19th-century mill engines see Watkins 1971.
45. Dickinson 1984, 11.
46. George Watkins Collection, SER 665, Royal Commission on the Historical Monuments of England, Salisbury.
47. Penn 1981.
48. *The Textile Manufacturer*, 1876, **2**, 153–7.
49. Watkins 1971, 102–5.
50. *The Textile Manufacturer*, 1877, **3**, 209.
51. George Watkins Collection, SER 821, Royal Commission on the Historical Monuments of England, Salisbury.

## Early twentieth-century mills, 1900–1926

1. Holden 1987–8.
2. Jones 1985, 190.
3. Holden 1987–8, 171.
4. Jones 1985, 60.
5. Gurr and Hunt 1989, 32.
6. Holden 1987–8, 163–7.
7. Nasmith and Nasmith 1909, 163.
8. Gurr and Hunt 1989, 57.
9. Jones 1985, 186.
10. Jones 1985, 159.
11. Freeman 1891, 230.
12. Jones 1985, 183.
13. Nasmith and Nasmith 1909, Chapter 3.
14. *The Textile Mercury*, 1903, **28**, 201–2.
15. Sington 1892; Nasmith and Nasmith 1909, 69.
16. Sington 1892.
17. Nasmith and Nasmith 1909, 161; see pp. 41–2.
18. Frank Wightman Collection, No 645, Q19/57/1–2, Greater Manchester Record Office.
19. The George Watkins Collection, SER 681 and 683, Royal Commission on the Historical Monuments of England, Salisbury.
20. Dickinson 1984, Chapter 2; Watkins 1971.
21. The George Watkins Collection, SER 146, Royal Commission on the Historical Monuments of England, Salisbury.
22. Watkins 1971, 104.

23. Register of Historic Steam Engines, 55 D81, 325, West Yorkshire Archives Service: Bradford.
24. Watkins 1971, 104.
25. The George Watkins Collection, SER 158, Royal Commission on the Historical Monuments of England, Salisbury.
26. The George Watkins Collection, SER 717, Royal Commission on the Historical Monuments of England, Salisbury.
27. The George Watkins Collection, SER 725, Royal Commission on the Historical Monuments of England, Salisbury; Longworth 1986, 60.
28. Dickinson 1984, 15–17; Nasmith and Nasmith 1909, 165, 285.
29. *The Textile Mercury*, 1910, **42**, 142–7.

## Inventory

1. Farnie and Yonekawa 1988, 173.
2. George Watkins Collection, SER 710, Royal Commission on the Historical Monuments of England, Salisbury.
3. Building Control Plans, Plan 18948, Bolton MBC.
4. Building Control Plans, Plan 19426, Bolton MBC.
5. George Watkins Collection, SER 789, Royal Commission on the Historical Monuments of England, Salisbury.
6. Deeds of Gilnow Mill, Conveyance of 1857, inspected courtesy of the owners, Nortex Ltd.
7. Crosses and Winkworth were the fifth largest cotton-spinning firm in the world in 1888: Farnie and Yonekawa 1988, 171–210.
8. George Watkins Collection, SER 594, Royal Commission on the Historical Monuments of England, Salisbury.
9. Nasmith and Nasmith 1909, 287; Dickinson 1984, 15, 17.
10. Plan of Land in the Barnfield Holme belonging to Robert Barlow and Joseph Blundell, 10 December 1792, ZAL/742, Bolton Archives.
11. Poor Rate, 1836, PBL/3/25, 142, Bolton Archives.
12. *Bolton Journal and Guardian*, 14 October 1904, 8.
13. Nasmith and Nasmith 1909, 167–8.
14. George Watkins Collection, SER 681, Royal Commission on the Historical Monuments of England, Salisbury.
15. Worrall 1884; and Worrall 1898.
16. Manchester Poor Rate, 1829, **1**, District No. 1, 86, M9/40/2/100, Manchester City Archives.
17. Swire 1824.
18. Examples in Yorkshire mills include Healey New Mill, Ossett, 1825–7, and Carlinghow Mills, Batley, 1831; see Giles and Goodall 1992. Another example in Manchester is the *c.*1840 wing of Great Bridgewater Street Mills (339).
19. Poor Rate, 1827–1901, District No. 4, Manchester City Archives; Kelly 1912, 314.
20. Schedule with the Conveyance dated 22 December 1856. Deeds of Brunswick Mill, inspected courtesy of the owners, Leslie Fink Ltd.
21. Specification of Sundry Works intended to be done in the Erection of a seven storey Fireproof Mill for Messrs Kelly and Gilmour in Bradford Road, February 1839, Deeds of Brunswick Mill.
22. For further information on Bannermans see Mortimer 1891.
23. *The Textile Mercury*, 1910, **42**, 142–7, Electrical Driving at the Bannerman Company's Brunswick Mill, Manchester.
24. Anon 1951, 17.
25. Building Control Plans, Plan 2623, Manchester City Council.
26. Boulton and Watt Collection, Portfolios 104, 449, 531, 1051,

Birmingham Library Services.

27. For the history of Chorlton New Mill, Manchester (323*), and other mills in Chorlton on Medlock see Clark 1977–8.
28. Tann 1970, 124.
29. Lee 1972, 12; M'Connel 1913, 8.
30. Lee 1972, Chapter 3.
31. Boulton and Watt Collection, Portfolio 167, Birmingham Library Services.
32. Similar towers used for the ventilation of contemporary mills are illustrated in Tann 1970, 117.
33. Building Control Plans, Plan 9038, Manchester City Council.
34. For the history of the firm of McConnel and Kennedy see Lee 1972 and M'Connel 1913.
35. Fairbairn 1869, 197.
36. Boulton and Watt Collection, Portfolio 465, Birmingham Library Services.
37. Plans of all the Spinning Factories in the Township of Manchester, *c*.1822, 9. John Rylands University Library, Manchester.
38. Fairbairn 1866, 181–5.
39. See illustration of the mill entitled 'Ancoats Doubling Mill', in M'Connel 1906, 26.
40. The engine house is identified in an 1899 block plan of the site: Building Control Plans, Plan 6376, Manchester City Council.
41. Building Control Plans, Plan 10131, Manchester City Council.
42. Building Control Plans, Plan 4716, Oldham MBC.
43. The machinery was by Platts of Oldham. See Platt-Saco-Lowell Papers, Order Books for scutchers, carding engines, drawing frames and mules, Lancashire Record Office, Preston.
44. Building Control Plans, Plan 1734, Oldham MBC.
45. Register of Historic Steam Engines, 55 D81, 325, West Yorkshire Archive Service: Bradford.
46. Gurr and Hunt 1989, 42.
47. Worrall 1910, 241.
48. *The Textile Manufacturer*, 1898, **24**, 421–3.
49. Gurr and Hunt 1989, 46.
50. For the history of the Kenyons of Crimble Mill, Rochdale (627*), see Muir 1964.
51. Sale by Auction, *Bury Times*, 14 May 1854, 5.
52. Information on the layout of woollen machinery in the mid 20th century was kindly provided by a former employee, Mr George Baker.
53. Worrall 1910, 287.
54. 1880 entry, Spotland Mill Valuation, CBR 5/158, Lancashire Record Office, Preston.
55. George Watkins Collection, SER 861, Royal Commission on the Historical Monuments of England, Salisbury.
56. Spotland Bridge New Mill, Rochdale (752*), is the name given on the First Edition 6 inches:1 mile OS sheet, surveyed 1844–7. Different sources give different names, however, and a number of other local mills also used the name 'Spotland'.
57. Spotland Mill Valuation 1863, CBR 5/158, Lancashire Record Office, Preston.
58. *The Manchester Guardian*, 16 October 1824, 3.
59. Building Control Plan, 1908, L/CS/M 11988, Salford City Archives.
60. Daniels 1915, 625–6.
61. Anon 1895, 33.
62. Holden 1987–8, 163.
63. George Watkins Collection, SER 158, Royal Commission on the Historical Monuments of England, Salisbury.
64. Deeds of Wear Mill, inspected courtesy of the owners, Leslie Fink Ltd.
65. A plan of the rebuilt mill, dated 1884, is held in the Building Control Plans collection, Stockport MBC Planning Department.
66. The fire, on 19 July 1831, was later described in the *Stockport Advertiser*, 25 August 1866.
67. *Ashton Reporter*, 29 March 1884, 1.
68. Worrall 1896, 65.
69. George Watkins Collection, SER 722, Royal Commission on the Historical Monuments of England, Salisbury.
70. Hill 1907, 253. See also: Answers of James Wilkinson, Parliamentary Papers (House of Commons), 1834 (167), *Employment of Children in Factories* XX, D1, 27.
71. Worrall 1884.
72. Haynes 1987, 27.
73. Poor Rate, 1836, Parish of Ashton under Lyne, 58; PUA/4/1, Tameside Local Studies Library.
74. Sales by Auction, *Ashton Reporter*, 20 January 1883.
75. Deeds of Good Hope Mill, Conveyance of 1896, inspected courtesy of the owners, G. Nixon and Co Ltd.
76. *Leigh Chronicle*, 2 October 1891, 8.
77. See obituary of Caleb Wright, *Leigh Journal and Times*, 29 April 1898, 8.

# Bibliography

Ainsworth, W. H. 1858. *Mervyn Clitheroe*

Allen, Z. 1831. *The Practical Tourist*

Anon 1858. The City of Men. *Chamber's Edinburgh Journal*, 251

    1888. *The Manchester of Today* **2**

    1895. *Lancashire. Men of the Period. The Records of a Great County. Portraits and Pen Pictures of Leading Men. Part First*

    1951. *The Mills and Organisation of the Lancashire Cotton Corporation Ltd*

Archer, J. H. G. (ed) 1985. *Art and Architecture in Victorian Manchester*

Armstrong, T. 1943. *King Cotton*

Ashmore, O. 1975. *The Industrial Archaeology of Stockport*

Ashworth, J. R. 1915. Rochdale Soot-Fall. *Transactions of the Rochdale Literary & Scientific Society* **12**, 50–3

    1918. National Scientific Research and what Lancashire has done for the Advancement of Electrical Science. *Transactions of the Rochdale Literary & Scientific Society* **13**, 69–80

    1919. Atmospheric Pollution in Rochdale. *Transactions of the Rochdale Literary & Scientific Society* **14**, 109–19

Aspin, C. 1981. *The Cotton Industry*

Atkinson, E. 1973. Slow Burning Construction. In *The Century Magazine* **15**, 1889, 565–79, reprinted in *The Industrial Progress of the Nation*, 309–37

Bailey, A. J. 1984. The Instability of Growth in a Leading Sector: The Economics of Cotton Firms during the British Industrial Revolution, 1795–1820. A paper presented at the annual conference of the Economic History Society, 6 April 1984, and cited by permission of the author

    1985. The Impact of the Napoleonic Wars on the Development of the Cotton Industry in Lancashire: A Study of the Structure and Behaviour of Firms during the Industrial Revolution. PhD thesis, University of Cambridge

Baines, E. 1835. *History of the Cotton Manufacture in Great Britain*

Baines, T. 1869. *Lancashire and Cheshire Past and Present* **2**

Barker, H. W. 1898. Cooling Reservoirs for Condensing Engines. *The Textile Manufacturer* **24**, 338–41

Barker, W. H. 1927. The Towns of South-East Lancashire. *Journal of the Manchester Geographical Society* **43**, 31–54

Benson, A. P. 1983. *Textile Machines*

Bergin, T. *et al* (eds) 1975. *Salford. A City and its Past*

Bourne, J. 1872. *A Treatise on the Steam Engine*

Brighouse, H. and Forrest, C. 1917. *Hobson's. The Novel of Hobson's Choice*

Burchell, R. A. (ed) 1991. *The End of Anglo-America. Historical Essays in the Study of Cultural Divergence*

Calladine, A. and Fricker, J. (forthcoming). *East Cheshire Textile Mills.*

Candee, R. M. 1989. The 1822 Allendale Mill and Slow-Burning Construction: A Case Study in the Transmission of an Architectural Technology. *I. A.: The Journal of the Society for Industrial Archaeology* **15**, 21–34.

Catling, H. 1970. *The Spinning Mule*

Chaloner, W. H. 1949. The Cheshire Activities of Matthew Boulton and James Watt of Soho, near Birmingham, 1776–1817. *Trans Lancashire Cheshire Antiq Soc* (1951), **61**, 132–5

    1954. Robert Owen, Peter Drinkwater and the Early Factory System in Manchester 1788–1800. *Bulletin of the John Rylands Library* **37**, 78–102. In Chaloner 1990, 135–56

    1990. *Industry and Innovation. Selected Essays*

Chapman, S. D. 1981–2. The Arkwright Mills – Colquhoun's Census of 1788 and Archaeological Evidence. *Ind Archaeol Rev* **6**, 5–27

Clark, S. 1977–8. Chorlton Mills and their Neighbours. *Ind Archaeol Rev* **2**, 207–39

Clarke, C. A. 1893. *The Knobstick. A Story of Love and Labour*

Coutie, H. 1989. The Cotton Famine in Stockport. *Cheshire History* **24**, 18–27

Crabtree, J. H. 1907. Modern Practice in Fire-Fighting. *Magazine of Commerce* **10**, 18

Daniels, G. W. 1915. Valuation of Manchester Cotton Factories in the Early Years of the Nineteenth Century. *Econ J* **25**, 625–6

    1927. Industrial Lancashire Prior and Subsequent to the Invention of the Mule. Reprint from *The Journal of the Textile Institute* **8**, 1–16

Dickens, C. 1854. *Hard Times*

Dickinson, H. W. 1963. *A Short History of the Steam Engine*

Dickinson, T. C. 1984. *Lancashire Under Steam: The Era of the Steam-Driven Cotton Mill*

Dodd, G. 1851. *The Textile Manufactures of Great Britain (British Manufactures)*

    1852. *Curiosities of Industry and the Applied Sciences*

Dodd, W. 1842. *The Factory System Illustrated*

Douet, J. nd. *Going Up In Smoke. The History of the Industrial Chimney*

Esher, L. 1981. *A Broken Wave. The Rebuilding of England, 1940–1980*

Fairbairn, W. 1865. *Treatise on Mills and Millwork. Part 2. On Machinery of Transmission and the Construction and Arrangement of Mills*

    1866. Description of the Removing and Replacing of the Iron Columns in a Cotton Mill. *Inst Mechanical Engineers*, 181–5

    1869. Rise and Progress of Manufactures and Commerce in Lancashire and Cheshire. In Baines 1869

Farnie, D. A. 1979. *The English Cotton Industry and the World Market, 1815–1896*

    1984. John Bunting (1839–1923). In Jeremy 1984–6, **1**, 506–10

    1985. John Rylands (1801–88). In Jeremy 1984–6, **4**, 999–1004

    1989. The Metropolis of Cotton Spinning, Machine Making and

Mill Building. In Gurr and Hunt 1989, 4–11

1990*a*. The Textile Machine-Making Industry and the World Market, 1870–1960. *Business Hist* **32**, No. 4, 150–70. Reprinted in Rose 1991, 150–70

1990*b*. John Worrall of Oldham, Directory-Publisher to Lancashire and to the World, 1868–1970. *Manchester Region History Review* **4**, 30–5

Farnie, D. A. and Yonekawa, S 1988. The Emergence of the Large Firm in the Cotton Spinning Industries of the World, 1883–1938. *Textile Hist* **19**, 171–210

Fitton, R. S. 1989. *The Arkwrights. Spinners of Fortune*

Fitton, R. S. and Wadsworth, A. P. 1958. *The Strutts and the Arkwrights 1758–1830*

Fitzgerald, R. S. 1987–8*a*. The Development of the Cast-iron Frame in Textile Mills to 1850. *Ind Archaeol Rev* **10**, 127–45

1987–8*b*. Albion Mill, Manchester. *Ind Archaeol Rev* **10**, 204–30

Fowler, A. 1979–80. Trade Unions and Technical Change: The Automatic Loom Strike, 1908. *North West Labour History Society Bulletin* **6**, 43–55

Fowler, A. and Wyke, T. (eds) 1987. *The Barefoot Aristocrats. A History of the Amalgamated Association of Operative Cotton Spinners*

Freeman, J. R. 1891. Comparison of English and American Types of Factory Construction. *The Textile Manufacturer* **17**, 175–9, 228–30, 276–8

Giles, C. and Goodall, I. H. 1992. *Yorkshire Textile Mills 1770–1930*

Gray, J. M. 1937. *The Weavers' Wage*

Greenwood, W. 1951. *The County Book of Lancashire*

Gurr, D. and Hunt, J. 1989. *The Cotton Mills of Oldham*

Hart, P. E. 1965. *Studies in Profit, Business Saving and Investment in the UK, 1920–1962*

Haynes, I. 1987. *Cotton in Ashton*

1990. *Stalybridge Cotton Mills*

Henderson, W. O. 1968. *Industrial Britain under the Regency. The Diaries of Escher, Bodmer, May and de Gallois 1814–18*

Hill, S. 1907. *Bygone Stalybridge*

Hills, R. L. 1987–8. Peter Ewart, 1767–1842. *Manchester Memoirs* **127**, 29–43

1989. *Power from Steam: A History of the Stationary Steam Engine*

Hodgkinson, E. 1831. Theoretical and Experimental Researches to Ascertain the Strength and Best Form of Iron Beams. *Memoirs of the Literary and Phil Soc of Manchester* **5**

Holden, R. N. 1987–8. Pear Mill, Stockport: An Edwardian Cotton Spinning Mill. *Ind Archaeol Rev* **10**, 162–74

Howarth, K. 1974. The Industrial Archaeology of Radcliffe and the Irwell Gorge. *Ind Archaeol* **11**, 14–34

Howarth, R. W. 1975. *List of Works and Extensions to Works Constructed to the Designs of Sydney Stott, Architect*

Hughes, S. 1853. *Treatise on Gasworks*

Hyams, E. 1957. *Taine's Notes on England*

Jacobs, J. 1969. *The Economy of Cities*

Jeremy, D. J. 1991. British and American Entrepreneurial Values in the Early Nineteenth Century: A Parting of the Ways? In Burchell 1991, 24–59

Jeremy, D. J. (ed) 1984–6. *Dictionary of Business Biography* 5 vols

Jewkes, J. and Gray, E. M. 1935. *Wages and Labour in the Lancashire Cotton Spinning Industry*

Johnson, H. R. and Skempton, A. W. 1955–7. William Strutt's Cotton Mills, 1793–1812. *Trans Newcomen Soc* **30**, 179–205

Jones, E. 1985. *Industrial Architecture in Britain 1750–1939*

Kelly & Co. 1912. *Directory of Manchester and Salford*

Lamb, R. 1848. The Manufacturing Poor. *Fraser's Magazine*, 9

1866. *Free Thoughts on Many Subjects* 2 vols

1872. *Yarndale*

[Lamb, R.] 1856. A Whitweek in Manchester. *Fraser's Magazine*, 631. Reprinted in *Free Thoughts on Many Subjects*

Lee, C. H. 1972. *A Cotton Enterprise 1795–1840. A History of McConnel and Kennedy, Fine Cotton Spinners*

Leigh, E. 1873. *The Science of Modern Cotton Spinning*

Lewis, J. P. 1965. *Building Cycles and Britain's Growth*

Lloyd-Jones, R. and le Roux, A. A. 1980. The Size of Firms in the Cotton Industry: Manchester 1815–41. *Econ Hist Rev* **33**, 72–82

Lloyd-Jones, R. and Lewis, M. J. 1988. *Manchester and the age of the Factory. The Business Structure of Cottonopolis in the Industrial Revolution*

Longworth, J. H. 1986. *The Cotton Mills of Bolton 1780–1985. A Historical Directory*

[Lowe, J.] 1854. A Manchester Warehouse. *Household Words* **9**, 268–72

M'Connel, J. W. 1906. *A Century of Fine Cotton Spinning 1790–1906*

1913. *A Century of Fine Cotton Spinning 1790–1913*

Macleod, M. *et al* 1988. *The Ditherington Flax Mill, Shrewsbury. A Survey and Historical Evaluation*. The Ironbridge Institute Research Paper No 30

Madge, C. and Harrisson, T. (eds) 1938. *First Year's Work 1937–8 by Mass Observation*

[Mallalieu, A.] 1836. The Cotton Manufacture. *Blackwood's Edinburgh Magazine* **39**, 407–24

Mann, J. de L. 1958. The Textile Industry. Machinery for Cotton, Flax, Wool, 1760–1850. In Singer *et al* 1958, 277–307

Mantoux, P. 1961. *The Industrial Revolution in the Eighteenth Century*

Mason, J. J. 1981. A Manufacturing and Bleaching Enterprise during the Industrial Revolution: The Sykeses of Edgeley. *Business Hist* **23**, 59–83

Mass Observation 1970. *The Pub and the People. A Worktown Study*

Middleton, T. 1952. *The History of Hyde and its Neighbourhood*

Mills, W. H. 1921. *Trafford Park, Manchester*

1924. *Grey Pastures*

Moorhouse, G. 1964. *Britain in the Sixties. The Other England*

Mortimer, J. 1891. Henry Bannerman and Sons Ltd. Its Origin, Rise and Progress. *Diary and Buyer's Guide for 1891*

1894. Cotton: From Field to Factory. *The Textile Mercury* **10**, 95–6

Muir, A. 1964. *The Kenyon Tradition: The History of James Kenyon & Son, Ltd, 1664–1964*

Musson, A. E. and Robinson, E. 1969. *Science and Technology in the Industrial Revolution*

Nasmith, J. and Nasmith, F. 1909. *Recent Cotton Mill Construction and Engineering*

Nicholas, R 1945. *The Manchester and District Regional Planning Committee. Report on the Tentative Regional Planning Proposals*

Orwell, G. 1937. *The Road to Wigan Pier*

Penn, T. Z. 1981. The Development of the Leather Belt Main Drive. *I.A.: The Journal of the Society for Industrial Archaeology* **7**, 1–14

Pole, W. (ed) 1877. *The Life of Sir William Fairbairn, Partly Written by Himself*

Redford, A. 1934. *Manchester Merchants and Foreign Trade*

*1794–1858*

Rohde, S. 1979. *A Private View of L. S. Lowry*

Rose, M. B. (ed) 1991. *International Competition and Strategic Response in the Textile Industries since 1870*

Rubinstein, W. D. 1974. British Millionaires, 1809–1949. *Bulletin of the Institute of Historical Research* **47**, 202–23

Ryan, R. 1937. *A Biography of Manchester*

Schinkel, K. F. 1967. *Aus Tagebüchern und Briefen*

Schulze, H. J. F. 1853. *Nationalöconomische Bilder aus Englands Volksleben*

Simpson, I. 1990. Power Looms and Poverty. *Stockport Heritage* **2**, 24

Singer, C. *et al* (eds) 1958. *A History of Technology. Vol IV. The Industrial Revolution c.1750 to c.1850*

Sington, T. 1892. *Cotton Mill Planning and Construction*, reprinted from *The Textile Manufacturer*, June 1892, 278–9

Skempton, A. W. and Johnson, H. R. 1962. The First Iron Frames. *Architect Rev* **131**, 175–86

Southey, R. *Letters from England* (ed, with an Introduction, J. Simmons 1951)

Stewart, C. 1956. *The Architecture of Manchester. An Index of the Principal Buildings and their Architects 1800–1900*

Swire, W. 1824. *Plan of Manchester*

Tann, J. 1970. *The Development of the Factory*

1974. The Textile Millwright in the Early Industrial Revolution. *Textile Hist* **5**, 80–9

Tattersall, F. W. 1914–20. *Cotton Trade Circular*

Tattersall, W. 1895–1913. *Cotton Trade Circular*

Tawney, R. H. (ed) 1968. *Studies in Economic History: The Collected Papers of George Unwin*

Taylor, W. C. 1840. Moral Economy of Large Towns. Manchester. *Bentley's Miscellany* **7**

1968. *Notes of a Tour in the Manufacturing Districts of Lancashire*

Thelwall, R. E. 1972. *The Andrews and Compstall Their Village*

Thompson, W. H. 1967. *History of Manchester to 1852*

Tippett, L. H. C. 1969. *A Portrait of the Lancashire Cotton Industry*

Tomlinson, C. 1854. *The Useful Arts and Manufactures of Great Britain*. The Manufacture of Cotton Yarn. Part 2

Tomlinson, V. I. 1975. The Coming of Industry. In Bergin *et al* 1975, 19–61

Unwin, G. 1924. *Samuel Oldknow and the Arkwrights. The Industrial Revolution at Stockport and Marple*

Ure, A. 1835. The Philosophy of Manufactures

1836. *The Cotton Manufacture of Great Britain* **1**

Vose, J. R. (ed) 1919. *Bolton: Its Trade and Commerce*

Walter, E. V. 1976. New Light on Dark Satanic Mills. *Communication*, 22–3

Watkins, G. 1971. *The Textile Mill Engine* **2**

Williams, M. J. 1987–8a. The RCHME/GMAU Joint Survey of Textile Mills in Greater Manchester. *Ind Archaeol Rev* **10**, 193–203

1987–8b. Gilnow Mill, Bolton, an Example of Detailed Recording by the Greater Manchester Textile Mill Survey. *Greater Manchester Archaeol J*, **3**, 129–39

Worrall, J. 1884–1963. *The Cotton Spinner's and Manufacturer's Directory*

# Index

Page references in **bold** are to illustrations or captions for illustrations